AS THE BUYING [...]
D[...]
savings plans, insurance policies and other "safe" investment plans even the future value of pensions and social security no longer insure your economic security.

YOU NEED NEW WAYS TO PROTECT YOUR FUTURE.

HOW TO PROSPER DURING THE COMING BAD YEARS

contains specific investment techniques to combat the erosion of your savings. Howard J. Ruff prescribes solid, easily understood, easily managed investment plans as hedges against inflation. He systematically details how and where to acquire them safely, and even how to profit from these decisions when the economy eventually stabilizes.

"This book frightened me. I don't know whether it's Howard's gifted writing or the simple logic of Howard's predictions, but I couldn't put it down and I recommend this book to everyone."
—*Dow Theory Letter*

"Sound advice to help an inflation-weary investor and an eloquent plea for fiscal sanity."
—*George Bush*

"Useful . . . well-written, readable, entertaining and instructive."
—American Institute for Economic Research, *Research Reports*

A LITERARY GUILD ALTERNATE

ATTENTION: SCHOOLS AND CORPORATIONS

WARNER books are available at quantity discounts with bulk purchase for educational, business, or sales promotional use. For information, please write to: SPECIAL SALES DEPARTMENT, WARNER BOOKS, 75 ROCKEFELLER PLAZA, NEW YORK, N.Y. 10019

**ARE THERE WARNER BOOKS
YOU WANT BUT CANNOT FIND IN YOUR LOCAL STORES?**

You can get any WARNER BOOKS title in print. Simply send title and retail price, plus 50¢ per order and 20¢ per copy to cover mailing and handling costs for each book desired. New York State and California residents add applicable sales tax. Enclose check or money order only, no cash please, to: WARNER BOOKS, P.O. BOX 690, NEW YORK, N.Y. 10019

HOW TO PROSPER DURING THE COMING BAD YEARS

Howard J. Ruff

WARNER BOOKS

A Warner Communications Company

WARNER BOOKS EDITION

Copyright © 1979, 1981 by Howard J. Ruff

All rights reserved. No part of this book may be reproduced in any form or by any electronic or mechanical means including information storage and retrieval systems without permission in writing from the publisher, except by a reviewer who may quote brief passages in a review.

This Warner Books Edition is published by arrangement with TIMES BOOKS, a division of Quadrangle/The New York Times Book Co., Inc., 3 Park Avenue, New York, N.Y. 10016

Cover design by Mike McIver

Warner Books, Inc., 75 Rockefeller Plaza, New York, N.Y. 10019

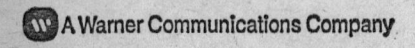

Ⓦ A Warner Communications Company

Printed in the United States of America

First Printing: January, 1980

Reissued: July, 1981

15　14

This publication is designed to provide the Author's opinion in regard to the subject matter covered. It is sold with the understanding that the Publisher or Author is not engaged in rendering legal, accounting or other professional service. If legal advice or other expert assistance is required, the services of a competent professional person should be sought.

The Author specifically disclaims any personal liability, loss, or risk incurred as a consequence of the use and application, either directly or indirectly, of any advice or information presented herein.

CONTENTS

Introduction   11

PART I: PROBLEMS

1 The Watershed Years   25
2 Inflation—The Great Transfer Tax   38
3 A World Turned Upside Down   65
4 Putting Governors on Thermometers   75
5 The Ponzi Chain Letter   82
6 East Side, West Side   98
7 The Old Homestead   117
8 Don't Bank on It   125
9 Power to the President   144
10 We Owe It to Ourselves   153
11 Sin-Tax   159

PART II: PRESERVATION

	Introduction	175
12	Gold and Silver Coins	178
13	Personal Debt	191
14	Pass on the Old Maid	195
15	Preparing for the Black Market	238
16	Panic-Proof	247

PART III: STRATEGY

	Introduction	321
17	The Break-Even-or-Better Strategy	323
18	The Golden Calf	331
19	"... A Girl's Best Friend"	347
20	"Do Thy Patient No Harm"	353
	Appendix	368
	Index	377

INTRODUCTION TO THE NEW EDITION OF HOW TO PROSPER DURING THE COMING BAD YEARS DECEMBER 25, 1980

The two-year period since I first completed HOW TO PROSPER DURING THE COMING BAD YEARS has been one of the most dramatic and volatile times in the history of the Republic.

The Iranians have seized our Embassy and, as of now, still hold 52 of our personnel. The Russians have invaded Afghanistan. For the first time in 100 years, we have rejected a duly elected, sitting president for a second term. Ronald Reagan and a whole new team of "New Right Conservatives" now occupy the White House and rule the United States Senate.

Gold has seen incredible highs and wild swings of as much as $120 an ounce in one day. We have seen silver go from $7 an ounce to $48 an ounce and back to $10 in the Nelson Bunker Hunt market fiasco.

1979 was the last year of the most incredible economic expansion in the history of the country and then in 1980, we took a sudden dip into recession, which is just getting up a real head of steam.

We've seen incredible growth in Federal debt and budgets, with inflation rates and interest rates over 20%. Such a prospect was considered the "wildest ravings of a Prophet of Doom" when I forecast these events.

There has been a remarkable change in attitude toward my kind of philosophy, as typified by a visit I made shortly after the publication date to a Minneapolis television station for a talk show. The announcer's introduction went something like this: "Today we are studying Psychoceramics, and we have with us a crackpot from California." Very funny!

A year later, when promoting the paperback, I appeared on the same station and this time the announcer, who had subsequently read the book and, to his advantage, followed some of the advice said: "Today we have with us one of America's most respected financial advisors." This was the same guy!

The press had fascinating reactions to the book. The

mainstream reviewers, including the book section of THE NEW YORK TIMES, simply acted as though the book did not exist. It was not reviewed seriously by anyone of substance and reputation in the publishing industry.

Columnists and editorial writers, however, took notice of it mostly by referring to me as a "Profit of Doom, making a fortune from scaring people." FORBES referred to me as the leader of a financial cult, "The Jim Jones of the Financial World." I thought this was a bit excessive.

My reaction to all this? Let's look at the record.

My wildest forecasts of precious metals prices, interest rates and inflation rates came true. Those who took the advice in the book made an awful lot of money. They beat the whey out of inflation. Those who didn't, took a whipping. There is no question that the strategies in HOW TO PROSPER were valid.

Now, why a new edition?

I found it necessary to update some of the strategies simply because the market prices have changed so dramatically that the old portfolios no longer make sense. They are obsolete.

We've come through a period where the bond strategy described in Chapter 17 has been profitably used to our advantage, and if someone were to read this book without understanding where we are in the economic cycle, he could utilize the wrong strategies at the wrong time.

The political realities are now different and have raised serious questions as to the validity of some of the concerns in the book. I felt they must be updated.

Rather than changing the text, in most instances we have added footnotes. This will enable you to compare the original text with the new information and market prices.

Revising this book was fun in one sense, because it was deeply satisfying professionally to be able to say, "I told you so. I was right."

On the other hand, because the trends which I forecast were often destructive of the long-term future of this country, it was a sad task to chronicle the progressive disintegration of the capital structure of America.

If, after you read the book, you feel the need for a more recent update, we would be happy to send you one free of charge. Just write to me: Howard Ruff, P.O. Box 2000, San Ramon, CA 94583. God bless you all.

INTRODUCTION

One day in November, 1968, I went to my office to attend a meeting at which I thought I was going to receive some help and advice from the people who managed the national company with which I had a speed-reading franchise. We were just beginning to emerge from a very difficult few months, resulting from a prolonged newspaper strike which hit without warning and prevented us from advertising during our peak months. We had been in financial trouble for some time, but things had started to improve.

When I walked out of that meeting, I was wiped out. My franchise had been cancelled and the struggle to save my company was over. My business was down the tubes. My banker had been notified and my accounts were frozen. I had $11.36 in my pocket. I had no money, no job and no unemployment insurance, because there isn't any such thing for small businessmen who go broke. My rather spectacular collapse hit the front page of the financial section of the San Francisco Bay Area papers and I was invited to resign from the Oakland Symphony Finance Committee, because I was embarrassing them. It was a terrible period in our lives. It had only been 5 months since the accidental drowning of our 21-month-old son, Ivan.

It was in the depths of that despair that a chain of events began that has culminated in this book.

My family and I decided that such pain, public humiliation and grief had to be put to some positive purpose, for others, as well as ourselves. So we went to work, armed with our determination to learn everything we could from that business failure so that it would never ever happen to us again. It was then that I resolved to apply to my life in the future the principles I had learned from a variety of sources.

There was my Mormon upbringing, which stressed prudence, avoidance of unsound debt, and a kind of 19th century rugged self-sufficiency.

I had spent years in economic studies, and several years as a stock broker, specializing in venture capital and municipal bonds.

My 25 years as an actor and professional singer had taught me to be persuasive and effective in the use of the language in front of audiences.

I determined to some day repay every debt, even though my legal obligation was discharged through the legal process of bankruptcy.

When Jesus preached the virtues of "a broken heart and a contrite spirit," I believe He meant that people generally do not bring about real change in their lives until they are traumatized by hitting a bottom of despair and misery from which there is no choice but to make basic changes in one's life and outlook, or follow a path to self-destruction. And from that bottom in my life came the determination, not only to never repeat the same mistakes that had made me vulnerable, but to help others avoid personal financial difficulties caused by their lack of understanding of the real world.

One major asset I retained from that speed-reading school collapse was my personal ability to read rapidly. I can handle most material very rapidly, and I have close-to-total recall. In five hours a day of reading, I process vast amounts of written material and run across things that most of you would never have a chance to get to. Bits and pieces of information click into place that would not have done so had I not covered so much ground in a short time, and I can quickly become a walking encyclopedia on almost anything.

I fought my way back through two undercapitalized business ventures, both of which are flourishing today, one of which was sold for a substantial profit which provided the capital to launch my newsletter and advisory service, the *Ruff Times*. In between, I became interested in flying and developed an obsessive interest in weather and climatology, which is something that every economic forecaster should know about. I also became fascinated with the subject of nutrition, which led to the establishment of a vitamin supplement and food storage distributorship (the business I sold in 1975), which equipped me for my research into food problems and food storage.

These events, plus my long interest in economics, have come together in the creation of this book and the *Ruff Times*. However, it was the business collapse that gave me the perspective, the drive and, hopefully, the character to bring me to this point where I can speak with authority from a pretty good track record as a forecaster and advisor. And that is where I am today—the author of this, my second book, the Editor, Publisher and principal owner of the fastest growing advisory service in America, and the host of a TV talk show called *Ruffhouse*, which is shown on more than 60 stations across the United States.

This book was originally conceived as a basic text for subscribers to my advisory service, and the occasional references to *Ruff Times* services are for their benefit. We live in rapidly shifting times, and, although I believe the principles expressed in this book will continue to hold true for your personal planning, short-term and intermediate-term trends can change, creating both risks and opportunities, and time tables can sometimes use adjustment. I decided to write a book that can stand alone, but my staff and I can keep my subscribers apprised of any changes in the economic climate or in my strategy. There are alternate strategies for these changes in the economic climate in Chapter 20.

Some material has been derived from my extensive files and the *Ruff Times*. Other material is re-introduced and summarized from my first book, but over half of it is new—derived from my further studies, interviews with guests on my TV show and my attendance at economic conferences. That which is repeated from previous works is repeated for specific reasons, and should be considered "an up-dated summary and review." This should be of great value to long-time subscribers and will also serve as a total overview for new readers.

You may read this some time after completion in the fall of 1978,* and some of the material may then be dated, and advice that was valid when it was written may need to be thought through again. As you will see, I make no claim to infallibility. It can be updated either through the *Ruff Times*, or, if you are carefully analytical, by looking back through all the basic principles in Parts II and III and applying them to changing conditions.

WHY DID I WRITE THIS BOOK?

Before I was an author, I was a father and husband and that's still my Number 1 role in life. I love my wife and my children, and they, along with my religion and an unalarmed conscience, should form an inseparable whole. I am concerned about the hard times I see coming, and my family will have to live in that world. I

---
*This new edition has been updated through December 1980.

want to prepare them to get through without physical discomfort and with fundamental Judeo-Christian values intact, and I'm working very hard to see that sound principles of ethics, morality, and economics are passed on to my offspring, because when I train my children, I'm training my grandchildren. Everything I write is, in the final analysis, my legacy to them. Of course, I want them to be proud of me, and I want to give them an example which they can emulate.

I also believe that my small amount of this world's wealth is a stewardship and I have a responsibility to protect it and magnify it.

Each one of you who takes my advice will create a little pocket of stability and emotional security which will stand you in good stead in hard times and will "panic-proof" your life. Every family which has its debt under control, investments which will beat the inflationary spiral, and all of the things that will make for social and financial stability, will make the world safer and more stable for Kay and me and our children.

You are reading this book because you are perceptive enough to sense that something is terribly wrong out there and you are one of millions of Americans with a growing sense of unease about the future. The institutions you always trusted are now giving you a queasy feeling, you are making more money but you seem to have less, and you know all is not well. I congratulate you for your insight. I share your feelings.

I believe that the nation is about to undergo its greatest test since the Civil War, and if we can elect more talented, honorable, free-market oriented men to office, the more likely it is that we will be able to steer the Ship of State through stormy waters and keep it afloat.

I also believe the nation will survive, and if enough of us do the right things, we may come out of this stronger than we went into it. I doubt if this book will transform the world, even if it sells a zillion copies, but maybe it can change just enough people's attitudes to tip the scales in a close case.

I also intend to challenge the conventional wisdom in economic forecasting and financial planning that has led us into this mess. Those sacred cows are outdated, inaccurate, Pollyanna-ish and unrealistic, and can lead you and this nation into personal and national economic bondage.

Those who are making and influencing our economic policy are either acting in their own economic or political self-interest, are fools, or are just plain wrong. The course that they have plotted can only end in fiscal chaos, and this book is an effort to chronicle these momentous events in advance. I want it to stand as a monument against this happening again in my children's or my grand-children's lifetime. That's how sure I am that I'm right, but I take no pleasure in my forecast.

POINTS OF VIEW

I have written from the point of view of an "Economic Ecologist." Ecology is the study of the inter-relationships of living organisms and their environment. The economy is also an "ecology." Most economists study only numbers and put them into computers and let the computer tell them what the world will be like. That leads to false conclusions, because it excludes the human equation. Economic forecasting is as much of an art as it is a science. If we do not study the whole "ecology"—man's religion and ethics, his sexual behavior, government regulation, and politics, as well as laws, money, and fundamental economics, we will not understand the economic environment and we will make lousy decisions with our own money. For that reason my scope will be broader than you might have thought in a book which purports to deal with financial advice, but I think you will be surprised when you find out how much impact human sexual behavior has on your property tax and New York City's bankruptcy.

As I said, I never have professed to be infallible, but my track record says I'm right far more often than I'm wrong. But I must protect you against my fallibility by giving you advice that won't hurt you and alternative plans if I am wrong or if my timetable is off. I must help you limit your risk, as the investment marketplace is always rational in the long run, but it can be downright paranoid-schizoid on any given day—and is often totally logic-proof for weeks at a time. Small losses caused by being a bit early or a bit late should be written off as premiums paid for an insurance policy against the worst case, just as all automobile insurance policies are mentally written off as protection against the crash you fully expect not to have. The Hippocratic Oath, to which every physician subscribes, says, "Do thy patient no harm," and that's my objective.

Everything that I am advising you to do I have done myself, within the limits of my financial resources, as I am comfortably well off but not wealthy. Those who will gain the most benefit from this book are those who have some savings or some assets, small or large, such as an equity in a home. You can benefit even if your resources are quite limited. You can start your personal and financial survival program with as little as $50 a month for a few months. Everybody can do something, if it's only to vote out of office those fools and mountebanks who keep digging our hole deeper.

Throughout the book you will find references to books, publications, services and products with some candid "consumers' guide" type comments. To assist you in your search for them, I have listed all of these at the end of the book, giving addresses, sometimes phone numbers, and prices when appropriate. Each product so listed, when referred to in the text, will be mentioned in the Appendix.

I will make commercial recommendations, but I receive no financial rewards from those recommendations. I only sell advice—none of the investments or products discussed in this book, so the one exception to my "no profit" stance is books, which are generally available from my publishing firm, Target, as some are obscure and hard to find, and, of course, my newsletter.

In some instances, both my interest and my expertise in some of these commercial areas arose out of my involvement in similar businesses. For example, out of my zeal for such products, I got into the food storage and supplement business in 1972 and designed one of the food storage programs I describe and recommend in Part II. I sold that business in November 1975 specifically to avoid the understandable confusion on the part of the media regarding my motives and so my recommendations would be fully credible. If I had not been in the trenches in that business, I would not have had the experience necessary to be a competent advisor on food storage, nor understood the various ways you can make serious mistakes in that vital area.

In each case, when I do recommend a firm and a product, I negotiate the best deal that I can for those who solicit my advice, consistent with maintaining the financial health of the recommended business.

These firms are all dependable. They are not the only good firms in existence, but I prefer to find one good solid company in each area, negotiate a good deal for my clients and monitor it closely to see that they conduct their business honorably and conservatively. Refusing all commissions has cost me a lot of money in the short-term, but I believe it has been a big factor in helping to make my firm the most successful "hard money" publisher in the country, and my financial reward will come in time from that. But better than that, I enjoy the love and respect of my nine children who know that their father gave up money for a principle.

A great American religious leader once said, "There is no success in the world that can compensate for failure in the home. And when all is said and done, if nothing else I ever do works, if I can achieve success in that all-critical area, my life will have been a success.

To this end, I dedicate this book to the following people: My magnificent wife, Kay; our children, Larry, Eric, David, Pamela, Sharon, Patty, Ivan, Timmy and Debbie; my faithful secretary and dear friend, Judy Kimball, who has been with me for seven years and has typed every word I have ever published; and my best buddy and business associate, Terry Jeffers, who manages our publishing company, Target Publishers, who has been a catalyst for my thinking and has seen that all of my plans were faithfully and efficiently executed.

I would also like to thank Dr. Gary North, editor of *The Remnant Review*, and author of *How To Profit From The Coming Price Controls* for his inputs on that subject.

And last of all, this is dedicated to my tens of thousands of newsletter subscribers who demonstrate their love and appreciation through over 500 letters and phone calls to our offices every day. So read on—while I do my best to persuade you. It won't hurt you a bit, and it might save everything you have if I'm right.

PART I
PROBLEMS

1
THE WATERSHED YEARS

Much of the American wealth is an illusion which is being secretly gnawed away and much of it will be completely wiped out in the near future.

The American experiment is, without a doubt, the most incredible social and economic phenomenon of all time. Everywhere I travel I see evidence of great wealth: hundreds of thousands of beautiful vacation homes, millions of boats, airplanes and expensive cars, roads jammed with motor homes, expensive restaurants with people standing in line for hours for the privilege of spending a lot of money, and the casinos of Las Vegas and Atlantic City jammed with wall-to-wall gamblers. Nothing in man's history has even come close to it, and yet the forces are already irresistibly in motion to bring much of it to an end.

Have you ever played the "Neighbor Game"? Your spouse says to you, "Dear, I wonder how much money Jones next door makes?" You consider the new boat, the Mercedes in the driveway, and the European vacation, and you say, "Well, he probably makes $60,000 a year." But you didn't estimate Jones' earnings, you only estimated what Jones *spends*, and the odds are that the Joneses are spending more than they make, and they can only do so as long as someone will lend them the difference. And the day may not be far away when a lot of Joneses, all caught in the same whirlpool of unsound, unsecured debt, won't be able to make their payments. And most of the Joneses and their creditors are going to be wiped out. Everything Jones has is "on the cuff"—mortgaged to the hilt. Debt is as American as apple pie, to say nothing of hot dogs and Chevrolet. We got here by borrowing. The Joneses did it, your city does it, your State does it, and Uncle Sam does it. Oh, boy, does he do it!! We got here by spending money that isn't ours, created from nothing, and while our spending power went up with our debt, the value of our assets is daily being ripped away by the inevitable result of our borrowing and spending—inflation. And inflation is the monster that will devour most of us. But it doesn't have to happen to you.

The purpose of this book is to persuade you that the United States is about to enter its greatest test period since the Civil War—an inflationary spiral leading to a depression that will be remembered with a shudder for generations, and whoever is President of the United States and presides over the collapse will be "the Hoover of the 70's and 80's," and the opposing party will be running against him for the next 50 years. There's a better-than-even chance that we will be well into it during the Carter Administration, in which case, he was elected President of the *Titanic*.* And if he should escape it, it will get his successor for sure.

No one knows exactly where the breaking point is, but it's coming, and soon. As this book is published, America is truly on the brink, and so is the rest of the world, because when we sneeze, the rest of the world gets pneumonia.

So what is in your future? A grisly list of unpleasant events—exploding inflation, price controls, erosion of your savings (eventually to nothing), a collapse of private as well as government pension programs (including Social Security), vastly more government regulation to control your life, and eventually an international monetary holocaust which will sweep all paper currencies down the drain and turn the world upside down. Paper fortunes based on lending will be destroyed and a new kind of investment and financial planning morality will put some very unlikely people on the top of the heap. And you can join them there, if you know what you are doing when the heap turns over.

You don't have to be terribly smart if you can identify the basic trends and make some very simple decisions with your assets—as long as you do it before the heap turns over. You might do it too

---

*I was assuming two Carter terms. Reagan has inherited the helm. He has my prayers and my sympathy, even though I helped to elect him. He will also inherit the blame.

early, but that's O.K. Do it now, and wait. You'll be vindicated soon. And I'd rather be a year or two too early, than a week or two too late.

Here's the most likely scenario.

In the next recession,* which will happen sometime shortly after the publication of this book, it will appear that deflation and unemployment are threatening the public welfare. Washington will react in panic fashion to attack the problem by cranking up the money and spending machine to "stimulate" the economy —a bit of "the hair of the dog that bit us." Job programs, matching funds, guarantees, loans, and social spending programs will be triggered by events, such as the need to replenish state unemployment funds (29 state unemployment funds are broke even before the recession starts), and keep major businesses from going bankrupt, to say nothing of saving the banks and bailing out broke cities and states which will be hurt financially by the spreading property tax revolt. This will result in a flood of newly created money, which is the engine of inflation. You will see a runaway inflationary spiral, to be followed by another government panic move—price controls.

Because of the impossible complexity of our society, price, wage and rent controls cannot be universally, fairly and intelligently administered. As a result, rising commodity prices, taxes, and the cost of government regulation, will squeeze some manufacturers to the point where they will stop making many mass-market products. The inevitable result of price controls is shortages. Milton Friedman has said,

---
*We saw the first dip of the recession in 1980. After an illusory "recovery," the second half, deeper and scarier, will come in 1981.

"Economists may not know how to stop inflation, but they know how to cause shortages. Simply impose price controls." This will lead to black markets and further breakdown in the respect for law and order on the part of middle class Americans. Today we don't have the patriotic fervor of World War II to ensure our voluntary compliance with the laws against illegal "Black Markets," as this is a period of great cynicism and deteriorating respect for law.

Controls will fail. These distortions in the economy, and the dollar floods coming from the printing press, will cause Americans to distrust their own paper money and get rid of it as fast as they can in an orgy of spending, similar to what happened in Argentina when their inflation was running at 800% a year and they were buying everything in sight. Eventually our credit economy will turn into a pure printing press economy. (I'll explain how in Chapter 2.) Sooner or later, the American currency will collapse, creating chaos in the marketplace. The government will probably make one or two abortive attempts to issue a new currency by "fiat" (official order) and this "fiat" currency will be rejected. Eventually things will get so bad that the government will be driven by desperation to re-establish a gold-backed currency, but because it has disposed of much of its gold hoard, gold will have to be revalued upward to a price adequate to back the new money—perhaps thousands of dollars per ounce. This will be the only way to establish a means of exchange that people can trust. Those who have no need for a means of exchange during the chaotic period (who have already bought several months' supply of all the things they will need, such as food, clothing, candles, medicine, automobile parts, etc.) will get along tolerably well. Those who have no acceptable means of exchange and no advance storage program will be terribly hurt and there could be great suffering. But eventually order will be re-established, and painfully the nation will climb back out of its pit, hopefully chastened and prepared to avoid the mistakes of the past for 50 to 100 years, but lenders—and unsound borrowers—will have been wiped out and paper fortunes will have disappeared.

If you're still with me after this rather gloomy prognosis, I'd like to tell you (1) how we came to this brink, (2) why this is the most likely scenario, and (3) what you can do to get through it, and even get wealthy. I will unfold the plan piece by piece in Parts II and III after I've scared the wits out of you in Part I. Then I'll summarize it for you in the last chapter.

This is no "bail - out - of - civilization - and - head - for - a - retreat - in - the - Rockies - with - a-machine-gun-turret-on-the-roof" plan. I don't believe in burning bridges behind you, because you will want to go back. And this program is not just for the rich. There are obviously some things that you can't do if you don't have some money, but the basics will substantially raise the odds on personal and financial survival and can be implemented by nearly everyone.

So, read on at your own small risk. I've recommended financial moves over the last three years that have worked out most of the time, and everyone who took all my advice is way ahead, on balance. But bear in mind that if you take my advice and it's wrong and you lose money, it won't cost me a thing. The responsibility is yours.

The program is simple in concept:

1. Identify the trends, the pitfalls, and the opportunities in advance.

2. Survive the initial chaos in good health.

3. Make the right moves ahead of time that will preserve your purchasing power, and that's not as hard as it may seem. I will give you a total strategy—a plan that should get you through to the other side in enhanced financial condition.

One crucial point: I am not forecasting the end of the world, the end of Western civilization, or even the end of the American dream. The nation has survived a Civil War, three total monetary collapses, and several depressions, to say nothing of the resignation in disgrace of a President and a Vice-President, and we have gotten through. The inherent strength of the American system is incredible. It is the Rasputin of world economies.

Rasputin, the Mad Monk, was a Siberian peasant who achieved great influence over the Czarina of Russia just prior to the Bolshevik Revolution. Many believed he was a holy man, capable of great miracles. He was certainly capable of prodigious excesses of appetites, including legendary sexual feats. Eventually, a palace conspiracy decided to murder him. First, they fed him huge drafts of poison with his meal that would have killed ten lesser men and he didn't even belch. He was stabbed and shot, and he still wouldn't die. They dumped him through the ice on the Neva River and he clambered back onto the ice, terrifying his would-be assassins. Finally, they managed to kill the man-monster and he stayed dead.

The American economy is the Rasputin of the 70's. It has endured incredible insults and fended them off with marvelous resilience. Despite the inflationary excesses of government and the creeping bonds of tyranny from government agencies, it is still the marvel of the world. My guess is that nothing can really kill it, although it will get terribly sick, but somehow, someday, it will come staggering back like Rasputin, as it did from the depths of the recent recession and the Depression of the 30's.

I am being continually bombarded by letters from those who have adhered to the teachings of those who advocate heading for the mountains or bailing out of the United States. I've read most everything they have to say and most of them reason from basically sound economics. I just don't agree with their conclusions.

I don't know how to prepare for the end of the world, so I'm not even going to try. At least not physically. About all you can do in that exigency is be spiritually ready for anything that comes, and that's a matter between you and God; however, I think that we should simply prepare prudently for the worst possible case for which practical preparations are possible. I know of some who have a ten-year supply of food hidden in the mountains and are prepared to live there forever in a shattered, anarchistic world of total collapse—a new Dark Age. Perhaps they are right, and I respect their convictions and their willingness to live by them, as long as it doesn't hurt anybody else or "scare the horses," as Lady Astor said. If retreats are your cup of tea, go to it, but they aren't mine. I am not going to set up a retreat and plan to "shoot the starving hordes" if they come after me. I will take my chances in a small town and assume that America can come staggering back like Rasputin. In the meantime, I will save and invest as much money as I can so that my family can be as comfortable as possible through these difficult times and be prepared to take advantage of the investment opportunities that will arise.

This can be a time of great oportunity right now, and more times of opportunity will come when things bottom out. Your job then is to be sure that you and your family have the security and the assets to take advantage of the opportunities now and on the other side of the gulf that yawns before us, so as to be influential in shaping the rather plastic world that awaits us. My message is one of realism and hope in roughly equal doses, coupled with The Plan.

COMING ATTRACTIONS

Now a word about what to expect from this book.

Part I describes the problems we face, forecasts what's coming, then presents the case for my scenario. You will learn why more and more people are beginning to realize that the traditional "widows and orphans investments" such as blue chips, utility stocks, bonds, certificates of deposit, cash value insurance, and even your I.R.A. and Keogh accounts are crummy investments for the immediate future and for some time to come. Some investments that would have been considered the riskiest in past years, are now the safest in this upside-down world. I will also identify the breaking points so that you can chart this unhappy scenario as it unfolds.

Part II deals with the basic strategy for personal survival through the most difficult early stages of the confused and disrupted marketplace.

Part III will tell you how to hold your own financially—to preserve the purchasing power of your investment assets. You win the inflation game if you break even in purchasing power, after taxes and expenses. It's a low risk, low-management-time strategy for maintaining your purchasing power through the inflation period in order to take advantage of bargains at deflated depression prices later.

I will also present some aggressive strategies requiring higher degrees of risk for those who have the right temperament to use some of their assets to take advantage of opportunities that are always created when chaotic change occurs. If you have the right attitude and have kept your purchasing power intact by following the strategies we'll discuss later, you can become wealthy, using those more aggressive strategies with many hundreds of percent return on your dollars, as you catch the three basic changes in direction—the inflationary take-off, the downward break, and the point when the recovery begins, or reasonably close to it. Exact precision in timing isn't necessary.

I do not write "for the edification of great experts," but for the "little guy" (or the "big guy," for that matter) who wants to make it safely from here to there and doesn't care how elegantly the theory is presented. There is a minimum of jargon and difficult-to-understand concepts. My goal is to make this program so understandable that everyone in your family will be able to understand this strategy.

1979 and 1980 was a watershed period. Gold and silver more than tripled during this period since the first edition. Many readers made fortunes as a result. I did too. 1981-87 will have even better opportunities. You ain't seen nothin' yet. Great fortunes have been made when rapid economic changes occurred in either direction.

I am frequently challenged by the question, "Rather than telling individuals to prepare for bad times, why don't you devote the same energy and influence to changing things—to turning things around and preventing these problems?"

The answer is that I do try, even though I have concluded that the trends are irreversibly beyond the point of no return, and by the time you've finished, you'll understand why. The juggernaut is headed for the precipice, and it doesn't matter whether we go soaring over the cliff with our foot on the accelerator (inflation), or skidding with our foot on the brake (deflation).

The world is best served by those who act in their own self-interest to protect themselves and their families, with due regard to basic principles of honesty, ethics and morality and the other guy's personal and property rights. For example,* if my recommendation to store wheat as part of your food storage program is followed by significant numbers of people in 1978 and 1979, it will merely strengthen the sick farm economy and dispose of the grain surplus problem. If and when the time comes when food is short due to uncertainty of the distribution system, which I believe is quite likely, the people who have stored food will not be competing for scarce goods, and there will be more for everyone else.

I am reminded of the story of the little girl who was very restless and couldn't think of anything to do. Her mother found a map of the world in a magazine and cut it out along the lines of each country into a big jigsaw puzzle. She told Mary to put it all together, thinking it would keep her busy for hours. Five minutes later Mary came back whining, "I don't have anything to do." Her mother went to check on whether Mary really was through with the puzzle, and sure enough, she was. So mother asked,

---

*Unfortunately, not enough people actually followed my food storage advice.

"Mary, how did you do it so fast?" To which Mary responded, "There was a picture of a family on the other side. I put the family together and the world turned out just fine."

The moral in that story? If each family will become solvent, self-sufficient and panic-proof, the world is better off and that's what this book is all about—becoming panic-proof.

2
INFLATION—THE GREAT TRANSFER TAX

> The story is told of the modern Rip Van Winkle who goes to sleep in 1978 and wakes up in 1988. His first thought is to find a pay phone and call his broker. He checks on his IBM stock, which was worth $25,000 when he went to sleep, and finds to his delight and amazement it is now worth $250,000. Just then the operator breaks in and says, "Your 3 minutes are up. Please deposit $30,000!"

I've borrowed this story from my first book, because it's still appropriate. That's what happens when inflation gets out of hand. And it will. To understand how that can happen, you must understand the nature of the inflationary beast, as it is the key to nearly every other problem we face.

Inflation is *not* an increase in prices, although prices do increase. IT IS A DECREASE IN THE VALUE OF YOUR MONEY. It means that every dollar buys less. This is not the first time it has happened. Inflation has brought down civilization after civilization. In the reign of Diocletian, around 300 A.D., the following letter was written by a Roman businessman to his agent in Gaul (France):

> Hurry and spend all the currency you have. Buy me goods of any kind at whatever price you find them.

The value of money was dropping relentlessly and he wanted possessions, not cash, because the Roman Empire had been hit by such violent inflation that, to quote Emperor Diocletian, there were

> increases in prices, not only year by year, but month by month, day by day, almost hour by hour and minute by minute.

Rome unsuccessfully tried to solve its inflation by controlling, not merely prices, but the entire lives of most of its subjects, locking them forever into fixed places in the socio-economic order. Rome solved it, in short, by transforming itself into a totalitarian state, as rigid and all-pervasive as any the world has known.

The Romans inflated the currency by mixing base metals with gold and silver in their coins, clipping them, and making them thinner or smaller, until everyone lost confidence in the money.

But that's old fashioned now. We have the printing press. The brilliant economist Ludwig Von Mises said "Government is the only institution that can take a valuable commodity like paper, and make it worthless by applying ink."

The classic modern inflation, of course, is Germany of 1923, when they printed billion Mark notes on one side to save ink. A classic story is told of the man who took a wheelbarrow full of money to the supermarket to buy a loaf of bread and he couldn't get the wheelbarrow through the door so he left it on the sidewalk, assuming that no one would steal the money because it was so worthless. He was right. When he went out to get his money, it was scattered all over the sidewalk and the wheelbarrow was gone.

We had a runaway inflation in China and in many parts of Europe after World War II. We've seen horrible inflation in Brazil, Peru, and Chile and we had an icy brush with the economic grim reaper here at home when the true U.S. inflation rate hit around 15% in 1974. England has been grappling with 12% to 25% inflation. In each instance, it has caused a decline in prestige and economic power, undesirable social changes, hardship, and, more often than not, dictatorship. The Peruvian government had to declare martial law and battle with rioters protesting 42% price inflation. Argentina is a military dictatorship with terrorist gangs shooting policemen, and policemen organizing illegal vigilante groups and executing suspected terrorist sympathizers. When their inflation rate hit 800%, banks were offering 120% interest with no takers, and there, as well as in Chile, the temporary solution was to try to keep the lid on by repression.

The question which naturally arises is—why did the Argentine and Brazilian currencies collapse completely? They seem to be getting inflation under control.

First, they are small economies existing in a world dominated by the dollar. They have the IMF, The World Bank, and the great multinational banks to bail them out. Through dictatorship and international rescue operations they have temporarily put a lid on their problems. Second, their scenarios are not fully played out yet. When the U.S. inflationary monster escapes its cage, who will recapture it? The IMF? The banks? When the world's dominant currency fades, everybody is in trouble and no one is big enough to bail it out. Greece could fall in a Roman world without unsettling that world, but Rome couldn't.

In China, the result was a Communist transformation into the most regimented anthill society the world has ever seen, and, of course, the German inflation of 1920-23 created a fertile womb wherein a Hitler could be nurtured.

What is inflation? How do we get it, and what does it do to us? And will we see it bust loose here in uncontrolled form?

The term "inflation" means one thing to the economist and another thing to the public. The economist knows that inflation is an increase in the money supply. We "inflate" the money supply by creating money, either through the printing press, through the fractional-reserve banking system, or the actions of the Federal Reserve, or a combination of all three.

When a country's money supply is fully redeemable in gold, there is built-in discipline as to how much money can be created. If a government knows it might lose its gold by redeeming too much paper money, the politicians have to be very careful how much paper they print. As a result, it eventually becomes the objective of politicians in all paper money economies to get rid of the gold standard and establish "fiat money" (unbacked paper, declared to be money by a government edict, or "fiat") so that more money can be created and more and more "benefits" can be "given" to its citizens to earn the gratitude of the voters. Alexander Tytler, a Scottish economist of the late 18th century, said that democracies decline when "the majority of the people discover they can vote themselves benefits from the public treasury." This is not likely as long as there is the discipline of gold-backing. Gold, that so-called "relic of barbarism," is maligned by the big spenders of today because it is their enemy.

Here's a simple analogy. If you went to an antique auction and you and everyone else in the room had $1,000 with which to bid, the highest price for which the antiques could be sold is $1,000. But if somehow you were able to put an extra $100 in cash or credit in the hands of some of the people in the room, the price of the antiques would go up, because there would be more money available to bid. The favored people who got the extra $100 would be the successful bidders and they would get the available goods. In the meantime, the purchasing power of all the money in the room, stated in terms of antiques, would be less, as the price would "rise." The antiques had not changed, but the people's ability to buy them had decreased. I'll have more to say about that auction later.

In effect, when government creates money and spends it into existence by bestowing it upon its favored groups, their purchasing power is temporarily increased and yours is diminished, because this new money filtering into the free-market auction place creates buying demand and bids up the price of everything. When your money cannot buy as much as it used to, the value of your money has declined and it is worth less. That's inflation!

Monetary inflation is a thief. It robs you who do not have wage escalator clauses in your union contracts or whose income is fixed. That $300 a month annuity that looked so good 20 years ago now assures only a not-so-genteel poverty. However, even those of you who have cost-of-living escalator clauses in your contracts are raped by inflation (and government is the pervert that does it) simply because the value of your savings is chewed away faster than you can earn interest. Inflation transfers your spending power to government as surely as if the government had taken the dollars away from you and spent them. Inflation gets at your savings, your bonds, your stocks and your check book balances. In short, any monetary assets denominated in paper dollars are stolen from you.

So inflation is truly a tax.

Government can create money by printing it and loaning it to veterans, minority businessmen, etc., or even foreign countries who will eventually bring it back to this country to spend, deposit, or invest.

It can increase the money supply through the Federal Reserve, by allowing the banks to keep a smaller percentage of cash deposits on hand while loaning larger amounts of newly created money. In fact, money has a tremendous multiplying effect through the banks. Here's how.

If you had $1,000 in the bank and I asked you how much money you had, you would say, "I have $1,000." The bank doesn't keep that money safe and untouched for you. It is paying you interest, so it has to earn some money with it.* Under the present rules, it can lend $850 of it to someone else. If you ask the person to whom they lent it how much money he has, he will say, "$850." You still claim you have $1,000, so your $1,000 has grown to $1,850 and no one has printed or coined anything. His $850 gets spent and ends up in other checking accounts, which the banks can also use as reserves against which they will loan additional funds—up to 85 cents on the dollar, and this continues until roughly only 5% of the money supply in this country is actually printed or coined and the other phantom 95% consists of computer bookkeeping.

Many economists (Milton Friedman, Arthur Burns, etc.) say that the money supply

---

*Under 1980 banking legislation, banks can loan even more. The money machine has even more horsepower.

should be expanded at the same rate as the expansion of goods and services, so these two factors will balance out, and it would not be inflationary. That's theoretically very sound. However, in the real world, human nature being what it is, and politicians being what they are, government cannot resist temptation, and, with its encouragement, the citizens vote themselves benefits from the public treasury. The politicians are unwilling to take the heat of voting to directly tax you to pay for all of it, so they create budget deficits, and Uncle Sam creates the needed money through the Federal Reserve, and the money supply increases at a rate faster than the real wealth. The net effect is an increase in prices, or, more properly, a decrease in the purchasing power of your money. The net result is that you have been taxed to pay for the deficit. The inflation tax is hidden and not understood, which makes it the favorite of government.

No politician likes to vote for a direct tax bill, because he can become the visible target of your anger. Look at the Jarvis-Gann tax limitation initiative in California as well as similar movements in other states. It succeeded because it was aimed at the most visibly repugnant of taxes—the property tax. Unfortunately, Jarvis-Gann also hit the most responsive efficient level of government, the local level. The property tax was an easy target, because it hits with such an immense impact. If there had been a *withholding* property tax, and no regular assessment notices to remind you how bad it is, and it just nibbled away at you a little bit at a time, there probably would have been no property tax revolt.

The Inflation Tax is like a ghost. You can't get a handle on it. The average person doesn't have the slightest idea who causes inflation, so government can blame big business and big labor when they respond to the government-created inflationary spiral by trying to keep their purchasing power or profits up to snuff. Wages rise, when prices are boosted to cover wages, and higher wages are demanded again to keep up with increased prices, etc., and they play a game of leapfrog which no one can win because there's no finish line.

As Pogo said, "We have seen the enemy, and he is us." It is our fault for two reasons:

1. Our ignorance. Few of us understand the process, so we let them get away with it.
2. Even if we understood the process, we would still like our personal benefits because they give us money to spend we did not have before, especially if you are one of the favored groups upon which government bestows its generosity. And, because your increased income gives you more borrowing power, you can increase your debt and spend more. And then you are one of the Joneses, living on borrowed money and borrowed time, and you are not about to give back your benefits.

According to a study by the North American Newspaper Alliance, approximately 56%* of the people in this country receive tax money and are largely dependent upon it.

---
*This study is now outdated. The percentage is even higher.

Disabled and Direct Support (including Dependents)	10,500,000
Retirees and Pensioners (including Dependents)	35,300,000
Public Assistance and Unemployed (including Dependents)	26,073,000
Government Workers and Dependents	47,251,000
Active Armed Forces Personnel and Dependents	5,137,000
Total people	124,261,000

And that does *not* include workers for government contractors (Lockheed, etc.), merchants and suppliers serving government installations and military bases, and those who use government services (farmers, small businessmen, private pilots, schools, etc.), and a zillion others, including all those who are looking forward to collecting Social Security some day.

Don't bet on a significant number of these people giving back the money. Government money is like a cancer that has spread through more than 56% of society. The odds are, it's got you, too. See if this composite biography sounds like anyone you know.

> A young man attended public school, rode the free school bus, and participated in the subsidized lunch program. He entered the Army, and then upon discharge retained his National Service Insurance. He then attended the State University, on the GI Bill.
>
> Upon graduation, he married a Public Health nurse and bought a farm with an FHA loan, and then obtained an RFC loan to go into business. A baby was born in the county hospital.
>
> Later he put part of his land in the soil bank, and the payments helped pay for his farm and ranch. His father and mother lived on his ranch on their Social Security; REA

lines supplied him with electricity. The government helped clear his land. The County Agent showed him how to terrace it, then the government built him a fishpond and stocked it with fish.

Books from the Public Library were delivered to his door. He banked his money and a government agency insured it. His children attended public schools, rode free school buses, played in the public parks, and swam in the public pools.

He was a leader in obtaining the new Federal building, and went to Washington with a group to ask the government to build a great dam. He petitioned the government to give the local air base to the County.

Then one day, after hearing that Carter's $500 billion budget for 1979 added up to $2,000 for every man, woman, and child, he wrote his Congressman.

"I wish to protest these excessive governmental expenditures and attendant high taxes. I believe in rugged individualism. I think people should stand on their own two feet without expecting handouts. I am opposed to all socialistic trends and I demand a return to the Principles of our Constitution and of State Rights.

Author Unknown. (Edited slightly)

WINNERS AND LOSERS

Inflation, like any other game, has some who win and some who lose. Let's list the losers first.

1. *People Who Lend Money*. This includes those who have deposits in the bank, cash value

in their life insurance policy, 1st and 2nd mortgages, and bonds—corporate, municipal or federal. It's very simple. They will be paid back in dollars of less value than the ones they loaned. If the inflation rate is 10% and you receive a 10% return on your investment you are breaking even. Or are you? Let's go back and look at that again. If you paid 20% taxes on your interest, here's how it would work out.

	$1000	invested (loaned)
+	100	earned interest
	$1100	total
Less	20	income tax
	$1080	
Less	108	purchasing-power loss (10% inflation)
	$972	remaining value of your capital
	$ 28	net loss in purchasing power (2.8%)

A slight loss, right? But, if you depend upon the interest for your living expenses and you spend the $80 (your after-tax earnings) to live on, where do you stand?

	$1000	invested (loaned)
+	100	earned interest
	$1100	total
Less	20	income tax
	$1080	
Less	108	purchasing-power loss (10% inflation)
	$972	value of your capital
Less	80	spent to live on
Grand total	$ 892	purchasing power remaining

You now have $108 less purchasing power than you started with—a loss of 10.8% per year.

So there you are, folks. Many of you have been taught to only spend your interest, and never touch your capital. Right? *Well, if you are spending your interest, you are consuming your capital.*

How high a rate of return do you have to have to break even? In a 10% inflationary world, assuming a 20% income tax rate (unrealistically low, but I don't want to load the case to make my point), you need almost a 20% return on your money to break even and earn a true 4% return, after taxes and inflation. Unless, of course, you reinvest all of the interest proceeds in which case you still need about a 15% rate of return to break even after taxes and inflation. And if your tax bracket is higher than 20% it's even worse.

Now, do you believe inflation rips off the lender?

2. *The Saver is a Loser* if he puts his money in a bank or Savings and Loan and earns a rate of return lower than the rate of inflation because he's really a lender. If he buys a Certificate of Deposit to get a slightly higher rate, his money is tied up for a long period of time, and he can be destroyed quickly if inflation really gets going into the 20% to 30% range.* Because spending beyond your means is basically immoral, and saving is basically moral and essential for the nation to be able to build capital for growth and investment, inflation forces us into lousy decisions, beginning with the conclusion that saving and lending is dumb, unless, of course, you don't understand the process and are dumb enough to continue to save and lend. Fortunately for the vote buyers and the borrowers, the lenders and savers haven't yet caught on.

---

*I am even more convinced this is a conservative inflation range for the next few years. We saw 20% briefly early in 1980.

3. *Pensioners Will Lose Big.* If you have set up an annuity or are counting on your Social Security, your company retirement plan, your state or city pension plan, or your Military pension, you will be in bad shape, because the purchasing power of those dollars will be zilch by the time you get them.

What about I.R.A. and Keogh plans? They are based on the assumption that if you can set aside tax-free money for retirement into an investment fund and have it earn tax-free dollars, when you do take it out years from now you will supposedly be in a lower tax bracket. With an I.R.A. (for wage earners) you can set aside up to $1,500 of your wages tax-free each year. The Keogh (for self-employed) limit is $7,500.

If they are such a good deal, why don't I like them?

First, I don't think it's a safe assumption that you will be in a lower tax bracket. Inflation is accelerating us all into higher tax brackets. The odds are you will be in an equal or higher bracket and the tax savings will be nonexistent.

Also, rising inflation will chew up capital faster than you earn interest, and you'll get back cheaper dollars than you put in.

These plans are inflexible. It is difficult, costly, or impossible to switch them from one kind of investment to another, and with the changing environment you need to be prepared to switch between hard money and paper. If you do, the tax penalties are severe. I am most concerned with the programs offered by insurance companies and savings and loans which are totally inflexible and oriented in the direction of paper investments. You are a lender. Even if the savings and loan and insurance companies don't go broke, the money is going to go broke, and you will be locked in. You will have climbed into a leaky lifeboat.

There are some Keogh plans using gold and diamonds, which makes them more acceptable. The only two I know of are Reliance Diamonds (see Appendix), who can help you with a diamond Keogh, and Investment Rarities (see Appendix), who can help you with a gold Keogh.

I'm not an expert on these plans. I'm just pointing out how they fit into the future as I see it. With the inflation in your future, they are simply guaranteed instruments of confiscation over the long haul.

Eventually, government will repudiate all of its debt by paying you off in worthless dollars. However, those who receive government pensions are a very potent voting bloc and they probably will have their benefits increased to keep pace with the inflation for some time, but eventually that will bankrupt the pension system because that burden will fall back on the rest of the taxpayers, and they'll revolt.

More about Social Security later.

THE WINNERS

I spend five hours a day reading newsletters, economic reports and newspapers, and I've concluded that most financial advisors don't understand money and none of them understand politics. We have to look at the winners, and the losers who think they are winners, in order to understand why inflation is going to keep going, and here they are, starting with the biggest winners in order of benefit.

1. *The Borrowers.* And who is the biggest borrower of all? Why, Uncle Sam, of course, with the cities and states next in line. They know they will pay off their debt in dollars worth far less than the ones they borrowed. In an inflationary spiral, the one who gets the money first and spends it is the one who gains the greatest benefit, because he spends it before it filters, multiplies and compounds through the economy, driving up prices. That's precisely what government does. It is also a calculated, deliberate policy to inflate at a "controlled rate." Inflation is a form of bankruptcy and repudiation of debt, so they try to do it a little at a time to avoid alarming anyone. When it gets out of hand, they will do like the German government did in 1923 when they paid off all those patriotic German bondholders to the pfennig with money which had the total spending power of one American penny. The government didn't go broke, the money went broke, and the people who bought those bonds (the lenders) got ripped off. Our government is following the same process. Don't expect government to cut its own throat by really cutting inflation. Government benefits too greatly.

2. Other winners are those who bought bigger houses by obtaining bigger mortgages. The bigger the house, the bigger the inflation

profits. As inflation increases the price level of their homes, they see their equity growing and they feel rich, and if they cash in at the right time and get off the debt pyramid, they truly are. They will pay back their mortgages with very cheap dollars. In fact, in a real runaway inflation, you might be able to pay off your mortgage with one week's or one month's salary.

This pay-off concept is presented beautifully in Benjamin Stein's novel, *On The Brink*, a story of a not unlikely future when a White House decision is made, once inflation gets out of hand, to deliberately accelerate it so that millions of Americans with mortgages and debts can pay them off with a few days' salary. The idea is political dynamite for a while, as there are more debtors than there are mortgage holders and landlords. At least, that is the way it is perceived. Everyone ignores the fact that the solvency of their banks, their pension funds, and their insurance companies are at stake, and in the economic ignorance of the American people, they enthusiastically jump on the idea.

3. Those borrowers who use the borrowed money productively and cautiously to invest in counter-cyclical investments do just fine. They will pay off their loans with cheap dollars, and build fortunes through leverage.

4. Those who invest early in chaos or disaster hedges do best of all, especially if they use leverage wisely. This includes gold, silver, antiques, collectible items—those things to which people instinctively turn when the value of paper money is diminishing in an attempt to beat

the loss of purchasing power that inflation brings, and in fact, that inflation *is*.

5. Those who merchandise these items. Anyone in the antique, art, stamp, coin, diamond, or food storage business should do very well during the runaway inflationary spiral, especially if they sell their businesses near the peak.

6. Investors in small town real estate. The quality of life in large cities will deteriorate, for reasons I'll explain later, and there will be an exodus of middle-class money, talent, businesses and investments to the small towns of America.

7. Anyone who gets through all this "even with the game" is a winner. He will have the resources to pick up some incredible bargains after the inflationary spiral has run its course and there's been an explosive complete collapse of the economy. There will be incredible bargains in stocks, bonds, real estate and a myriad of other things, which we will discuss later for those who had the foresight just to preserve their purchasing power.

Inflation is a destroyer, but more than that, it is a genie that once let out of the bottle can never be put back.

INFLATION OR DEFLATION?

As this book is written, there is great controversy among the "hard money" investment advisors as to whether or not we are headed for more inflation or a destructive deflationary depression like the 1930's. Remember the Maginot Line? When the Germans outflanked the Maginot Line with paratroops and fast-moving Panzer divisions, the guns were pointing in the wrong direction. Like the generals who built the Maginot Line, the deflationists are fighting the last war. Because the American decision-making generation is still re-living the last great deflationary depression of the 30's, our most predictable reaction will always be to inflate the currency to fight deflation and depression, just as the Germans have so far refused to inflate (thank goodness!) because they are still fighting their "last war" against the great inflation of the 1920's. We will not see deflation before a hyperinflation has run its course. The people who propose that we will allow deflation simply do not understand politics or the human equation. Government will spend more than it collects in taxes and the Federal Reserve will accommodate their inflationary money requirements.

Let's examine why there will be no deflationary depression until after inflation has devoured us.

Once inflation reaches a certain point, governments conclude, and quite rightly, that they must continue to inflate or die politically. If they do not inflate, their inaction will cause a deflationary depression, and it will be obvious who caused it, and no politician wants his name associated with that.

The only way you could have deflation now is if the government deliberately stopped creating money at a rate needed to meet the demand for money. Remember, deflation means an increase in the value of money. You can only increase its value by having less of it. You can only have less of it if politicians and money managers suddenly get the guts to reverse the process and kick us into a deflationary depression as a deliberate act. That just ain't agonna happen, although they may try cautiously for a while until unemployment rises, business falls off, and the resulting political and economic pain triggers Uncle Feelgood into cranking up the money machine again.

Price inflation now has a life of its own, independent of the monetary simulus that started it, because most everyone has a cost-of-living escalator built into his labor contract, and businessmen raise prices in anticipation of future price and wage inflation. Prices can even increase in the face of monetary contraction.

When price inflation reaches a certain point, it causes disruptions in the economy that can only be solved with more money, and then only temporarily. For example, if you have 20% to 30% inflation, the whole American business and distribution system, which extends credit for 30 days, could periodically and randomly be interrupted. Take wheat, for example. The farmer sells grain to the elevator operator, who sells it to the miller, who sells it to the bakery, who sells the bread to the distributor, who sells it to the supermarket chain, who accepts your check. At every point along the line, each link in the chain buys and sells on 30 day credit. If money is losing value at the rate of 20% to 30%, the party who extends 30 day credit has an inflationary loss on his accounts receivable of 2% to 2.5%. Remember, those who extend credit get ripped-off by inflation, so he either (1) starts charging interest on what used to be net accounts, (a cost which has to be passed on to the next level), or (2) he demands cash, creating a need for an increase in the money supply to prevent interest rates from exploding out of sight, or (3) he just raises his prices. These price increases are compounded several times as they move through each step in the distribution chain until the effect on the retail price level is explosive. All three of these factors are inflationary, with a bias towards the printing press, and we can quickly move from a credit economy into a printing press economy.

It used to be thought that you could extinguish the inflationary fire by raising interest rates and taxes to reduce spendable income and cool off demand, while discouraging borrowing and expansion. However, our fire extinguishers are loaded with kerosene, as taxes and interest are merely passed on in the price structure to the next level. In fact, taxes help make inflation permanent.

There is no way a businessman can deflate prices when so many of his costs are inelastic. During the depression of the 30's, the businessman or manufacturer had only two primary cost factors to be concerned with—labor and materials. Because the prices of these things were collapsing, he could reduce retail prices, and he did. You didn't have much money but you could buy a loaf of bread for a nickel. Today, a businessman has inflexible and rising costs, including the costs of government regulation, property taxes, social security taxes, high interest rates, high wages protected by union contracts and minimum-wage laws, price-supported commodities, etc., and all these costs have to be passed on in his prices. Because of this, rather than reducing prices to stimulate demand, when demand drops in a recession or depression, he plans to manufacture and sell fewer units and raises his prices to make more money per unit. That's why during 1974 and 1975, when unemployment was high and the economy was coming to a screeching halt, we still had the highest rate of inflation the nation had seen in almost a century. So inflation is intractable, and don't let anybody "kid you otherwise." Unless, of course, government slashes spending, sells its printing presses, stops regulating, eliminates price supports and minimum wage laws, and deliberately throws us into a gut-wrenching, election-blowing depression. Eisenhower held inflation to 1.4%—and lost both Houses of Congress, so don't hold your breath.*

Here's another possible scenario, explaining how we can become a "printing press" economy, or, in other words, how the government could be forced to start grinding out paper money.

Principle No. 1. The Germans went from a credit economy to a printing press economy in a little over three years. Basically here's how it happened.

As government deficits created demands for continuing increases in the money supply,

---

*Now that the Republicans have gained control of the Senate, we'll see if Reagan and his friends on the hill can do the tough things and hold that control in 1982. I'm hopeful, but dubious.

interest rates began to rise along with the price inflation rate. The rise in interest rates led to a fall in the value of bonds. (That's further explained in Chapter 3.) Worsening economic conditions led to more demands on government, larger deficits, more inflation and higher interest rates (as high as 10,000%), and eventually the bond markets collapsed entirely. The government, however, could not cut back on its spending because of the political demands of the people, so, rather than issuing bonds, which no one would buy anyway, they simply "monetized their debt," which means that, rather than going into the capital markets and borrowing the money to fund their deficits, they printed the money directly.

Principle No. 2. In our present economy, the government tries to fund its deficits by going into the capital markets and borrowing from the existing money supply. While trying to maintain a relatively steady growth in the money supply of around 3% to 7%, with little success. As the demands on government increase during recession, and the taxing system runs smack into the tax revolt, the deficits will begin to explode. Soon the government cannot meet its borrowing requirements from the capital markets without driving out all other borrowers and creating a horrendous depression, so they are forced to increase the money supply. But they can't increase it enough to ease the interest rate pressures. As interest rates continue to rise, bond prices collapse and soon it becomes impossible for the government to borrow money, as people begin to thoroughly distrust any fixed-interest debt instruments (just as most of my clients and I do now). The government then has an interesting choice: cut the budget, reduce spending, and cancel government programs, plunging us into deflationary depression and take the political flak, or go directly to the printing press. I am betting they will go directly to the printing press. There is no example in history of anyone having done otherwise, except military dictatorships, and fortunately, a military dictatorship would be hard to fully implement in this country. We don't have a national police force and we don't have a large, dependable army to enforce it.

Principle No. 3. There are forces already in motion which will increase public demand on government sufficient to cause the deficit to explode in the next few years.

As the dollar crashes, as it has been doing, foreign investors in American government securities will bail out and the Arabs will try to pull their short-term deposits out of the New York banks. The government, in order to rescue the banking system, will be forced to resort to the printing press to replace that lost money.

If the tax revolt spreads and Jarvis-Gann type laws became the order of the day, the states will find themselves running terrible deficits, and their credit ratings with the bond rating agencies will fall apart, as has already happened in some California cities and counties. The states will then be faced with either truly cutting back on services, or simply dumping their problems on Washington. The federal government, after an appropriate period of denials and protests, will comply, as the Administration cannot do otherwise and have any hope of being re-elected. This can only be done with printing press money. As we move into the recession and our cities and states find themselves in deeper trouble, it's going to require massive amounts of federal money to guarantee their bonds and to provide the necessary unemployment insurance and other benefits. Twenty-nine states exhausted their unemployment insurance funds during the 1975-78 expansion! What's it going to be like when we get into a deep recession?

When the depression strikes, the Lesser Developed Countries will default on their debt to the large banks, and the Federal government will have to trot out more money to bail out the banks. We are the lender of last resort for the entire world, due to the loans the big multinational banks have made to these countries, and the government will not allow those banks to go broke, even at the cost of hyper-inflation. They *are* the monetary system of the world.

Cities, states, and the Federal government in the next recession will be stuck with a monstrous problem of declining tax revenues and increasing demands on government to alleviate the suffering caused by recession, unemployment and business slowdown and to keep the blood out of the streets.

While all of this is going on, this insane witches' brew of problems will be stewed in the pot of more inflation, as all of this printing press money flooding the economy will result in high-velocity spending, with people frantically trying to keep up with the cost of living by buying before prices go up, but losing ground, and we will be faced with the spectre of inflation and depression at the same time. If you don't think that can happen, take a look at Germany in the early 20's. Take a look at the United States in '74 and '75. They are different, only in degree, not in kind.

The argument of the deflationists that the collapse of the bond markets is deflationary, is not borne out by history. In fact, it is just the opposite. In the 1930's we were in a deep, *deflationary* depression and bond prices, particularly government bond prices, were at all time highs. In fact, they were so high that they sold at negative yields. Paper money increased in value and would buy more. Government securities were considered the safest investment of all. In the German *inflationary* depression however, the bond markets collapsed in 1920. If that were deflationary, you would not have had the runaway paper money inflation of 1920 through 1923. Historically, the bond markets collapse in inflations. In deflations, bond values increase.

Those who argue deflation are basically saying that paper money will increase in value, which means that would be the best holding of all. History records no instance of a hyper-inflationary spiral ending with a substantial increase in the value of paper money. And I don't think it's about to happen now.

Will Rogers said, "Invest in inflation, it's the only thing that's going up." And that's a very sound principle. If you have to periodically buy something on a regular basis, and prices rise, you are hurt by inflation. But if you already bought a lot of it when it was cheap, then you can watch your wealth increase and you are on good terms with the inflationary monster.

Parts II and III of this book will tell you how to do it. There are ways to ride to wealth through inflation, while limiting its damage.

3
A WORLD TURNED UPSIDE DOWN

If an unsophisticated widow goes to a conservative financial advisor or trust officer of a bank, trying to get income with safety from a $100,000 insurance policy, he will probably give her a "conservative" portfolio consisting of AAA government, municipal, and corporate bonds, Blue Chip stocks such as General Motors, AT&T and the like, and perhaps some utility bonds or preferred stocks. If he's really daring, he might suggest 10% second mortgages or a few AA or A rated bonds for higher yields. Some money would go into long-term C.D.'s and a small amount in demand deposits. Over-all, if he did a super job, she might get 8½% yield, which would give her $8,500 in income to supplement her Social Security check.

That's the conservative way to do it. If anything went wrong, the advisor would be blameless, as he was "conservative." But you have been conditioned to live in a money world that no longer exists. What you and that bank trust officer don't realize is that the financial world is turned upside down. That portfolio will eventually destroy you, as surely as if you periodically walked into the bank and burned some of your money. And inflation is the villain.

Let's look at each of these investments in an inflationary period.

THE STOCK MARKET

The stock market has been deathly ill since 1966. At that time the Dow Jones Industrial Average peaked a little over 1,000 and it has been struggling ever since, with at least two massive retreats in between, to break permanently over that 1,000 mark again. If it does, we'll all cheer. Or rather, you will. I won't, because it's no big deal. If you adjust stock prices for inflation, in order to regain the purchasing power equivalent of the 1966 Dow Jones today, the Dow Jones would have to go to almost 2,000.*
Put another way, after adjusting for inflation, the Dow Jones at 1,000 is really around 500† in 1966 terms. Now, if you still think that 1,000 D.J. would be a good deal, then you haven't been listening. Up until 1966, anybody could make money by buying good quality stocks and holding on. General Motors, AT&T, U.S. Steel—those were "widows and orphans" stocks and many a conservative portfolio prospered during

---
*Make that 2,500 now.
†Make that 400 now.

that postwar era. However, those "conservative Blue Chips" now fluctuate widely, and though they have always paid their dividend, at any given time you could have substantial capital losses. The market price stability of the "widows and orphans" stocks is a thing of the past.

The only way to beat the game today is by trading, but the odds are against you. As Harry Schultz, the world's highest priced financial advisor, told me at a conference in the Bahamas, "you can make money in anything as long as you are willing to short the market when it's going down and buy when it's going up," and he's right, with certain qualifications. This kind of in-and-out trading requires a temperament which can coolly cut losses and allow profits to run. Most traders lost money, even in bull markets, because they do not have the temperament for the marketplace.

1. They are afraid to buy when prices are low and everyone is discouraged, which is precisely the time they should be buying. Their temperament will not allow them to do it.

2. When they have made a bad choice, they are afraid to "take a loss." I don't know how many times I've had people say to me, "I can't afford to sell that stock. I can't afford the loss. I have to wait until it comes back." Then they end up letting their losses run on, or they sell at the first sign of break-even. I can't think of a better way to lose money than to cut your winnings and to let your losses run. That ain't the way it's supposed to work. Stock market profits come to those who have the temperament to

deal with the marketplace. If you have the guts to handle it, the stock market has some real possibilities, as long as you are prepared to be an in-and-out trader. Those who recommend the widows-and-orphans-buy-and-hold approach to the stock market today are fools. If you don't have the temperament to trade, stay out!

Why is the stock market behaving in this way? Inflation. The stock market, as my friend Dick Russell, publisher of *The Dow Theory Letters* (see Appendix), is fond of saying, tends to sum up everything that everybody knows about anything and the market is usually wiser than the analysts. Stock prices, over the long haul, tend to discount reality. By that I mean that if there's something wrong with earnings, or the economy, and we can't quite put our finger on it, the market seems to sense it, and stocks often appear to be "under-valued" for good reason. I believe that most corporate earnings are grossly overstated. Here's just one reason.

Under our present tax laws, corporations are not allowed to set aside sufficient depreciation reserves to truly meet the inflationary cost of replacement and modernization of plants and facilities. These understated, inadequate depreciation allowances tend to make earnings look much better than they are. The market somehow knows that, and the "price earnings ratio" that the market is willing to put on a stock has been dropping steadily for some years. If the true replacement cost were reflected in corporate earnings reports, you would understand why the stock market is down. Inflation in construction, real estate, heavy equipment, computers, etc., is villain number one. And the market also knows that the future for business is dubious at best when inflation rages.

BONDS

If you care to understand why bonds are a lousy investment for widows and orphans, you need to understand how the bond market works. I'll keep it simple and try not to go down deep and come up dry.

Bonds are I.O.U.s issued by some corporate or governmental entity. They are generally sold in $1,000 denominations. If you buy one when it is issued, and redeem it at maturity, 20 or 30 years later, you will have received regular interest payments, generally by clipping a coupon and redeeming it at your bank or at the company that issued the bond, and you will be repaid the face or "par" value in dollars. That used to be the most conservative way to invest, if the issuer's credit merited a good rating. But then that "Ole Debbil" inflation rears its ugly head and ruins your financial Garden of Eden.

I've already explained in Chapter 2 how you lose money in fixed-return investments through inflation unless you receive impossibly high interest returns, and that's bad enough, but let me show you what else happens to your money in an inflationary spiral. Long-term lenders always want an interest return that protects them against the expected future rate of inflation, plus 3% or 4% real return on their money. If you needed to sell your 6%, $1,000 bond, which yields $60 in gross interest, you wouldn't be able to sell it for $1,000 if interest rates generally have risen above your 6% yield. Would you buy a 6% bond if 8% bonds were available? Sure you would—at a discount! If interest rates generally should rise to 10%, and new 10% bonds are available, your bond could only be sold at a huge discount. It could drop to a market value of as little as $600, because of the $60 fixed return interest coupon would give a 10% return on that $600 purchase price. The longer the term, the deeper the drop. So, these are the basic principles.

1. Interest rates always rise in a period of runaway inflation.

2. When interest rates rise, the market value of a bond will fall. If you want or need to sell, you could take large capital losses, If you hang on, you take your inflation beating year by year, which, even in a "controlled" inflation, is like being nibbled to death by ducks. But when inflation really explodes to 30% or 50% or 100% a year, you are wiped out in a big hurry.

The same thing is true of C.D.'s, insurance cash values and, in fact, *anything that gives you a fixed return*. The rate of inflation eventually gets to you and chews up any possibility of profit.

To repeat, if you spend the interest to live on, *you are actually consuming your capital, as your interest return must be reinvested just to partly keep up with the inflationary loss and keep your capital intact.*

Remember, inflation is a transfer tax, a means by which government transfers wealth from those who have savings and capital to those favored groups to whom it wishes to grant benefits. It is a dishonest transfer of wealth, even more sure and infinitely more insidious than direct taxation and it is a deliberate policy of government.

My Uncle Buck used to tell the following story: "We had a horse back on the farm that ate so much oats one winter it was eating us out of house and barn, and we were pretty poor, so we decided to teach him how to eat sawdust. We started out by mixing a little sawdust with his oats and each day we added a little more and a little more and a little more, until pretty soon we had him eating over 65% sawdust."

At this point, he always stopped, and I would step right into his trap. I said, "Uncle Buck, how did the plan work out?" Uncle Buck said, "We don't know. About that time, the darn horse died and ruined the experiment."

A LITTLE ADVICE

In an inflationary environment, the only possible justification for owning bonds, C.D.'s, cash value insurance, or anything that returns interest at anything less than roughly twice the rate of inflation, is if you have so much money that you can afford to watch it erode away under the assumption that you only have a few years to live, and you will be gone before your money will. Don't count on it. At the rate things are going, you will probably outlive your money.

In a later chapter, I will cover the opportunities to be enjoyed in bonds when interest rates are falling. Just as bond prices fall when interest rates are rising, the market value of bonds rises when interest rates are falling, and there are some great capital gains to be made at the right time, and that could become part of our basic strategy sometime down the road when the recovery begins. If you only knew one thing—which way interest rates were going—you could get rich buying and selling bonds. But for now, just smile politely when the trust officer tells you to buy bonds.

All this presents you with a real dilemma if you are depending on income from your investments for living expenses. What can you do? Well, there are several good choices, but just to keep you in suspense, I will not discuss them now. I'll get into that in considerable detail in a later chapter, as, in this part of the book, we are dealing with problems, not solutions.

The principle is. In a period of rising interest rates, the shorter the maturity, the less chance for capital losses.

In a period of *falling* interest rates, long maturity paper, like 30 year government bonds, increases in market value. Not only could you get a high rate of interest return if you buy them when interest rates peak, but you get potentially spectacular capital gains as interest rates fall and the prices rise. This will only work if we come out of the next recession without the Big Crash, and interest rates and inflation ease up, as they did in 1976 and 1977. But it's possible we could have one more up-cycle before that big event, and we should have our strategy ready. If we hyper-inflate now and then move into the final deflationary phase of the cycle, forget it! All bets on bonds are off if the whole darn financial system has come unglued and government has repudiated its indebtedness by paying off with inflationary dollars. And don't laugh. That's exactly what the Germans did. Borrowers paid off their indebtedness at that time and Professor E. W. Kemmerer, in his book *Money*, published by Macmillan in 1937, tells this funny-sick story about the inflation risk to creditors.

> In the latter days of the inflation, when it was feared that there might be a stabilization of the Mark at a value higher than the prevailing one, creditors were reported to have been seen "running away from debtors and debtors pursuing them in triumph and paying them without mercy!"
>
> ... Farmers and urban home owners paid off their mortgages at the cost of a few days' labor or a few bushels of grain. But what the debtor gained, the creditor lost, and creditors were often the most worthy classes in the community, as, for example, the small investors that put their life savings in government bonds or in the bonds of the large corporations—the middle-class clerk or artisan with a savings account, the owner of a life insurance policy upon which premiums had been paid for many years or the widow or orphan living upon the income from trust funds invested in bonds or mortgages. The savings of these people were practically wiped out as well as those of the wealthier classes.

If you are a lender, you might end up being paid off by a ruthless debtor who insists you take depreciated money. After all, inflation is merely a form of gradual bankruptcy by government, the largest debtor of all, so that he can pay you in money worth far less than that which he borrowed from you. And other debtors can use the same strategy.

Another reason to avoid bonds is that the finances of cities, states and corporations will be terribly strained as increased social costs run head on into the tax revolt, consumer spending turns down, businesses pull in their horns, and illusory profits are peeled away.

Now if you don't like what is in this chapter, don't blame me. Blame the guys that did it. We all think we benefit from some aspect of government spending, so we are the engine of inflation.

4
PUTTING GOVERNORS ON THERMOMETERS

Let's go to another auction. Fifteen people are bidding on a piece of industrial equipment. Beside each of them is a bucket filled with paper money, and to make a bid, he must reach into the bucket and pull out the bills immediately prior to making his offer. Then you notice a curious phenomenon: From time to time a man steps behind one or another of the bidders and deposits varying quantities of newly printed money into each man's bucket. Prices climb higher and higher, and as they do, the man scurries faster and faster, refilling first this bucket and then another. Several of the participants seem to get most of the money, but everyone gets extra bills from time to time. They reach in, grab a fistful of bills, shout out the ever-climbing price, and snarl at each other when the bids climb still higher. They are frantic. They all want the item. Some drop out of the bidding, discouraged, but six remain. "This is crazy," they all say. "Prices have never been this high before," they gripe. "This has to stop somewhere." Then: "The government ought to 'Do Something' about these prices."

Eventually, the government "Does Something." Another official steps up to the auctioneer's microphone, while six people are still bidding, and he announces: "That's it, ladies and gentlemen. No further bids." He freezes the price.

But there is only one item for sale, and six bidders want it. But higher bids are now illegal.

So who gets the item? An old friend of the auctioneer? Someone who has been coming to his auctions for many years? A big-ticket spender? Someone who has done some favors in the past for the auctioneer? How about the person who winks and touches his diamond ring? What about that fellow who has a pile of marketable spare auto parts in his garage? Or what if the auctioneer wants the item himself? And who can best make the judgment?

To settle it, the government official may call the other official over to him—the one passing out all the paper money—have him peel off a few bills, and pay the auctioneer the ceiling price. "We will see to it that the person who needs this most will get it." But who needs it most? The government man decides. He has just become the new auctioneer.

Insane, you say. Of course, but that is exactly what we saw under Nixon's price controls, and what some of us remember from World War II, and that's what we'll see in the future. The free market is a giant auction. The man passing out the money is the federal government (or its central bank). The second official is the head of some price control agency. And the disappointed bidders will be us.

With the government controlling prices, creating shortages, and destroying profits in the legal markets, more and more products will be shifted toward the illegal "midnight auctions" of the covert free enterprise system—the Black Market. Price inflation will continue around, past, and beyond the legal price-controlled markets until the price-control system breaks down from lack of compliance—like prohibition—but the damage has been done. Those who are dependent on the legal, visible, official, government-controlled semi-auction markets will have to do without. They will not be able to purchase what they want at the officially sanctioned prices.

If you want to understand the free market system, remember the auction analogy. If you want to understand price inflation, remember the government official with the fiat money. And if you want to understand price controls, remember the phrase: "No further bids."

DISGUISING THE INFLATION

Printing money has always been a governmental

specialty. It's the one thing they do well. In the economic division of labor, mankind has developed a familiar pattern: citizens produce goods and services, while governments produce pieces of paper with ink on them. The person who believes that our government cannot continue to inflate the money supply does not know much about history or politics.

Governments are run by politicians, and politicians do not want to face the full political repercussions of mass inflation. At the same time, they are afraid of taking the single most important step that must be taken if we are to save the dollar, namely, reduce government expenditures until there is a surplus in the Treasury, and then steadily repurchase all government bonds and bills until there is no government debt remaining in the hands of the public or in the accounts of the Federal Reserve System. One economist, Gary North, believes that the person who calls for a balanced federal budget is an unsuspecting Liberal. We ought to have budget surpluses in order to reduce the mountain of federal debt.

The largest component of the long-term federal debt structure is the Social Security System. Most experts agree that system is statistically bankrupt. Politicians have three choices: (1) raise FICA taxes to unacceptable levels by direct taxation, (2) repudiate the whole program, or (3) inflate the currency to meet their obligations. Guess which one is politically acceptable? But since Social Security and federal pension payments are indexed to the cost of living, inflating the currency to pay off these massive multi-trillion-dollar obligations will inevitably backfire, since the flood of "fiat" money will raise prices, requiring increases in benefits, requiring more fiat money, and so on, mandating mass inflation. The politicians, however, will soon impose a politically acceptable short-run cure: freeze all prices, thereby freezing the cost-of-living-index. This way, the government can shut off the cost-of-living escalators, create all the paper money it requires to make the social security payments, and theoretically there will be no threat of increased Social Security System deficits as a result of the rising cost of living.

Of course, black market prices will become astronomical, but that's the only way you can buy what you want. However, black market prices are never, ever inserted in the official cost-of-living index of any nation. Then the bureaucrats and politicians can blame black marketeers for the total devastation of the *real* income of the Social Security System's so-called beneficiaries. In short, good-bye pensions, annuities, and cost-of-living escalators; hello poverty.

PRE-CONTROLS STRATEGY

If you are now persuaded about all this, then you have to give some consideration to a preliminary self-defense strategy. It will involve a systematic program of saving—real saving—meaning a systematic abandonment of conventional forms of saving. Ultimately, it involves a program of "mini-warehousing" of durable goods.

When will controls be imposed? This is a political question and there are no magic formulas that can be used to predict a particular President's response to the public's response to inflationary economic conditions, but it is sensible to prepare beforehand.

What are some of the warning signs?

The most important leading economic indicator of impending price controls is a sustained period of double-digit (10% or more) price inflation in the Consumer Price Index or its 1978-79 parallel. (The government created a new index, so there was a transition period—1978-79—in which two official indices were in use.) If double-digit annual rates are sustained for over six consecutive months, there will be increasing political pressures to Do Something Right Now. If the rate is close to 12%, then it might be a year before controls are imposed—though I would not bet my survival on having a full year—but if the rate is above 15%, it will be a lot shorter—maybe it will have happened by the time you read this.*

The most significant political leading economic indicator has already appeared: an official guarantee that the President will *not* impose price and wage controls, just like Richard Nixon. President Carter announced on April 11, 1978, in a luncheon speech to the American Society of Newspaper Editors: "There are no easy answers. We will not solve inflation by increasing unem-

---

*We lucked out—so far—probably until 1982-83. I still believe we will see controls—Reagan and a Republican Senate notwithstanding. The public demand will be overwhelming.

ployment. We will not impose wage and price controls. We will work with measures that avoid both these extremes" (p. 4 of White House release). A few minutes later he also declared: "It is very important that Congress act now on the proposed Hospital Cost Containment Bill as the most effective means that we can take toward reasonable hospital prices" (p. 7). The news media made no comment on the obvious contradiction of the two statements.

Other signs that controls are coming would be polls announcing that over 50% of the public favors controls. A major industry or union refusal to capitulate to "jawboning" would be another bad sign. If discounts from listed prices start drying up, we have another indicator (this applies primarily to purchases by manufacturing companies). When long-term interest rates start rising to levels above 15% (meaning mortgage rates or prime quality corporate bond issues), the government will probably move into action. Raw materials shortages or a series of strikes that remain unsettled for several months are also conditions that cannot be ignored by the politicians.

Enough of these signs are presently visible that controls are possible before the next presidential election, or in the first years of the next Administration.*

Fortunately, there are ways to beat the game in advance, which I will explore later.

---

*See footnote on previous page.

5
THE PONZI CHAIN LETTER

The inflationary process is a secret, cynical rip-off, but sometimes the truth peeks "out of the closet." Look at the following discussion of Social Security which I extracted from the Congressional Record. This exchange took place during the Social Security hearings between Senator William Proxmire and a Mr. Cardwell of the Social Security Administration.

> SENATOR PROXMIRE: There are 37 million people, is that right, that get Social Security benefits?
>
> MR. CARDWELL: Today between 32 million and 34 million.
>
> SENATOR PROXMIRE: I'm a little high; 32 to 34 million people. Almost all of them, or many

of them are voters. In my state, I figure there are 600,000 voters that receive Social Security. Can you imagine a Senator or Congressman, under those circumstances saying we are going to repudiate that high a proportion of the electorate? No.

Further, we have the capacity under the Constitution, the Congress does, to coin money, as well as to regulate the value thereof. And therefore, we have the power to provide that money. And we are going to do it. It may not be worth anything when the recipient gets it, but he is going to get his benefits paid.

MR. CARDWELL: I tend to agree.

Let's go back to that conservative financial advisor that we talked about in Chapter 3. If you ask him to set up a plan for your retirement, he will probably include your Social Security benefits in your future income projection. You gave that money to the government through payroll deductions to hold in trust for you and they will give it back to you. Right? Wrong!

We've discussed the probability of being paid in worthless dollars, but we've only uncovered the tip of the Social Security fraud iceberg. It's the most dishonest, reprehensible, deceitfully unsound scheme ever foisted by government upon a trusting public—a fraud so huge that the imagination is inadequate to grasp it.

Try this True/ False quiz:

T F Payroll deductions for Social Security

go directly into the Social Security trust fund.

T F Those deductions from your pay check will be used to pay your retirement benefits.

T F It is important to decide whether or not Social Security benefits should be paid strictly from payroll tax deductions or from the general fund.

T F The Social Security trust fund has diminished several billion dollars in recent years.

T F When the trust fund is dissipated, the government will have to start printing currency or borrowing money to pay benefits.

If you marked all of these "False" you score 100%. All of your basic assumption about the Social Security fund are probably false.

As we examine why, bear in mind that the national economy has become dependent upon the Social Security System. It disburses more funds than any other governmental subdivision. It is our biggest single tax. The impact of changes in Social Security payroll taxes or benefits is immense, and if we increase either, the effects on the economy are complex and ultimately negative.

Pensioners are trapped in the system. Most are totally dependent upon it. Millions of people would be in for real suffering if the Social Security System were to go broke, or if benefits were to be cut, or not increased to compensate for cost-of-living increases.

NOW YOU SEE IT, NOW YOU DON'T

When the government forces your employer to deduct Social Security taxes from your paycheck, all of this money, along with your employer's "contribution," go into the General Fund. It is not held separate from other funds. It is all used for current expenses. In lieu of the money that should go into the trust fund, the Treasury Department issues government bonds, notes and bills to Social Security, and they constitute the whole fund—approximately $15 billion in September 1978. The trust fund has never seen any of that money, only these pieces of paper which represent that the government has created money and spent it, and will print more if necessary.

These securities are a liability of the United States Treasury and are secured by "the full faith and credit of the United States government," which means the printing press. When the fund disburses its monthly benefits, it merely calls upon the Treasury to issue checks and money is printed to cover it. *All* the money being paid has to be newly created at the time of payment. The government would do this even if there were no government securities in the Fund. The cost to the taxpayer in inflation would be the same. It's just that everyone feels safer if there are pieces of paper saying the government promises to do this, but it really doesn't make any difference. The so-called Social Security trust fund is nothing more than a glorified set of bookkeeping entries. Just for form's sake, if it issues more money than was collected for FICA, the Treasury merely retires some of those notes, bonds, or bills, and the "Trust Fund" shrinks.

How valuable is a Treasury security held by the Social Security System? If you were to write yourself an I.O.U. for $1 million, add it to your financial statement and take it to the bank to obtain a loan, they would laugh you out of the bank. We cannot create real wealth by giving ourselves our own I.O.U. The Social Security Administration is a division of the United States government holding I.O.U.s of another division of the United States government, with no collateral. This paper represents no value at all. It is not an asset. As a result, the debate over whether the Social Security System should be paid from the general fund or from payroll taxes is simply a discussion of cosmetics—the appearance of things. Already Social Security money is being paid from the general fund by the creation of additional money through the banking system. As long as the government's finances are in deficit, that will always be the case. The so-called depletion of the so-called trust fund is not the real threat to the system. The principal threat is the rising tide of pension payments, supported by fewer workers, and the budget-busting, inflationary impact on the taxpayers. The over-all federal deficit has been increased by whatever amount the Social Security fund is out of balance.

The Social Security System depends upon the confidence of the people that their payroll deductions will be paying for their retirement. That's not true, and never was. The government indulges in bookkeeping games and we are conned. Social Security payroll deductions are simply another method of raising money to fund the government's needs. Your FICA payroll deductions went for defense, Agriculture, FTC, EPA, etc., as well as Social Security benefits.

AND NOW THE BAD NEWS

But the real fraud is the fact that the system is really a gigantic chain letter. Chain letters operate under the assumption that when you add your name to the bottom of the list and send your dollar to the guy at the top, enough other suckers will add their names under yours so that eventually your name will rise to the top and you will get money from those at the bottom. It pays off only if others fall for it. Sooner or later it sputters to a stop and the last guys in lose out.

The Social Security system operates under the same premise. The money taken from you is used to pay benefits to those who are currently receiving benefits, including many who have paid nothing into the system, as the system is being used to achieve social benefits other than the original intent. Because of that, plus cost-of-living increases in benefits, which have outstripped increases in payroll deductions, it is not being operated on a pay-as-you-go basis. The result? The supposed "depletion of the trust fund" which we already discussed. If this were honestly labeled, the admitted Federal budget deficit would be much larger. (See Chapter 11.)

You hope the system will hang together

long enough that when you reach retirement age, others entering the system will be willing to pay enough that you can be paid when you get to the top of the chain letter. You are totally dependent upon a continuous flow of new money from new workers entering the Social Security system. There used to be ninety workers supporting each person in the Social Security program. Now there are three. Fifteen years from now (if the system is still functioning by then—dubious at best), there will be only two. You are making a monstrous bet on your children's willingness to bear that tremendously increased burden, especially because the government is going to buy your vote by increasing your benefits to keep up with the inflation they created, thus adding to our kids' burden. Soon we will reach the point where they don't dare take any more out of people's paychecks, lest it cause a revolt. So they will pay you by the "inflation tax" and, of course, this chews up the value of your money, and even though your benefits will increase, your purchasing power will shrink.

PONZI REVISITED

This is a perfect reflection of a classic fraud case some years ago when a man by the name of Ponzi raised funds from investors by promising huge payoffs. He did nothing productive with the money and earned no profits for his suckers, but he paid huge dividends by borrowing from other investors so that he could continue making these payoffs. The pyramid eventually collapsed of its own weight and Ponzi went to jail only because he didn't have a printing press and couldn't collect the inflation tax. That's considered illegal when private citizens do it, but it's considered "compassionate" social engineering when government does it. As long as the number of new suckers is sufficient to balance the books, then the fraud holds up. But if the number of paying "marks" diminishes to the point where they cannot or will not balance the books, then the system eventually is exposed for the fraud it is. We have gotten away with it for a long time, but now it has become an obvious cause of large government deficits and inflation, and will soon become an out-of-hand political issue. The whole monetary system is then in danger.

CRACKS IN THE PLASTER

Jesse Cornish said in reference to the coming depression, "I think we will see the cracks in the plaster before the roof comes down." I'd like to show you a few of those cracks in the plaster.

First, more people are living longer into their "golden years" and this great voting bloc is treated very carefully by our legislators who continue to increase their benefits faster than payroll deductions. Every medical advance that prolongs life is an enemy of the system. An effective, widely accepted cancer cure would devastate it, because each unanticipated retiree is an enemy and a threat to the system. Even with current mortality rates, too few will be paying for too many.

The baby boom of the 40's and 50's which brought a large number of workers into the system in the 60's and 70's is about over, and fewer worker bees will enter the hive while the number of recipients will increase enormously, and the birth rate is still slowing to well below the replacement rate. If they continue to increase the deductions to maintain the appearance of solvency, the economy will grind to a halt because of this terrible drag on spending power of the American worker.

In addition, the system is threatened by the withdrawal from the system of several states, cities, etc., for whom participation in the system has always been optional. Over 235 such governmental bodies have withdrawn their employees from the system because it produces such poor benefits for the amounts paid in. Alaska recently withdrew and New York has decided to withdraw, and any of their employees who had been paying into the system for less than ten years will lose everything they paid in! Their Social Security benefits go down the drain. It also means fewer people entering at the bottom of the chain letter.

Our senators and congressmen are pretty smart, however. They realize how unsound the system is, so they have their own sound, healthy, fully funded pension program, and their cost-of-living escalators built into their wages and their retirement. Then they can continue cynically voting for inflationary programs and more Social Security taxes and monthly checks because they are insulated from the problems that they have caused. Just remember that, the next time you vote for a big spender.

I am not so much worried that the Social Security system will collapse but the Social Security system will be the cause of the nation's bankruptcy, because it is the single largest obligation of government, and the debt defies description.

According to the 1977 Federal Statement of Liabilities (issued by the Treasury Department every two years), the Social Security system has approximately $4 *trillion* in unfunded obligations. That means it will have to pay out $4 trillion more in benefits to those who are presently covered by the system than it will collect in wages. That's roughly equal to 75% of everything that everyone in America owns.

SELF-FULFILLING PROPHECY?

I've been accused of destroying the very confidence in the system that keeps it alive by telling you all this. It's the old dilemma of whether or not to tell the terminal patient he's dying. I trust the truth. What choice do I have? Sooner or later the problems will be recognized, and the jury-rigged, dishonest, counterfeit, funny-money currency system will collapse of its own weight, whether or not I talk about it. My concern is for you. You must plan your life on the certain premise that Social Security will be of very little help to you, and it may have done a lot of harm.

First, it has discouraged saving, because it

takes money away from *you* that you might have saved, and most people feel that "the Social Security will take care of us." The system has made Social Security "junkies" out of us because even the most sophisticated financial advisors seldom seriously question that the Social Security will be there when needed.

But there is no question in my mind that eventually the Social Security system will overwhelm our monetary system through inflation and the loss of confidence in governmental promises—if the other problems we will be examining don't get us first. Those who will be hurt most are those who were promised the most. The system is immoral, dishonest and unethical and we have become hooked on it. The only way to save the system and the economy would be to slash benefits, which would not only be cruel at this point, but politically impossible. But the greater cruelty is yet to come when the system collapses of its own weight.

Now, what should you do about it? Here are Ruff's Recommendations:

1. Plan your future as though Social Security didn't exist.

2. Realize that if you accept your Social Security check when you don't really need it, you are taking it from some poor guy who had it ripped-off from his paycheck last week. You are not getting back what you gave the government. They spent that a long time ago. Your money is long gone. You are taking it from other overburdened taxpayers. What's the difference between that and welfare? As a matter of principle, even though it is Quixotic and

probably won't accomplish any good in the long run, I'm planning my life to not accept my Social Security check. I'm not sitting in judgment of those who have no other means of support, because I have no objection to helping those in real need, but I do believe that those who accept it and don't need it are only contributing to the collapse of the system.

One other alternative, is to accept it and give it to those who are going to have to pay for it—your children. Let them convert it into the kind of "hard assets" that will survive the trouble ahead, or contribute it to the political campaigns of those who share this free-market, limited-government, economic philosophy, who might help us get the Ship of State through the troubled waters without capsizing. Solve the dilemma as you choose, but please recognize that Social Security is welfare, pure and simple. Your taxes were given to others as "old age welfare" and you will collect "old age welfare," taken from others. The government will transfer that wealth from them to you, either by the FICA deduction or through the inflation tax which is, of course, the cleverest way to transfer wealth.

And incidentally the next time you get all starry-eyed about population control or no-growth, just remember what it means to the pension programs of the nation if the birth rate continues to drop and our productive capacity stops growing and there are fewer suckers for the chain letter.

Social Security leaves us nothing but bad choices. If the system goes broke, we face the specter of our parents starving if we can't take care of them. If they do increase taxes sufficiently to maintain the appearance of solvency, they place a burden on the economy it cannot endure. This is only of the reasons why I've consistently said over the years that we've long since passed a point of no return where there are no political remedies that will give us a soft landing in the abyss into which we are falling. All you can do is batten down the hatches and get ready. If that makes me a prophet of doom, so be it, but the Social Security System will bankrupt the country.

Somehow you must cut and scrape, and set aside a little each month in case you should live until the system fails or the taxpayers revolt or inflation explodes faster than the benefits increase.

If you are approaching retirement age, don't plan to depend upon Social Security. Work a few years longer and sock something away as a cushion. If you are in your 40's or 50's, make your retirement plans as though Social Security didn't exist. For you it doesn't.

If you are still comparatively young, and your parents are approaching retirement age, plan on caring for them if they can't care for themselves. They deserve it.

And there is a special place in hell for the liberal politicians, economists, intellectuals, social dreamers, and other fools, who made 200 million people totally dependent upon an irresponsible, inevitably bankrupt plan, while dissipating the nation's assets. Whatever good has been accomplished by Social Security thus far, and it is considerable, will be off-set many times over by the hardship that will come when inflation reveals that the Emperor has no clothes.

Now, some more bad news. Many other pension plans are poorly funded and will let you down when you need them most.

We are back again to our inflation monster. Even if the pension plan is fully funded, you lose. Even if the penson fund doesn't go broke, the money will go broke, and it won't support you in any where near the style to which you are accustomed.

Many pension plans are "under-funded." Oakland, California, found not long ago, that because they had not set aside sufficient money to fund their employee retirement plan, that for the next twenty years they would have to set aside an amount equal to 120% of the current payroll just to build that system back up to snuff and haven't figured out yet how they are going to do it.

The New York City employees' pension funds have been bludgeoned by politicians and Congress into giving away much of their admittedly swollen retirement fund by buying New York City debt paper. The trustees knew what a terrible investment it was, and before they agreed to buy New York bonds it took an Act of Congress to relieve them of any legal liability for taking this irresponsible action and violating their fiduciary responsibility in 1966 and 1968. They took real money and turned it into New York bonds, which is something a heck of a lot less. Abe Beame would still be Mayor of New York if he had a printing press, but he didn't, so he isn't.

New York City employee pension funds are in the same category as Social Security because Uncle Sam is eventually going to be forced to assume that obligation, which is the good news, but it will suffer the same inflationary fate as the Social Security obligation, which is the bad news.

Many corporate retirement plans are unfunded or underfunded, but I'll belabor the point again: It's not the government or the company or the city or the state that I'm worried about. The money will go broke.

One point. Most pension funds are invested in stocks and bonds, as are much of the resources of the insurance company whose annuity you bought. Even the Swiss bank that you thought was a good, safe place to put your money, probably has an awful lot of your deposit invested in the American stock market. Doesn't that make you feel just super?

As I read back over this chapter, it actually frightens me a bit, so it must be scaring you out of your wits. Don't give up hope. Keep reading. There are ways to take advantage of all this and I'll keep reminding you of that as we go along so you won't slit your wrists prematurely.

Before we leave the subject, *The Journal of Commerce* on November 21, 1977, reported some comments by economics professor Michael Wachter of the University of Pennsylvania's Wharton School. He said, "Most people under 35 have virtually no chance of collecting Social

Security and should avoid the system if they can and save for their old age." Mr. Wachter was an economic advisor to Jimmy Carter during his campaign and he says he is scared by the tendency of families covered by Social Security to save less than those who aren't. He said: "The government ought to be preparing the younger generation to face the fact that the Social Security won't pay for them, but they can't because then people would not go on paying the higher premiums.

> ... the belief that the government retirement system troubles were caused by the recent recession is a hoax," he says. "Although the failure of the system already is apparent ... it will be clear to everyone within 20 years ..."

And I say that Professor Wachter is a screaming optimist. His timetable is too long.

I suggest you transform any fear created by reading this chapter into a burning anger for the ignorant clods who sold this program to the American public, and I say this with full knowledge of the billions in benefits that have been paid to old folks to date. That temporary benefit, viewed in the context of the grand scheme of things, will be forgotten, and only the memory of the tragedy that is building will be remembered for generations.

6
EAST SIDE, WEST SIDE

As we search for weak points at which the first cracks will appear as a result of the inflationary strains, our attention is drawn irresistibly to our cities. The on-going soap opera being played out in New York City is perhaps the most significant financial event of the last half of the twentieth century. Why aren't we more alarmed? It's just that we've heard so much about it, it's lost its impact.

Most of our large cities are in weakened condition. New York just got there first. As inflation gains momentum, the large cities of America will be plagued with deteriorating public safety, loss of credit rating (partly due to the tax revolt) and cuts in essential services, with skyrocketing sales and business taxes, and continued urban blight. This will cause a middle class exodus from the cities to the small towns of America, which will be the beneficiaries of this exodus.

The purpose of this chapter is to help you understand what the future holds for you if you live in a large city. Forewarned is forearmed. Most of my suggestions as to what you should do about it will be covered more fully later on.

HOOKED

A few years ago when I was in the food supplement business, I also was engaged in nutritional counseling while working with orthopedic surgeons to help prepare their patients nutritionally for surgery, as well as to accelerate their post-operative recovery.

A young man whom I had attempted to train in vitamin sales knocked on my door one night. His eyes were dilated, his speech was slurred and it was obvious he was under the influence of something. He was high on heroin. I knew he had spent some time in prison because of drug-related crimes. He wanted help. I had told him that I believed that through diet and massive use of vitamins it is possible for an addict to get through the withdrawal period with substantially reduced symptoms. He had just had a "fix" and pleaded with me to help him kick his habit.

There was nothing ahead of him but bad choices. He could continue to take his heroin and increase his dependency, steal to support his habit, get sicker and sicker, and eventually die of an overdose, or he could go through a painful withdrawal, with no assurance that he would stay clean, even after the ordeal. He refused to try the cure. When I saw him months later he was a shell of a man. He was on methadone but he was like an automaton. He was unproductive. He had lost his sex drive. He was still trapped. The only difference was that his present addiction was legal. He was indifferent as to whether he lived or died.

Mayor Abe Beame of New York City said in reference to federal money, "They were the pushers and we were the junkies." Our cities are like a junkie whose connection is threatened. They are addicted to money—borrowed money, pension fund money, federal money, tax money. The addiction has made them sick. It has damaged their capacity to function, and the only thing that will keep them from terrible withdrawal symptoms is more money, and the "connection" will be cut off, via the tax revolt and a collapsing bond market. And when it starts to hurt, they will use every legal and political gun they can to get a new "fix."

There is no course of action open to us that will avoid terrible trouble in our cities. I don't know whether they will go with a bang or a whimper, but it means the most significant restructuring of American life style and population patterns since the Homestead Act of the nineteenth century and the great dustbowl-caused migrations of the 30's.

The cities will be among the first victims of inflation and monetary disruption. They are the most dependent upon the swill in the public trough. They will be one of the first of the large dominoes to fall.

WHY ARE THE CITIES THE WEAK POINT?

They are the most addicted, and their withdrawal symptoms will be the worst. Our cities have offered welfare and unemployment insurance, among other benefits, which have drawn the poor, the uneducated, the economically dislocated, the lazy and the criminal. This has created a set of circumstances which perpetuates their problems.

The great dustbowl drought of the 1930's resulted in an exodus of farmers and workers to California. This was a natural, healthy free-market response. Labor would move to where there was income. And in those old-fashioned days, income meant jobs. That pool of labor may have laid the foundation for the marvelous expansion of the California economy.

Today, welfare and unemployment insurance act as magnets, just as California jobs did then. This new exodus, rather than laying the foundation for new prosperity, merely concentrates the burden of care for unproductive people upon the backs of the taxpayers in cities. The free labor market has been distorted by our misguided attempts to help. Because we were not able to tolerate short-term suffering, we have given ourselves intractable long-term problems by muffling the self-correcting signals of the free market.

City problems are apparently being perceived in a subliminal way by many of their inhabitants. All of our large cities, with the exception of Houston, are losing the tax-paying middle class, at the rate of about 1% a year. The population exodus is a symptom of deep-rooted structural rot. Rutgers' Dr. George Sternleed says, "You can't support the poor without the rich. Every time some taxpayer moves out of the city, the poor are left even poorer, and this is happening in every large city in America."

We actually face the possibility of a nation with no important cities. What are the implications?

City problems are like a whirlpool, sucking in other parties, such as banks, Uncle Sam and city pension funds. New York City municipal employees think they have a pension fund worth billions of dollars. They don't. Much of their money has been poured down a rat hole, as discussed in the previous chapter. Even the best solutions offer nothing but withdrawal pains. Laying off city employees merely means adding to the unemployment rolls. Economy moves may be counter-productive as they worsen the already bad climate for business and lower the tax base. It also creates a kind of resentment that lies there like tinder waiting for the right spark to set it off.

WHEN THE LIGHTS WENT OUT

Chaos is possible in our cities as a result of social anger and inflation-disrupted markets. We are less than ten years away from the last round of riots, and conditions are becoming ripe again.

Don't forget the night in 1977 when the power went out in New York. It seems that the ghettos of New York are not exactly placid outposts of civilization.

We look back fondly on the earlier blackout of 1965 with nostalgia. Back then the mood of the city was healthy and amiable, and less than a hundred persons were arrested. A lot of people just stayed home and made "love, not war," and 280 days later, the maternity wards were full. There was no serious looting or rioting.

But in 1977 the damage was in the billions. Over 3,500 people were arrested, and it would have been a heck of a lot more except the police stopped confronting and arresting people.

The shocking thing is that most of the looters didn't feel they were doing anything wrong. And many of the so-called upright citizens were actually urging teen-agers on, asking to "get me one of those," or, "I could sure use a new bed." And in the spirit of carnival, the kids obliged.

With the unerring instinct of the liberal for the wrong solution, Joseph Kraft, the syndicated columnist says, "the real lesson is that we haven't spent enough money to solve New York's problems, and we need more programs aimed specifically at the poor in the cities." As we will see, things aren't that simple.

Government is not the solution, it's the problem. The more it tries to help, the worse things get.

A significant segment of New York is a deteriorating jungle where civilization has ceased to exist, and so is the core of many of our larger cities. The lesson of the looters is that our cities are vulnerable. What else could touch off rioting? Another energy failure? Municipal bankruptcy? Cuts in welfare checks? The assassination of a black leader? U.S. involvement in South Africa? Recession and rising unemployment with wide-spread lay-offs? Water shortages? What we've learned from New York is that the nation's big cities are rapidly becoming lousy places to live, and the expensive close-in suburbs will get the spill-over of problems.

The blackout only lasted 24 hours. Can you imagine what would have happened if it had gone on for a week, with people cooking in old wooden tenements with open fires, and lighting with unshielded candles? Most buildings couldn't get water above the fourth floor because the pumps wouldn't work, and as bad as it was, it was nowhere near as bad as it could have been if it had gone on for another day or two.

City neighborhoods have moved towards one-race groupings—inbred, hostile ghettos with a garrison mentality toward the rest of the world. We have lost most of the gains we have made in social relations and this holds the seeds of race war.

The quality of life in large parts of many cities is diminishing. The great exodus of corporations, jobs, and middle class whites from the cities is leaving an eroding tax base, and a growing fiscal deficit. Crime in most big cities is perceived as being out of control, which has accelerated the exodus. Schools have ceased to teach and our cities are turning out functional and economic illiterates who do not understand how the system works, and they are the voters who elect those who will have their hands on the spending throttle—the very people who are destroying the cities through their misguided legislation and wooly-headed generosity with your money.

We have accumulated a staggering mountain of municipal debt. As we have seen, history records no instance of public debt of this proportion having been paid off in anything other than worthless paper. It has become a game of Old Maid. They will continue "rolling over" their debt until no one is willing to lend, and the last investors are left holding lousy paper, or until conditions force Uncle Sugar into paying off (guaranteeing) their debt—again with printing press money. This has happened in New York, and will soon happen in other cities across the country. This can endanger the safety of the nation's banks, and ironically, they are one of the villains.

HOW GOVERNMENT "HELP" DESTROYED A CITY

Here's an example of what our friends in government can do to a city, as reported by *Fortune* magazine. It has lessons for your city.

The South Bronx has over half a million inhabitants, and the place is literally burning up. In the last seven years, there have been over 95,000 fires, more than 33 fires every night. There is solid evidence that one-third of them were deliberately set.

The population has dropped by 20% in the last 5 years.

So few criminals go to jail that crime clearly pays.

Welfare handouts have diminished incentive and promoted the break-up of families.

Rising minimum wage laws have foreclosed job opportunities for those with minimal skills.

Long before the South Bronx became a social sink-hole in which civilization has all but vanished, government systematically, though inadvertently, helped to wreck its economic life. Piecemeal urban renewal efforts wasted millions of dollars in capital improvements, while the burden of high and rising taxation encouraged businesses to take their money, jobs and taxes, and run. A hopeless tangle of city mismanagement has, on occasion, sent rehabilitation teams and demolition crews to the same building on the same day.

Over 30% of the families are on welfare, and most of those have no fathers in the home. About half of the 16 to 21 year olds have dropped out of school, and 60% are unemployed. And this is only 3 to 4 miles north of Manhattan's elegant upper east side, and may be the closest men have come yet to creating hell on earth. Every evening, adults coming home from work walk quickly, keeping a sharp look out, knowing it is just a matter of time until they fall prey to a junkie, mugger, or one of the 89 organized street gangs in the neighborhood, some armed with automatic weapons. Some observers who have toured the area emerge shaken, saying it reminds one of Berlin or Dresden after World War II. The place is battle-scarred and bombed out. In block after block, amidst apartments that are still inhabited, stand similar buildings, vacant and abandoned, their windows blown out by the heat of fires.

The infection that started the destruction of the South Bronx began in 1943 when government enacted the Emergency Price Control Act, which froze rents at their March 1943 levels. Over the years, tenants came to regard low rents as a right, so the New York politicians continued local rent control, even after it became plain that the law was wrecking the entire city stock of rental housing. About 90% of the buildings were built before 1915. They needed new heating systems, plumbing, wiring, window frames and roofs, which cost money. With some exceptions, the "rich greedy slum-lord" is a myth. Mostly, the landlords were small businessmen who lived and worked in the neighborhood and invested their life savings in a single piece of property. The level of maintenance declined precipitously, as taxes and the cost of repairs increased, and rental income was frozen at money-losing levels.

Soon tenants started moving out, either to more attractive parts of the Bronx, or to the low-down-payment home with the big FHA or GI government-insured mortgage on Long Island or in Westchester County. Soon there was an increasing number of old vacant apartments for as little as $20 a month. Blacks began pouring in from the rural south, and Puerto Ricans flew in by the plane loads from their impoverished island. Two million came between 1945 and 1974. There were jobs in New York that paid attractive hourly wages and they knew that if they lost their jobs or couldn't find one, there was always welfare. For example, in 1960, an average family on welfare in Mississippi got $27.11 a month. A similar family in San Juan received no assistance at all. In New York, the average family could collect $101.41. And for a poor Puerto Rican, $101.41 in 1960 dollars, was a lot of money. Most of the newcomers settled in the South Bronx.

The next problem was an increasingly unattractive business climate. New York forgot the direct link between a good climate for business and the existence of jobs. They looked upon businessmen as the enemy. Whenever the city needed new revenues, they soaked the business community first. In 1966 for example, the city imposed a 5.5% corporate income tax on top of federal and state income taxes. In 1974 the levy was raised to 10%. To supplement these revenues, the city adopted a nightmarish array of permanent inspection fees. By 1970 it was charging up to $77 a year to inspect each boiler in every factory in commercial buildings. Gas stations were hit with an annual fee of $600 a year for inspecting their underground tanks. Piled on top of one another, and on top of general taxes, they created powerful incentives for businessmen to move. By 1974 the

South Bronx had lost one-third of the manufacturers who were there in 1959, and all of the jobs they provided.

In the 60's the job market began to collapse. Welfare rolls swelled 500%. Payments were structured so they provided an incentive not to work. If the head of the household took a job, the benefits automatically dropped by one dollar for every dollar earned. Since the job was unlikely to be lucrative, and was probably unpleasant, many welfare recipients decided not to work at all.

Assaults went up 420% in 10 years, and burglaries, 700%. The criminal justice system began to break down and the odds of being jailed grew so small that crime began to pay.

By the 60's the forces that would wreck the South Bronx were firmly in place. Housing was being ruined by rent control. Businesses were being squeezed by rising taxes, low paying jobs were made unattractive by welfare, and black and Puerto Rican immigrants continued to arrive and be packed in by the Welfare Department.

It was inevitable that these destructive forces would reinforce one another and would reach a critical mass. But instead of exploding in riot like Watts did, the South Bronx deteriorated quietly. The Federal Government poured money into it to reward it for its peaceful behavior, treating the South Bronx like a favorite nephew, and that sealed its fate.

From Washington came $3 million for an experimental social services center, $16 million for a family health care center, $77 million for a model cities program, and $250 million for a new hospital. One aim of The Great Society was to provide jobs for the poor. Hundreds were hired by a bewildering array of federally funded organizations. Many of these newly minted bureaucrats were illiterate. But they pushed paper around and drew up grandiose plans. To no one's surprise, the plans that emerged didn't work. Soon, entire buildings were abandoned, and the outflow of working tenants and business and jobs became a hemorrhage. An unofficial estimate, which may be understated, shows that 5,400 apartment units were abandoned during the first four months of 1975.

Within a year the South Bronx began to burn. Too many people had too many incentives to throw a match. Some landlords, whose abandoned buildings brought in no rent and literally could not be given away, began setting insurance fires.

The market value of a piece of income property is relative to its net income. When it is showing a loss, and there is no chance of improving the income, you can't even give a building away, because the buyer would get stuck for the delinquent taxes.

An equally potent incentive to arson that is devastating in its revelation of the bureaucratic mind, was offered to the city dweller.

Welfare recipients in deteriorating buildings naturally want to move. The regulations forbid the payment of moving expenses to welfare recipients who had not lived in the same place for at least two years. There was one glorious exception to this rule, and is posted in big block letters in neighborhood welfare offices. Any tenant burned out of his apartment automatically gets a grant—from $1,000 to $3,000—to cover the cost of new clothing, new furniture, and moving. Burned out families go to the top of the waiting list for public housing projects.

James Dumpson, administrator of the city's Human Resources Administration, says he has no choice.

"The law says that if a family is found in need, the administrator of the Human Resource Administration shall give assistance. I don't determine who set the fire."

Then the building strippers set to work setting first in apartment buildings and removing copper tubing, plumbing fixtures, electric wiring and anything else they can sell after the building is cool. Sometimes they would strip the building first, then set fire to cover their tracks. Gutted buildings were swiftly occupied by drug addicts, who often burn down buildings in the process of melting their heroin when they are spaced out of their minds. Youngsters do it for fun or as little as $3 to $5 for a torch job. Arson is among the most difficult crimes to prove, since the evidence is usually destroyed in the blaze.

The authorities are outnumbered by the law breakers and outmaneuvered by the defense lawyers, and New York jails are so overcrowded that most suspects are freed on their own recognizance and commit additional crimes. Right now, the odds of serving a prison sentence after a felony in the South Bronx are less than 1 in 100. The situation is now so bad that a Police Commander used it to persuade a subject to surrender. The incident occurred in April 1974 when police surrounded an apartment house where the armed man was holding an adult and three children hostage after a family quarrel. He called out, "There's no way you can escape, give yourself up."

"No way. I ain't gonna get arrested and go to jail."

"Have you ever been arrested before?"

"Yeah. Ten times."

"You ever been sent to jail?"

"No."

"What makes you think you'll get sent up this time? Come on out of there before someone gets hurt. We'll arrest you, we'll book you, and you'll get arraigned, and you'll go free like always."

The gunman surrendered and never went to jail.

The first big expense a lot of landlords eliminate when they get pressed is real estate taxes. New York allows a three-year grace period before foreclosure proceedings may be started. Sometimes it takes longer. Many landlords walk away from their buildings because they can't sell them and they can't pay the taxes. One landlord owes the city $352,000 in back taxes. "I would like to pay my taxes," he says, "but I've got to pay my fuel bills and they have tripled since 1973. What can I do?"

New York has been wading through a five-year continuing soap opera, tip-toeing from crisis to crisis, because the costs and shackles of government and the promises of politicians have created insoluble problems. And the end result will be either the collapse of city finances (and I wouldn't want to be there on the day the welfare and unemployment checks bounced), or the federal government will temporarily bail it out through guarantees of its debt paper. Guarantees mean that profligate politicians will have been rewarded by suddenly being blessed with the most salable municipal paper of all, because Uncle Sugar guarantees it! Suddenly, the worst becomes the best, and the sound, well-run cities will have to fight for what's left over in the municipal bond borrowing place, until political pressures force Washington to assume the whole mess, and in the next deep recession they will be forced to make good on a lot of defaulted municipal paper. And that will be inflationary. Remember the printing press?

New York City is not the only city that has problems. This is a spreading plague. As we saw in the South Bronx, help programs from Uncle Sam are the kiss of death. The jungle which we have created in New York is a harbinger of what awaits us in the rest of the large cities of America. Every city is dependent on borrowing in the Municipal Paper markets, or some form of federal money, either through matching funds, government job programs, government rent of office buildings, military and Federal employment, grants, and a thousand open and concealed programs. When we move into the depression, after inflation has increased the cost of goods and services that the cities must pay for, they will be caught in a squeeze. The demands for welfare, unemployment insurance, and other aid will explode, while at the same time tax collections will diminish, made worse by the tax revolt, and population, jobs and companies will continue the exodus to small town America and the Sunbelt and big city credit will be impaired. There's not a single city in the United States with over a million population which will not be in financial distress to some degree or another by 1980, according to *Business Week* magazine. All the big cities are in decline. They are all adding services and increasing public payrolls, while the economic base deteriorates. The spreading local tax revolt will reduce income, and the reversal of the spending process will be immensely disruptive. That doesn't mean we shouldn't cut taxes. That just means we had better brace ourselves to deal with the problems those cuts will create, which, as bad as they are, are probably better than the problems we will eventually have if we continue on our inflationary present course.

WARNING LIGHTS

Economist Thomas Millar of the Urban Institute in Washington lists nine municipal danger signals. Among them: substantial long-term out-migration, loss of private employment, high debt service, high unemployment, high tax burden, increasing proportion of low-income population.

Some of the cities displaying these dangerous signs are Buffalo, Boston, Cleveland, Detroit, Newark, New York, Philadelphia, St. Louis, Oakland, and Los Angeles. Others that are better off but still in trouble are Cincinnati, Chicago, Baltimore, Pittsburgh, New Orleans, San Francisco, and Milwaukee.

Most cities can get by with their problems as long as the economic cycle is in an upswing. It's when the country gets in trouble economically that the problems are exposed.

If cities and states cannot raise taxes, or borrow what they need, they will slide inexorably into a New York City dilemma—either cut spending and services, something that the interest groups will resist furiously—or collapse financially. As the prosperous urban and suburban whites head for small cities and towns, driven by fears both real and imagined, looking for the stability of a previous era, this will create an explosive boom in places such as Bakersfield, Salt Lake City, Boise, Davenport, and Albuquerque, as these newcomers will buy homes, land, farm equipment, food, and furnishings with their rapidly depreciating currency.

If you are comfortably situated at least 20 to 30 miles from the welfare ghettos, the odds are you'll be physically safe. You don't have to run for the backwoods or Switzerland. The U.S. and Canada will be the best places to be. When we drop into depression, the whole world drops back into the stone age for a while. We will recover first and suffer the least damage. The democratic tradition is the most likely to survive here in the U.S.

What should I fear, then?

I would fear living too close to a welfare slum during the first few weeks of big city collapse, because they are going to be mad, and I know who they're going to blame. I would want to have a place to go to, away from the city during that brief period after welfare and unemployment checks stopped, or during the possible inflation riots, or when the distribution system breaks down.

The future of America is in its small towns. That's where your money should be invested. That's where safety will be and that's where life will be least disrupted as the monetary system undergoes its uncertain gyrations. And I'll have more in-depth stuff on that subject in the next chapter.

7
THE OLD HOMESTEAD

I didn't want to get into a discussion of real estate as an investment until you had read the previous chapter on cities, because it wouldn't have made sense.

Real estate is the most frequently requested subject for discussion in my mail and on the Hot-Line, to say nothing of the innumerable talk shows I've been on, because it touches more people's lives than any form of money deployment.

At this point I only want to discuss the home you live in, and touch on some general investment principles.

Is there a decent future for real estate, and should you continue a real estate investment program in light of the problem we have discussed earlier?

The answer is a highly qualified "yes," depending on *where* and *what the* property is and *how you finance it*. Some Real Estate investments are going to clobber anyone who owns them, and others will take you through the troubles in reasonably good shape. You must understand your objectives, and don't shrug that off as a cliché. You can have some rapid capital appreciation with great safety in the limited time we have ahead of us, if you know what you are doing. You can also invest conservatively to get your purchasing power from here to the other side of the depression, relatively intact.

We have a basic strategy which will be discussed in depth in Part II so here I'll limit myself to an analysis of what the future holds for your home.

TAKING MY OWN ADVICE

In August 1977, I concluded it was time to bail out of the expensive suburb in which I lived, because I felt that most of the explosive capital appreciation was behind us in our area and it was about to peak out and reverse itself.

A recent study by Walter X. Burns and Charles D. Kirkpatrick of the marketing forecasting division of Lynch, Jones and Ryan, has come to the same conclusion. They say that the mania in house prices, is nearing its peak and the outlook is for a "Humpty-dumpty crash in the immediate future." As reported in the *Dallas Morning News*, they said,

> But the rapid rise in housing prices cannot really be attributed to population growth, scarcity of land, inflation or greatly increased family income. Rather we think we have an old-fashioned mania on our hands. To date, all of the criteria for a mania have been met except for the eventual collapse.
>
> When?
>
> It looks like the house price mania will break in the very near future.
>
> How bad might it be?
>
> The percentage declines after manias are usually enormous. We believe the decline might match the 80% drop in stock prices which followed the crash of 1929.

I agree, insofar as the expensive suburbs and the cities are concerned. I had watched my home appreciate at a rate of 15% to 25% a year for some years, and I had a huge equity which could be lost if the "mania" were to turn around so I decided to follow up on my own advice and look for a small town where the inflation in real estate prices was in its first 15%, rather than its last 15%. I picked a small town in the Central Valley of California which is surrounded by a diversified agricultural economy and concluded that it would be one of the beneficiaries of the middle-class exodus from the cities described in the previous chapter. I bought a home and settled down to stay.*
If I am wrong about the collapse of prices in the cities, I won't be hurt, because if prices

---
*Oops. I found an even better small town in Utah in 1980 and *really* settled down to stay.

should continue to inflate there, it will also continue in my town. And I was able to buy a heck of a lot more house for the money, and ended up with an improved cash position.

In fact, in an inflationary spiral you can improve your cash position dramatically by moving once or twice, because you can generally get into the second or third home with only slightly more down payment than you had in the first one, and your "inflation equity" money, now turned into cash, can be put to work in some other counter-cyclical investment, and you have a double-whammy improvement in your finances. Figure it out. If you bought your home five years ago for $50,000, with $10,000 down, you can sell it now for over $100,000, take out about $65,000 equity cash, buy a home of about the same size in a small town for $75,000 with a down payment of $15,000, and have $50,000 to invest. You might even manage to have a paid-for home, if you plan it properly.

Typically, the most dramatic investment success that most of you have had was from something that wasn't really planned as an investment—the home in which you live. You were utilizing the principle of leverage, and have received a high percentage of appreciation, even if you didn't know what you were doing. You probably have had a 500% return on your money. Here's how it works.

Leverage means utilizing the principle of a lever in making money. Archimedes said, "Give me a lever and a place to stand and I can move the world." You use a little bit of your money (the down payment) and a lot of someone else's (the mortgage) as a "lever," and the rate of return on your invested money is greater. Look at this.

You have $100,000 to invest. If you buy a piece of property for $100,000 cash, and eventually sell it for $130,000, your $30,000 profit is a 30% profit on your $100,000 investment. However, if you buy it with $10,000 down and a $90,000 loan and sell it for $130,000, your $30,000 profit is a 300% return on your $10,000 invested, and you could have used your other $90,000 to buy nine such income properties, and you can make ten times as much money, and spread your risk. In this example I've ignored interest costs (deductible of course) which reduces profits somewhat, but I wanted to keep the example simple.

Leverage can increase your risk as well as your profit when you use it with volatile investments such as stocks, commodites, etc., because they fluctuate downward rapidly, and you could end up with a margin call which you can't meet, and be forced to sell: however, leverage can be safely used in a rising or slowly fluctuating market with no margin calls, and that, over the past several years, has been real estate. And it will continue to be so in small towns. And you will never get a "margin call." Just keep up your payments. And you pay off the loan with ever-diminishing dollars. You can safely use leverage in any well-chosen investment where you are not subject to a margin call.

I think you should consider moving to a

small town—looking beyond the ring of expensive big city suburbs until you find a place where equivalent home prices are substantially below those in the community in which you live. Then sell your home and move. Either make the smallest possible down payment, or pay for it in full. Nothing in between makes sense. Later on I'll tell you what to do with the leftover money. There are lots of alternatives.

I know that many of you who read this book are simply not going to take my advice about moving out of the city. You enjoy the cultural opportunities, the public transportation, the closeness to work and the urban way of life, and you are prepared to take your chances. If this is your decision, then I have some suggestions for you also.

If your job, your profession or personal inclinations won't permit you to move from the city, then at least consider getting your money out, or move further from the explosive "welfare ghettos." Sell your place and rent an apartment, or refinance your home to the hilt and invest the proceeds in the counter-cyclical investments that will protect you in the coming downturn, as described later.

This gives you a smaller equity to lose, if prices should collapse, or if your income should be cut off, or if deteriorating social conditions should lead to wholesale insurance cancellations. If you do sell, the last thing you want to do is become the holder of a mortgage (a lender), even if you feel you can always repossess the property if the purchaser goes broke. Remember, the danger is that the money is going to go broke, and you might be one of those creditors pursued relentlessly by debtors and paid off in depreciated dollars.

Virtually all big city and expensive suburban real estate investments are high risk for the future due to the deteriorating quality of life in the cities, the inevitable reduction in urban services such as police, fire protection, etc., and escalating insurance costs. In the meantime, prices in small town America will probably remain relatively stable or even rise in the face of a collapsing real estate market in the big cities.

In the general price inflation that is coming, big city real estate is a deflationary exception. Real estate prices have gone up for years, but so did the stock market until 1966.

Your decision to sell is a very personal one, depending on whether or not your home equity is your principal asset, or whether you want to ignore my advice even if you believe it, simply because you like to live where you live now, and you don't care about your home's market value. But remember, casualty insurance cancellations are a very real threat in a deteriorating social environment. You might buy a home in a small town and rent it out until you need to go there.

In the meantime, speculative real estate in the big cities would be best disposed of now. I'm referring to industrial, commercial and residential investment properties, as well as raw land. Even if I'm wrong, or I'm early in that recommendation, the safer trend over the long haul is with small-town America.

When the financial panic begins, most of the troubles will be concentrated in the big cities. When it is over, there will be some tremendous bargains and you may want to come back some day, but in the meantime, I would prefer to observe from a distance.

8
DON'T BANK ON IT

Just imagine you are the Finance Minister of an Arab monarchy. You have to please your king who has the power to cut off your hand (or your head) in the public square if he wishes to. Your job is to see that he gets the maximum return from his oil revenues. You have put his money into short-term deposits in New York banks, who, in turn, have loaned it out to insolvent countries. You thought this was a great idea at the time because that would leave the banks on the hook—responsible for both the loans they had made and the money you deposited. But now the price of those things which your King has been importing (heavy construction equipment, building materials, high technology, etc.) are inflating between

15% and 25% a year, so his dollars are getting chewed up by inflation. In addition, the dollar has been sinking against virtually every other currency in the world and you are in the uncomfortable position of informing your monarch that he needs a 20% to 25% increase in oil prices just to break even.

If you think you feel sick now, look at your alternatives.

1. You can hedge your dollar losses by buying gold, which you have done covertly for some time anyway. As the dollar sinks, gold will tend to rise and compensate for your losses, but there isn't enough gold around to hedge you against the monstrous amounts of dollars that you have earned and have to place somewhere. But you do what you can.

2. You can stay with the dollar and tough it out and hope that your ruler doesn't lose his patience during the several years you think it will take for the U.S. government to correct its balance-of-payments deficit, balance its budgets and bring the dollar back to some semblance of strength—if ever.

3. You can carefully pull your money out of the New York banks and throw it into some other currency, but you had better do it just right or you will throw the dollar and the U.S. banking system into a disastrous tailspin before you can get most of your money safely out, and your losses could be beyond imagining.

The threat of withdrawal of Arab money from the New York banks is only one of several major potential banking problems as this book is written. I'm not alone in thinking that our

126

banking system is, to put it mildly, in delicate condition and racing towards the most serious tests it has faced since the 1930's, if a not unlikely combination of events should occur in the period from 1978 to 1985.

There's no point in getting overcomplicated about how banks work, but I think a few fundamentals would be useful. Understanding the nature of the system might give us some guidance.

The United States banking system is dominated by no more than fifteen banking groups, most of them controlled by giant holding companies. They are The First National City Bank of New York, Chase Manhattan, Chemical, Manufacturers Hanover, Marine Midland, Morgan Guaranty, Bank of America, Wachovia, Continental Bank of Chicago, The Mellon Bank, Security Pacific and Western Bank Corporation. These are the banks where nearly all of the thousands of smaller banks in the country do their banking. This is where all the money and credit in the United States come together. They are the key log in the jam. If you pull it out, the entire system crumbles.

These banks make money by borrowing it from depositors at one rate and loaning it at a higher rate. The spread between these interest charges represents their profit. However, it's not really that simple, because the banks can, in effect, create money out of thin air, just as the United States government can.

Let's go back to that $1,000 bank deposit that we talked about earlier. They can loan $850 of it to one of their other customers. He puts it in his checking account somewhere in the banking system where it counts as new bank reserves, and they can loan out 85% of that, and so on. They have literally created money from nothing. As a net result, most of the American money supply is represented merely by bookkeeping entries in bank computers.

Banks can get in trouble from both sides of their balance sheets:

1. Their outstanding loans could default, or
2. Their savings accounts and Certificates of Deposit (C.D.'s) could be withdrawn (or not renewed) in a banking panic, and, of course, that is the classic "run on the banks," as we've seen that only about 5% (or less) of their deposits are on hand in cash. The rest is loaned out or invested.

Banks operate on the assumption that all times are relatively normal and that nothing could ever happen which could endanger either their assets or their liabilities sufficiently to cause a "run" or abnormal loan losses. They count on public confidence and what some writers have called "the sticker principle."

If you, as a depositor, ever got worried about your bank and decided to go down and take out your money, as you approach the door you would probably notice a small oval sticker which says, "Deposits Insured to $40,000[*] by the Federal Deposit Insurance Corporation, an agency of the U.S. government." So you would say to yourself, "Well, perhaps I shouldn't worry, Uncle Sam will protect me." So you leave your money there and go home.

---

[*]Now it's up to $100,000, although the trust fund hasn't increased proportionately.

Let's look at that protection and see what it is really designed to do.

The FDIC guarantees over $750 billion in bank deposits. The total amount of money in the FDIC insurance fund is only about $6 billion, but it has statutory authority to borrow up to $3 billion more from the treasury in case of an emergency. This gives the FDIC a total of $9 billion with which to pay off depositor claims if banks should go broke. That means that there is only $1.00 of insurance coverage for every $83 on deposit, or stated another way, for every $1,000 you have in the bank, there is $12 to insure it. It would only take 1.2% of the nation's deposits to be wiped out through banking failures and the entire FDIC fund would be penniless.*

In 1975, the FDIC used over 40% of the total fund in the Franklin Bank failure rescue operation. Most of those funds have since been recovered, but I'm concerned about the amount of money that was needed at the time of the problem.

If one or two of the nation's top ten banks got in bad trouble, there wouldn't be enough money in the FDIC funds to save them.

Not only is the government liable for $40,000 for each insured account, but it is the government's policy to cover every last dollar when a bank fails. This means the FDIC's $9 billion could be exhausted even more rapidly. Is the FDIC just being nice to us—going the extra mile?

No. It was revealed by John Hensel, the FDIC Regional Administrator for National

---

*All the figures in this chapter are 1978 figures. It's worse now.

Banks in the California Region, at a seminar sponsored by Security National Bank (one of the banks on the Federal Reserve's problem list) that this generous policy was to compensate for the official policy of not disclosing the conditions of a problem bank to prevent runs and failures. The innocent public continues to open accounts at an insolvent bank, buy their C.D.'s and their stock, not knowing of their troubles. If the bank goes under and the FDIC does not pay off 100%, they could be liable for damage suits from bamboozled depositors and innocent investors.

Hensel admitted that this could threaten the insurance fund since it has not been set up for such exposure.

In April 1974, the FDIC chairman, Frank Wille, admitted that the FDIC had no way of foreseeing a banking problem, saying, "We are trying to develop a classification system which will tell whether a particular banking institution previously unclassified may have become a 'problem bank' since it was last examined."

And they are no closer to making that measurement now than they were then.

Mr. Wille assured us that, in regard to the FDIC rescue funds, "We could handle several large bank failures." And he hastily backed off, "but not a general run on the banks."

That ought to be an eye-opener, especially when one considers who said it. If you don't think a general run on the banks is possible, listen to what Mr. Wille had to say shortly after that.

"Like it or not, the nation's banks are all

affected by any significant failure that occurs within the banking system."

Senator Proxmire, Chairman of the Senate Banking Committee, said on February 1, 1976:

> A relatively limited economic setback could result, conceivably, in the failure of some of the nation's largest banks.

When one bank goes down the tubes, if it is big enough, it can take other banks with it. The banking panic of the 1930's began with the failure of a bank in Austria. Banks borrow short-term from one another, and they honor checks drawn on other banks and allow depositors to draw on those checks before they have cleared the issuing banks. A sudden and abrupt failure of a major bank could produce chaos at the clearing houses and have a devastating effect on all banks.

But the real uncertainty occurs when depositors become aware of bank problems and begin to react with general concern about the banking system. In a real panic, they won't attempt to distinguish between sound or unsound banks. All banks could become suspect. The classic public fear reaction is to withdraw money from banks. The only thing that prevents people from doing it is their belief that the banks cannot fail.

On April 21, 1975, *Business Week* observed.

> The banking systems' problems are serious with an overhang of very shaky loans the most

visible ones. 'Last summer scared the pants off some of these bankers,' says John C. Poppen of Booz, Allen and Hamilton, the management consultants. Banks, and such non-banking holding company subsidiaries as finance companies, leasing companies, mortgage bankers, and real estate investment trusts, literally funded everyone that needed money in the last decade. They used up their own deposits, and then sold C.D.'s and holding company commercial paper, and borrowed Federal funds to keep the game going, creating loan/deposit and capital/asset ratios that were simply intolerable.

The risk got so great that banks in 1974 had to charge off an unprecedented $1.8 billion to cover loan losses and there are still billions of dollars in loans in considerable trouble—$10 to $12 billion in loans to real estate investment trusts.

The generation of bankers that rose to power in the early 1960's have never known a truly sick economy. They took their ability to survive the minor economic disturbances of the 1960's as proof they could survive anything.

Last year pulled things apart. Inflation turned strong demand for bank money into frenzied demand, but more lending forced the banks to borrow still more, and by mid-1974 the system was stretched dangerously thin: too much questionable lending, too much borrowed money, too little capital to support swollen assets and monetary growth that has slowed to a dead zero.

In 1975, if the controller of the currency had required the banks to mark down all of their assets to market value, there would have been no capital left in the banks of America, and they would have been technically and legally insolvent and forced to shut down. Can you imagine what happened to the market value of their bond portfolios when interest rates soared to 12-15%? And yet they were carried on the books at the purchase price or par value.

Their tanker loans and loans to such credit-worthy borrowers as New York City, Lockheed, and Penn Central, if they had been forced to be written down, would have come close to making them insolvent. They loaned close to $100 billion dollars to insolvent countries, either directly, or through their foreign subsidiaries, and then made further loans, either directly or through The International Monetary Fund and The World Bank, just so those countries could stay current on their interest payments, and technically those loans could be carried on the books as "good loans."

The strong recovery from the recession of 74-75 saved the system, and now bank earnings are looking pretty good again. But all it will take is a return to the conditions of 1974 to raise the risks for several of our biggest banks to unacceptable levels, and inflation is the villain.

When interest rates climb, everybody gets mad at the banks for profiteering, but bear in mind that it also causes huge losses in the market value of their bond portfolios. Also, when general interest rates rise well above the rates which banks are willing or legally allowed to pay on deposits, a process called "disintermediation" sets in. Depositors withdraw money from the banks looking for higher yields elsewhere, and they can find them in such relatively safe investments as Treasury bills. This is a form of "bank run."

Here are the banking danger areas:

1. A modern day run on the banks. One or two "Top Twenty" banks could get into serious public trouble, as people withdraw deposits and refuse to renew C.D.'s at maturity, looking for higher yields and safety, probably in gold, silver, diamonds, foreign currencies and government securities. If it were publicized, this could result in a panicky stampede.

2. Over $200 billion in foreign loans. Many of them are to countries which would have defaulted long ago if further loans had not been made to them so they could make their interest payments.

One of those unstable countries could undergo a coup d'etat by a revolutionary group which would refuse to honor the debt, or perhaps a group of the poorer countries might get together and say, "We want a larger piece of the world's wealth, or we will default on our bank loans." Such grumbling has already been heard.

3. A rash of recession/inflation-caused corporate bankruptcies. This is precisely what we will see in the next recession, and this could be the triggering mechanism for a full-fledged bank panic.

4. The Arabs giving up on the dollar. They could try to switch into deutsche marks,

Swiss francs, Japanese yen, gold, commodities, and American real estate, rather than short-term deposits in the New York banks. They have anywhere from $75 to $100 billion in deposits in those banks, most of them with 90-day maturities or less, and those banks have committed the classic error of "borrowing short" from the Arabs, and "lending long" to almost everybody. (That means accepting short-term deposits and making long-term loans.) If that short-term money is not pulled out with great skill, heroic restraint, and a lot of luck, we all will have bad trouble.

THROUGH A GLASS DARKLY

The true condition of the banks is difficult to determine as so much of their business is done through overseas subsidiaries which generally do not have U.S. reporting requirements. We do know that the largest multinational banks like Bank of America, Chase Manhattan, and First National City Bank of New York have approximately 60% of their loans and over 60% of their earnings from overseas, and in foreign currencies. They are truly "citizens of the world." They don't just use the world's monetary system, they *are* the world's monetary system, and to determine their true status is not easy.

Forbes on July 24, 1975, devoted an issue to an analysis of the banks from an investor's point of view.

> Banks do not have to disclose as much about their operations as most other companies do.

> The idea has always been that public confidence in bank deposits is more important than investor confidence in their stocks. Information that might lead investors to sell their stock might also frighten depositors into pulling out their money. A declining stock market is one thing, a bank panic is something else again. Anything that might set off a bank panic is something to be discouraged.
>
> That policy which both the Federal Reserve and the Controller of the Currency support is, of course, vehemently opposed by the S.E.C. ...

Two big banks in 1975 considered running the disclosure gauntlet. Manufacturers Hanover Trust Company twice pulled back from a S.E.C.'s disclosure requirements. Chemical Bank beat an equally rapid retreat. To date, I know of no bank which has successfully issued equity or long-term debt issues to raise external capital. They are afraid of those disclosure requirements.

Investors are suspicious. Analyst John Lyons, of the bank stock firm of Keefe, Bruyette and Woods, observes that New York bank profits in the aggregate were up 30% in 1975, but that, "Potential loan losses are an absolute unknown, and in specific cases they could wipe out earnings."

The FDIC, Federal Reserve and Controller of the Currency were so concerned about the extent of the problem in 1976 and the disclosure thereof, that they successfully defied a Congressional subpoena demanding disclosure of Federal records of all U.S. banks with more than $1 billion in assets.

Let's go back to our Arab finance minister and see what he might do. As this book goes to print, the Arabs are, for the first time, showing signs of great interest in currencies and government securities other than ours. They are a major factor in the upsurge of gold prices and they are buying Japanese securities. They have been buying some Swiss francs and some British pounds and, as a result, most of these currencies have been exploding upward against the dollar. The continued inflow of Arab money into New York, which kept our balance of payments deficit from being worse than it would have been, may now be ended. The monstrous transfer of wealth to the oil nations has not totally destroyed the dollar, only because the Arabs were recycling their profits back into this country, mostly through the aforementioned short-term deposits. They don't even have to pull their money out in order to destabilize us. All they have to do is stop pouring money in, and that seems to have begun.

5. Let's not forget about the cities. The New York City experience gave banks their biggest scare since the bank panic of the 1930's. Several billion dollars worth of municipal bonds were in actual, if not technical, default. Congress has voted to guarantee some $1.6 billion worth of New York paper, and that will throw the entire municipal borrowing marketplace into a tizzy because the good cities that took care of their finances and

didn't overspend will now have trouble floating loans in competition with that Government guaranteed paper, while the frogs like New York have turned into princes by virtue of those guarantees. Most of the rest of the cities in the United States will eventually be standing in line, looking for the same consideration, and Uncle Sam will pick up a huge contingent liability that will come due during the next depression. You can bet your life that this will ultimately be paid with inflationary, printing press greenbacks during a hyper-inflationary spiral.

Most of these problems can be papered over as long as the economy is in an upswing, as it was in '76 on into '78, but when it turns down, any or all of these problems can become critical and the banks could be assaulted from every direction at once.

When things really start going sour, here's what the banks do.

1. They shore up public confidence by showing high earnings. Thanks to the miracle of modern accounting, losses can be shown on the balance sheet by the reduction of "loan loss reserves" and not as a debit against earnings, so we can see some glorious earnings reports from some very sick banks. Also, a loss this year need not be all charged off against this year's income (only 20% a year for five years) then they make some "bridge loans" to insolvent debtors to buy time and hope for the best.

2. They launch a massive P.R. campaign

to tell the world how sound the banking system is. Runs must be avoided at all costs. Money running around from one bank to another looking for safety is like water sloshing around in a boat. If there's enough of it the shifting weight can capsize the boat and they know this. Money leaving the banking system entirely is even worse. Cash ratios are so low that no banks can tolerate heavy withdrawals for long without a massive infusion of help from the Fed or the FDIC. Public confidence is so critical that anything goes in an effort to maintain it.

3. They demand secrecy. Disclosure could be fatal, triggering withdrawals. The political power of the banks to avoid disclosure is incredible.

4. The Federal Reserve has said, "We will simply allow the banks to continue to include in their capital those defaulted loans and notes as though they were not in default." That ain't honest.

What will actually happen if the banks get in trouble? There aren't any good choices.

First, the federal government will probably mount a huge rescue operation. They will print, if necessary, hundreds of billions of dollars to help certain large banks meet the demand from depositors. More inflation pressures! The banks could also invoke their right to refuse to give you your money upon demand, if they really need to, and it would take years to restore confidence again.

The following statement of policy is pretty typical of most banks.

Depositor(s) may at any time be required by Bank to give notice of an intended withdrawal, not less than 60 days before a withdrawal is made. The intent of this provision is to protect the best interests of the Bank and depositors alike, and it will be enforced *only in cases of financial excitement* [my stress added] or when it may be deemed expedient by the Bank's Board of Directors.

The First National Bank of
McMinnville, Tennessee

They can also stave off defeat for a few days by declaring a "bank holiday."

Under an Executive Order issued by any president, they can immediately freeze all transfers of funds from the banks, pleading "national emergency."

At best, it would mean great inconvenience for you as you would have to wait for your money, and by the time you get it, it may not be worth much. At worst, it could mean failure of the currency, and no acceptable means of exchange and the total loss of your money.

Now, you have some practical problems. What should you do? I don't know when the banks are going to be in trouble, or even if they will go broke for sure. I don't know how soon after publication you will read this book, or how far along the road things will be by the time you get your hands on it. All I know is that the risks are high. If, on any given day, only 5% of the depositors of the banks demanded their funds, even the strongest banks could fail. Obviously, conditions would have to deteriorate substantially before this kind of panic could happen, but we've already learned that inflation is precisely what can cause this. So here are my recommendations:

Don't buy C.D.'s. Only a small amount of money needed for the orderly conduct of your financial affairs should be kept either in your checking account or in demand deposit accounts. All the rest of your necessarily liquid funds should be in Treasury bills, or the Money-Funds described elsewhere in this book. The T-bill market will be the last market to go broke and that would give you time to get your funds out. This is the equivalent of cash. Most of your assets should be in the counter-cyclical investments that we will discuss later. Your bank deposits are being battered by inflation anyway, so why accept the risks of the banking system.

Some people have suggested that if you had money in the bank where you also had a loan outstanding, and the bank went broke, that you could argue that the money in the bank would off-set the loan and you would suffer on loss.

That sounds like a great idea, but when a bank fails nowadays, sometimes the assets (loans) are bought by another bank and the liabilities (deposits) are assumed by the FDIC, so you could have your loan in one place and your deposit in another, and it might not offset. The best bet is just to avoid banks except for necessary transactions so you won't have to worry about it.

Don't worry about whether your bank is a

good one or a bad one. If your bank is small and one of the first to go broke, the FDIC will probably rescue it, and you will merely go to the bank one day and find that it has been merged with another bank through secret negotiations with the FDIC and the Controller of the Currency and you will be able to get your money without any difficulty. It's when the entire system is in danger and shuts down for a while that everybody is in trouble, regardless of what bank you patronize.

SAFE-DEPOSIT BOXES

Is a safe-deposit box really safe? It had better be. That's where I have all my gold coins. The contents are my property, not that of the bank, and can't be attached by the bank's creditors unless you have a loan in default at the same bank, or a delinquent bank credit card account. Your deposits can and will be lost if enough banks are in sufficient trouble to overwhelm the FDIC. But safe-deposit box contents are yours.

If the bank should go broke, you may have trouble getting to your box because the doors will be shut for a few days, but after the dust settles and the panic is over, you will have access to your box. Maintain a separate inventory of everything for insurance purposes. Don't keep your will there because in many states it is illegal to remove anything in the case of a death of one of the co-owners until appropriate authorization from the courts.

Your will should be on file with your attorney or in a safe place at home.

The banks most likely to re-open after a panic are the flagship banks of those big banking groups we listed earlier. The nation will have to restore a monetary system of some kind and it can only do it through the banking system and those are the ones which would represent the highest degree of safety for your necessary dealings, even though they happen to be the ones which are most exposed to some of the bad loans. But remember, again, even if the bank doesn't go broke, the money will.

It is not my intention to tell you that the banks are going to go broke immediately. That would be foolish. I just want you to know how vulnerable the banks are to the kind of financial earthquakes that are inevitable and that the risks will rise as we move into recession and as inflation accelerates. There are many better ways to earn money than by putting it in the bank and there are many safer places to put your money. It is foolish to give them any more of your money than necessary. As we have seen, if you loan a bank your money at 7% or 8%, you are getting ripped off by inflation, and if you spend the interest, you are consuming your capital. Keep as much distance from the banks as you possibly can. They may be dangerous to your financial health.

9
POWER TO THE PRESIDENT

Now that you have absorbed this long litany of trouble, it is about time to assess what government will be doing in response to these problems as they develop, because government is the biggest fact of life in our financial, social and economic environment.

They know what's coming, and they're ready for it. If you don't believe me perhaps we should look at some of the government's contingency plans for the kind of troubles about which we are talking.

There is a mechanism already in place which is already the law of the land, which would give the President total dictatorial powers to solve any problem, real or anticipated.

THE DOOMSDAY MACHINE

During the last days of the Ford Administration, Congress cancelled several Presidential Executive Orders that had been around since World War I, including several declared by President Roosevelt, which gave the President dictatorial powers. At the same time, they approved another Executive Order, #11490 which can be put into effect by the President of the United States by declaration, and I quote from the Order, "*. . . in any national emergency type situation that might conceivably confront the nation.*" Under Congress' Mandate, the President can invoke this at his own discretion and then it can be reviewed by Congress after 6 months. If you read this 35 page Executive Order carefully, you will realize that it gives the President the power to do almost anything. He can ration fuel, control wages prices and rents, prevent transfers of money seize gold, silver and stored food, or by simple declaration do almost anything which the government can put together the machinery to implement. That statement implies some significant practical limitations, but let's look at the statutory powers inherent in this frightening document which is now the law of the land, only awaiting declaration.

It's called "Executive Order #11490—Assigning Emergency Preparedness Functions to Federal Departments and Agencies (As Recommended)." It gives almost every governmental agency specific instructions and powers in case of a national emergency. At my first reading, it seemed fairly innocent, in that it seemed to be directed toward contingency planning for nuclear war, but as I looked more closely, it had teeth, under a very loose definition of "national emergency." Each agency is to conduct their day-to-day operations with the emergency plan in mind.

In case of such an emergency, virtually all power comes under the Director of the Federal Preparedness Agency, which is subordinate to the General Services Administration. This man becomes, literally, "deputy dictator," operating under direct authority of the President of the United States ". . . in any national emergency type situation that might confront the nation." (Section F.E.C. 102 a)

> In accordance with the guidance approved by, and subject to evaluation by the director of the Federal Preparedness Agency, they are to be prepared to implement, in the event of an emergency, all appropriate plans developed under this order.

Section 105 indicates that

> . . . plans so developed may be effectuated only in the event that authority for such effectuation is provided by a law enacted by Congress or by an order or directive issued by the President, pursuant to statutes or the Constitution of the United States.

Such a statute has already been enacted by Congress, granting the President such authority, so it is the law of the land, if the President chooses to make it so. If you don't scare easily, read on.

HIGHLIGHTS

According to the Order, the Department of Defense will develop

> ... plans and programs for the emergency control of all devices capable of emitting electro-magnetic radiation.

There goes the old C.B.!
The Department of Interior

> ... shall prepare national emergency plans and develop perparedness programs covering electric power, petroleum and gas, solid fuels, minerals and water. Under the heading, "Production," they are to "... provide guidance and leadership to assigned industries or ensure the continuity of production ... and cooperate with Congress in the identification and evaluation of essential facilities.

Total control and seizure of industry!
The Department of Commerce is to

> ... control the production and distribution of all materials, the use of all production facilities, the control of all construction materials and the furnishing of basic industrial services, including (A) Production and distribution and use of facilities for petroleum, solid fuels, gas, and electric power, and the Secretary of Commerce shall develop control systems for prior-

ities, allocations, production, and distribution as appropriate, to serve as allotting agents for materials and other resources . . .

That's rationing! And therein lies the President's power to take control of all energy sources!!

MORE HAIR-RAISERS

The Department of Labor shall

> . . . develop plans and procedures for wage and salary stabilization and for the national and field organization necessary for the administration of such a program in an emergency, including investigation, compliance and appeals.

This is the President's statutory authority to impose wage and price controls, and a police-state structure to enforce them, without further Congressional action, and inflation is the "national emergency" that might trigger the Executive Order.

Now we get to something really scary, and that's in the description of the responsibilities of the Federal Bank Supervisory Agencies in Section #1701. They are to provide for the ". . . regulation of the withdrawal of currency and the transfer of credits, including deposits and share account balances."

This happy little clause says that they can simply freeze all of your money if it is sitting in a financial institution. Of course, this is explained away as the need for government to "prevent hoarding or panic buying." Actually, what it prevents is the rational response of those who have a natural dislike of having their assets confiscated. And here's another little joker thrown at us by the General Services Administration. They are to

> ... develop plans and emergency operating procedures for the utilization of excess and surplus real and personal property ... including ... the disposal of real and personal property and the rehabilitation of personal property.

That could mean seizure, confiscation, "land reform," and redistribution of wealth.

The SEC can effect

> ... the temporary closure of security exchanges, suspension of redemption rights and the freezing of stock and bond prices if required in the interest of maintaining economic controls.

You might not be able to unload your holdings in a collapsing investment marketplace.

And how does this grab you? They can prevent

> ... the flight of capital outside this country in coordination with the Secretary of Commerce.

So don't think you can just grab your money and send it to Switzerland. You can bet your life that the Swiss won't let you bring your money back here either. They will obviously retaliate in kind.

Well, those are the highlights. This is the ultimate weapon held by the President of the United States in the event of any of the crises we have discussed. But he needs an emergency in order to accomplish this. This Executive Order, it should be emphasized and repeated, can be implemented "in any national emergency type of situation." And who knows how that might be defined. Congress cannot review it for a period of 6 months. The only thing standing between us and a dictatorship is the good character of the President and the lack of a crisis severe enough that the public would stand still for it, and we've just devoted several chapters to describing the crises which have a high probability.

There are obviously some practical problems in implementing this. I don't think that government could get away with all of it because it would require a monstrous national police force, which does not exist. Our military would be extremely undependable under emergency conditions, principally because a large percentage of our military comes from the poor and the disadvantaged, and that class is the group which is going to be most angry about conditions, because they are the ones to whom the most promises have been made—the promises that will have to be broken, and I wouldn't want to depend on soldiers to put down looting and civil strife among their peers and families in an inner city.

The aspects of this plan that we should fear the most are those where the government can apply leverage at crucial points in the system. I'm referring primarily to the banks and the large energy companies. The most likely events will be the freezing of funds and the rationing of fuel, plus wage and price controls.

Least likely to be implemented would be the actual seizure of individual holdings of food, gold and money as that would require a police force way beyond the capability of this government.

This Executive Order, in my opinion, sums up the entire argument against registration of C.B.'s, and guns, and the advisability of conducting your survival item transactions, as described in Part II, with cash, as the banks microfilm all your checks and would be able to trace all transactions through the bank—or, more likely, demand that the bank search for them.

When I said in earlier chapters that the Ship of State would be sailing through stormy waters, I wasn't just referring to economics. Economics creates instability where the public demands a "strong man" and all we need is the right (or wrong) man sitting in the White House who would be inclined to take this authoritarian position for the "best good of the country." Even if the measures were temporary, and the President voluntarily returned the nation to its state of freedom, it would have brought about terrible dislocations in the economy—distortions which are likely to become institutionalized and planted in cement through government controls.

You might want to read this chapter again. Bear in mind that I am not talking about a possibility. This Executive Order is reality. It is the law of the land, only waiting to be declared. If you agree with me that the problems I have discussed could be construed as a "national emergency," justifying the imposition of such an order, then I think you have to conduct your life as though it were possible, even if you're not prepared to admit that it is probable.

You should purchase those items which will tend to be in short supply under a system of price controls (and we'll be discussing that later), and you should conduct your financial transactions with as much privacy as possible, leaving as few tracks as you can. You should have your money out of those areas which are essentially government controlled, and I'm referring to banks, the stock market, even the commodities market, at the first sign of trouble.

10
WE OWE IT TO OURSELVES

The Treasury Department publishes a bi-annual "Statement of Liabilities and Other Financal Commitments of the United States Government," showing all the liabilities of the U.S. Government. It is generally distributed only to Congressional leaders and a few government officials. The most recent statement is as of September 30, 1976. It's 31 pages long.

The so-called "National Debt" of approximately $650 billion is disposed of on the first page. That $650 billion is only the tip of the iceberg. Icebergs have about 15% of their bulk visible above water, but this one has only about 12% visible. That $650 billion is only the amount represented by U.S. Government Securities on which the government is paying interest—its "funded debt," which means that there is approximately $650 billion of government debt instruments, such as Treasury notes, bills, and bonds.

What in the heck is in the other 30 pages? About *$6 trillion* in other liabilities, that's what!

Just for openers, there is $190.6 billion in government guarantees to insure private lenders, including some things I've never heard of before, such as The Housing Guarantee Fund, Foreign Military Sales Funds, Overseas Private Investment Corporation, the Farmers Home Administration, Agricultural Credit Insurance Fund, etc. Some of the numbers are pretty big. The Rural Electrifiction Administration guarantees $4 billion of credit. The Maritime Administration, through their federal ship financing funds, insures about $5 billion. The Rural Housing Fund is $11 billion. The Low Rent Public Housing Program guarantees $13 billion and the F.H.A. guarantees over $93 billion.

These insurance commitments, when added to banks, savings and loans ($316 billion), student loans, etc., are $1.6 trillion. It might be interesting to point out that the government insurance commitments to save the banks if they get in trouble makes Uncle Sam the lender of last resort for the entire world, because of those banks' international loans. To save the banks we will have to save all those rag-tag, bob-tail countries and it might take all the money we can print. Also, bear in mind that the government generally has to insure loans only when they are so weak that no one would make them without government guarantees. That gives me the same feeling the astronauts had when they were reminded that the missile on which they were riding had been built by the lowest bidder.

There is a fascinating footnote at the end of the Insurance Commitments section:

> In several instances, incomplete data have been submitted by certain agencies since their accounting systems have not yet been developed to the point where they are able to provide the required information. In other instances the data furnished were on the basis of estimates by the reporting agencies.

And you can bet your sweet life that those figures are understated by untold tens of billions of dollars.

One interesting category is only listed in a footnote under the Social Security program. It is the Federal Supplementary Medical Insurance Trust Fund. The notes indicate that, since this program is operated on a one-year term insurance basis, with the premium rate being adjusted by the Secretary of H.E.W. so as to finance the cost of the program, ". . . this system is not susceptible to long-range actuarial analysis." I believe that liability is over $1 trillion. Even without that, the Social Security total deficiency, on an actuarial basis, is over $4 trillion, according to a footnote on page 22.

Increasingly enough, the net admitted actuarial liability of all these annuity programs was not totaled in the report. I wonder why? I had to do it myself. It came to $4.6 trillion and it may be grossly understated.

Let me repeat that Grand Total of all liabilities again. Over $6 TRILLION!

As Dick Russell says, the country is mortgaged to the hilt. There is no unencumbered capital in America. The mountain of debt, public and private, including the federal debt, is much greater than the total wealth. The federal obligation alone is 20 times more than the total money supply. History records no example of any nation accumulating debt in anywhere near these relationships to the total national wealth without eventually bringing down the entire economy and being repudiated through admitted bankruptcy, or liquidated, using the preferred form of bankruptcy—inflation. My guess is that we will liquidate our debt through the inflation process as the Germans did in 1923.

How can Uncle Sam accumulate such a mountain of contingent liabilities and yet get away with telling us that the national debt is only $650 billion? Well, it relates to accounting methods.

The story is told of a Frenchman whose hobby is ballooning who decides to practice his favorite sport one Sunday afternoon. He miscalculates the wind and gets blown across the English Channel and lands in a field someplace in England. As he is lying there half-stunned in the basket, an Englishman rushes up and says, "What happened?" The Frenchman says, "Where am I?" The Englishman replies, "Why, you are in a basket in the middle of a field." To which the Frenchman asks, "Are you an accountant?" "Yes I am, how did you know?" said the Englishman. The Frenchman replied, "Because the information you have given me is completely accurate and totally useless."

Arthur Anderson, the largest accounting firm in the world, recently completed a study of the U.S. Government's accounting methods. They urged the government to do just like corporations do—use an accrual system that matches assets with liabilities. According to Anderson, if they use standard corporate accounting figures for fiscal 1974, it would show that the U.S. Government really ran a 1973 budget deficit of $95 billion, not the $3.5 billion they reported. This kind of accounting would highlight for the public and our legislators, particularly the free-spenders, just how horrible this situation really is.

Congressman Phil Crane, a man whom I respect mightily, introduced a bill in the Congress proposing truth in government accounting. It died. He also proposed a second bill which required state and local governments also to adjust their accounting the same way. It died. Some state and local governments couldn't float any more bonds if they showed how bad their finances really are.

One of the arguments that's always been used in favor of public debt is, "We owe it to ourselves," meaning that it is quite harmless.

Surprise! That's no longer true. Remember the 20% of our Federal debt which is in the hands of the Germans, the Japanese, and the Arabs? Now that's good news and bad news. The bad news is they have us by our economic throat. At the present time they are friendly, but I don't think by any stretch of the imagination you could refer to any of these as our "traditional friends." And now the good news. The government will liquidate its debt through inflation, and our creditors will be left with a handful of useless paper. Can you now catch the vision of inflation from the Government's point of view? And can you now see why the Germans refuse to inflate their economies at our request, and why they complain about our inflation?

By no stretch of the imagination can the United States government be called solvent. The big question is: How long can it continue to get away with it? Only until such time as the public refuses to give them any more money, having discovered Uncle Sam is a dead-beat who has already borrowed several times more than he can ever repay.*

---

*All the numbers in this chapter have been increased in the more recent 1978 Statement of Liabilities. The trend is the same and accelerating. I haven't seen the 1980 statement.

11
SIN-TAX

John Adams once said that, "Our constitution was made only for a moral and religious people. It is wholly inadequate to the government of any other."

What does that have to do with money, economics and survival?

A heck of a lot. Any society's economy must be interpreted within the framework of its governmental and social systems. What John Adams meant was that this nation was based upon shared values (which are also shared by many who are not "religious"). Edmund Burke elaborated still further on this principle: "Men of intemperate habits cannot be free. Their passions form their fetters."

This nation has worked because there was

a general consensus that we had a responsibility to the general good and that every man was responsible for his personal welfare, that individuals were to be charitable to those who were unable to care for themselves, and there was no sympathy for those who would not work. We were willing to take up arms to defend our country. We believed that we could pull ourselves up by our own bootstraps and that life rewarded those who struggled. We looked up to those who achieved and did not punish success by excessive taxation. We were willing to sacrifice security for the opportunities that complete freedom offered us—along with the risks. People avoided "the dole" because to be dependent was humiliating, and this attitude motivated great achievements and was a strength to society in general.

We believed in secure, stable money, and several times through hard experience we have learned what happens when we violate this principle, as our currency system has collapsed more than once, but the side effects were relatively limited in the past because of the higher degree of decentralization and independence.

There was a general consensus as to what was "right" and "wrong" in ethics and morals. Family was honored as the time-tested basic structural unit of society and the "three-generation" family was the mainstay of our society.

I could go on and on about basic structural changes. It is the intangible, "spiritual" consensus that determines the strength of the society. This nation can become ungovernable as this consensus dwindles. I agree with John Adams that our constitution is "wholly inadequate to the government" of any people who do not, in a general sense, accept these basic principles. Our founding fathers operated on the principle that true freedom requires voluntary restraint.

I would like to point out some areas in which this consensus is becoming unraveled and zero in on the critical ones—those that are most likely to give us societal changes that are beyond our ability to adapt to, or cope with, or pay for.

The sexual revolution represents a great threat to our economy. It may be the one factor that can cause all of my optimistic forecasts of economic recovery to go astray.

Every society has basic structural factors that everyone takes for granted which must remain stable. In *Fiddler on the Roof*, Tevye understood this when he sang about tradition. Everyone in his society had a role and knew that role and performed it well, so they had a stable and balanced society. And when new values came into the society at too high a rate, their little village crumbled around their ears, helped, of course, by outside forces.

The changing value that concerns me most as an economic factor is the sexual revolution, because it is an assault upon the basic nurturing unit of society—the family—and it has financial consequences that are awesome to contemplate.

Professor Urie Bronfenbrenner, of the Psychology Department of Cornell University, recently observed that the American family is falling apart. Violence and vandalism are rampant in our schools and more people are living alone and these disturbing trends must be reversed if we are to survive as a nation.

> Changes of this magnitude have never occurred before except in times of great national upheaval like wars, depressions and floods.
>
> The family will either become more important again or we will go down the drain like Greece and Rome did. As soon as the family fell apart in Greece and Rome, so did the whole society.

Now, what does family have to do with money?

In a traditional family structure where parents are loyal to each other and devoted to their children, societies remain stable. Families stay together, and divorce is infrequent. Basic reverence for family and ancestors maintained relative social stability for centuries in Japan and Germany. The nuclear family was the basic motivating force in the colonization and development of our country. The sexual revolution is an assault upon that institution.

I have long been convinced that the religious restrictions against extra-marital or premarital sex, which are common to the Christian and Hebrew scriptures, are more for the protection of society than for the regulation of life of the individual. If you stop to consider it, it becomes apparent that all of the rules of sexual behavior such as the rules against incest and adultery seem to be designed to prevent sexual rivalry within the family. The laws against premarital sex are designed to prevent children from being brought into the world without a stable "nuclear family" environment to nurture them.

These were reasonable, rational attempts to control behavior for the greater good of the society. Whether you believe they were man-made or inspired by God, they were wise laws.

In short, much of what organized religion calls "sin" is a set of essential behavioral standards, the violation of which will de-stabilize society. This is not a simple matter of opinion or a moralistic position. As we shall see from some of the statistics, violation of these standards leads to fiscal instability, confiscatory taxation and to inflationary ruin. We have no choice but to study human moral and ethical behavior, along with traditional economics, when we try to understand the present and forecast the future.

SEX, FAMILY AND TAXES

Throughout history, advanced civilizations have had very restrictive, somewhat puritanical sexual codes during their ascendency and peak.

Codes of sexual behavior were sometimes "honored in the breach" but even when they were being violated, it was understood that a standard was being violated. Civilizations in decline tend to reach the point where the violation becomes the common, socially acceptable behavior among the upper and middle classes.

The family is not only the nurturing unit of society, it is the means by which the values of one generation are passed on to the next and by which the inexperienced young are protected against the consequences of their errors in judgment. The quality of the family determines whether succeeding generations will be neurotic, criminal, unstable, and a burden to society, or whether they will be strong, responsible, moral, independent and emotionally and spiritually stable contributors to society. When we train our children, we are, in effect, training our grandchildren. Adultery brings jealousy and sexual rivalry which can poison or break up the family unit, or, at the very least, make it a loveless environment in which to raise a child.

Adultery is also as much of an integrity problem as it is a sexual "sin," because the adulterer has to lie, sneak and violate his most sacred promises. I don't believe anyone can have a deceitful double life without spiritual and emotional damage which has to reflect itself in tensions in the home.

When society relaxes its attitudes against pre-marital sex, as we have done today, there is an explosion of unmarried family units without long-term legal or emotional commitments. There were 1½ million such unmarried family units, mostly teenagers, begun in 1976.

I have noticed with great interest that the climbing divorce rate has flattened out. Don't get too thrilled with that. It's simply because the most unstable elements of our society which are most likely to divorce are the ones starting those unmarried household units, and they are the ones which will break up, leaving fatherless or motherless children, and no statistical tracks.

I know what it is like to grow up without a father. My dad died when I was six months old and I never knew him. When I became a father I had no role model. I had to learn how to do it all by myself. The result was a lot of mistakes. When society condones casual sexual relationships that create children without a father-role model, with little girls being starved for male affection, and little boys not experiencing "father-son male bonding," the end result is generally promiscuity, illegitimacy and its accompanying burden on society. Society ends up paying the bill.

I think I turned out okay, and I'm sure others did also, but the odds were against us.

Loosening sexual morality always ends up hitting society in its pocketbook. The exponential growth of welfare costs and property taxes can be directly traced to the sexual revolution, and it is the major contributing factor to juvenile crime, alcoholism, abortions, drug addicton, and disrupted schools that can no longer teach, but can only "police," and badly too. And you pay for it!

These value systems have lasted thousands of years for reasons other than their existence in sacred documents. Traditional sexual morality has survival value for societies. I am looking at it strictly from the perspective of an economic observer. I haven't decided whether relaxation of these values is strictly a symptom or a cause of a declining civilization, but it is, at the very least, an accompanying factor to the rate of decline.

This raises an interesting question. Does

society have a right to enforce its traditional morality by laws as a protective measure to save itself, if that enforcement interferes with the human right to "sin"? The answer to that question is that if the majority of the people in a society have chosen to violate these stabilizing standards, passing laws won't help. Again, we get back to John Adams' invisible consensus. The key factor was everyone's agreement that certain areas of life could not be regulated by law, and they would be responsibly regulated by the people themselves. When the people cease to regulate themselves, society finds it impossible to come up with fair laws that are acceptable to society, and society and the individuals are the losers. To attempt to control human behavior by law in areas of personal morals raises grave questions, while at the same time, to permit the flaunting of aberrant behavior and give it social respectability raises equally grave questions, and I feel threatened no matter what we do. That is why the anti-homosexual crusade is profoundly disturbing to me. Homosexuality is an assault on the family institution, but laws attacking homosexuality are an assault on freedom, and I feel in jeopardy when social trends have placed society in a position of having to choose between these two horrible alternatives.

So we have a classic example of rights in conflict.

Any society that does not gain a general consensus that sex is reserved for heterosexual marriage is going to reap a harvest of unstable, confused children and relationships that shift like the sands, leaving children the bewildered, twisted victims. But if Adams' invisible consensus has broken down, a free democratic society cannot enforce laws regarding sexual behavior without becoming a police state.

In my church counseling responsibilities, I've seen over and over again how the lack of an effective role model for children leads to unstable second and third generations. Marriage is a tough enough learning ground for amateurs, even with a role model. I hope that when my children marry, they will be able to look back on a loving and stable relationship between and with their parents. I hope they learned from me how to be a father and leader in the home and how to love, respect and cherish a wife. I hope they will have learned from my wife how to deal with stress and disagreement in a mature way, and how to raise children in a firm and loving manner.

All we can really do to insulate ourselves is to create oases of sexual stability and fidelity in our homes and churches. If we don't, the next unstable generation will bleed us dry in welfare costs, crime, drug addiction, alcoholism, violence, police costs, fire costs, legal fees and gigantic government efforts to deal with these problems. If we sow the wind, we will reap the whirlwind.

For example, 50.3% of the newborn black babies in this country were illegitimate. Among the whites, the illegitimacy rate has nearly doubled, from 4% of all births in 1965 to 7.7% in 1976. According to Peter Schuck, a deputy assistant secretary of H.E.W., "There is definitely a high correlation between out-of-wedlock births, welfare costs and many of our most pressing social problems."

$11.7 billion is spent yearly in Federal, State and local Aid to Families with Dependent Children, which is the welfare program for poor families with no father at home. The Urban Institute in Washington, D.C. said that women who began their drift toward dependency as teen-age mothers cost taxpayers about 6 billion dollars a year in welfare payments.

Only 50% of the unwed mothers manage to get even a temporary job during the first four years of motherhood, and 9 out of 10 land on public assistance rolls, which is five times the rate of married mothers. Too often the children run wild for lack of supervision and mothers become mired in a life of poverty, alcoholism, drug addiction and child abuse.

Psychologist Bronfenbrenner says, "These people are going to put a growing burden on our society, not only to sustain them but to repair the social and economic damage they do."

The Carter Administration offered a new bill on adolescent pregnancy prevention and care which would finance more counseling, contraceptives, classes and day care for pregnant and unwed teenagers which will cost about $60 million a year. That would bring to $344 million the total that H.E.W. is asking Congress to spend on teen-age pregnancy, which is an increase of $148 million over the current level.

The total cost to society is impossible to determine exactly, but it is safe to say it adds up to between $500 and $2,000 per tax-paying family per year.

A society that collectively makes a wrong decision in these areas is a society on a collision course with financial and social disaster, to say nothing of the moral or religious implications. No moral authority can be exercised over a society that is not voluntarily granted to its leadership by its citizens, regardless of laws.

Based on the above principles, and strictly on economic grounds, I am opposed to pornography, sexually explicit films and television, and bringing children into the world without the emotional and legal commitments of marriage. I am especially concerned about publications advocating the "new morality," such as *Playboy*, *Penthouse*, etc., which have gained such respectability that you can buy them in any drug store or 7-11 in America. Their publishers have paid premium prices to get respectable authors to write articles on serious subjects to provide the rationale that many people need in order to justify buying sexually explicit material. Its very respectability makes it more dangerous, in my opinion, than the grossest hard-core pornography, because it is so generally available in places which are considered respectable.

I am concerned about the consequences of a man moving into middle age, who every day is comparing his wife, as she adds wrinkles and pounds, with the forever-young, physically perfect center-fold, and finds that his loyal spouse does not measure up to this fantasyland ideal. No woman can compete with that, and it may well be that this fantasy may be the reason for much male sexual dissatisfaction and infidelity, and for much unhappiness in the home.

Fortunately, sometimes this problem is self-correcting. The pendulum swings both ways. The 1920's were a period of great sexual license and rapid moral change. Isadora Duncan, with her free-love philosophy, was a great heroine of her times. The movies were really very explicit for their times and there was a very large underground market for hard-core pornography on film. When we went into the depression of the 30's, however, most everyone became concerned with the fundamentals of barely eking out an existence, and the nation swung into a puritanistic backlash in our schools, the movies, and the arts. Illicit sex had to go underground where it belonged. This puritanical period lasted almost twenty-five years.

The good news is that the age in which we now find ourselves may be just another swing of the pendulum, albeit considerably worse than the 20's. The pendulum will probably swing back when we go into the next crash, because people simply will not have the time, leisure, or emotional energy for the kind of hedonism with which we live now.

By now you understand the fundamental concept of the economic consequences. It was really brought home to me when I had to spend about $15,000 caring for three children of a woman friend of our family who had joined the sexual revolution. These children, who were brought up without a father, ended up in my lap, as she simply could not keep her family together for a variety of reasons and came to Kay and me for help. Her sexual behavior had a price tag for me. We have had several foster children in our home, and in nearly every instance, there were sexual problems in their homes. Some authorities believe that virtually every prostitute was sexually molested in the home by a close relative. It is a personal and national tragedy to know that more than 50% of the black babies born in this country are illegitimate, and nearly all of them will end up being wards of the city, state or county, and the direct and indirect costs have to be numbered in the hundreds of billions of dollars and eventually in the trillions, not to mention the enormous waste of precious human potential. And if that isn't an economic issue, I don't know what is.

PART II
PRESERVATION

INTRODUCTION

We've wallowed in trouble long enough. I don't deliberately set out to be pessimistic, but it would be foolish to be unrealistic, and someone has to define the problem. You must be aware of the problems or you won't act. We all need some personal and financial defensive positions. I don't expect to have a fire in my house but I expect to have a fire drill. I don't expect to crash my car but I own insurance.

These problems do not mean the end of Western Civilization. I've said it before and I'll say it again. The nation will recover. I know that some reviewers will choose to misinterpret this as a "doom and gloom" book, but I must make it clear that I am as persuaded of the ability of the country to survive all these problems, as I am of the problems themselves. The function of this book is to help you to prepare, and you won't do that unless you can clearly see the potential danger.

Not only is there a silver lining in this cloud as far as our government and our nation is concerned, but there are silver linings for you personally. Every one of these problems has within itself the seeds of personal solutions for you and your family.

Let's repeat what Will Rogers said. "Invest in inflation, it's the only thing that's going up." Whether or not inflation is good or bad for you depends on whether or not you own some of those things which are inflating in price. If most of your assets are invested in those things which do well during inflationary spirals, you are personally insulated from the worst effects. I can't pretend you will escape all of the effects of a national or worldwide depression because you will be exposed to increased crime, possible civil disorders, and even dangers to the Constitution itself. And obviously that will affect all of us, no matter how rich we might be, but over the long haul, as we fight our way through these problems, I am convinced that we can be standing on the right side of the financial balance sheet and we can end up with our assets intact, as well as our personal health and safety. If you live in the right place and have a reasonable amount of self-sufficiency, and the distribution machine misses a few beats, you'll still be O.K.

Part II deals with the most fundamental aspect of my total program. This may be the only relevant advice for some of you, because (a) some of you won't have enough money to go beyond it, and (b) some of you have taken the financial moves already, having perceived these problems, but you haven't dealt with the survival steps.

I will be concerned in the next few chapters with personal survival and safety, and being sure that you do not over-react to the realities. There are a lot of "gloom and doom" guys out there who would have you bail out of society and get a place in the mountains with a machine gun turret on the roof. I don't believe that's necessary.

So let's move on to a sensible plan that does not burn your bridges behind you and gives you some flexible alternatives if my timetable is off or if it doesn't turn out exactly as I think. It's possible to be right about the problem but miss the boat in judging the implications. The program must be flexible and you must grasp the principles which will enable you to adapt your strategy to changing situations. But the advice in Part II will not change. It's fundamental advice that I would give you, even if the odds favored good times ahead.

Incidentally, the order of Chapters in Part II may seem a bit odd, in that I start with Ruff's Recommendation #2. That's because I wanted to leave the most important survival recommendation until last—for emphasis.

12
GOLD AND SILVER COINS

Ruff's Recommendation No. 2. Have one-half bag of "junk silver" coins per person, and, if possible, an equivalent dollar amount in gold coins for your "survival" position.*

The human consciousness of gold and silver as real wealth is expressed in language, legend, fairy tale, cliché, and value judgment. It is natural to speak of silver linings, the "golden boy," the Midas touch, the pot of gold at the end of the rainbow, etc. No matter how cleverly governments assure us that paper and ink are real money, whenever a small but significant percentage of the world's population gets worried, they want gold or silver. It doesn't take much interest to bid up the price, as there isn't much of it around.

---
*That recommendation is now ¼ bag per person because the price of silver has more than tripled since the first edition.

Gold and silver are counter-cyclical to paper investments. That means that price-wise they move in the opposite direction to paper. When paper-based economies are booming and everyone is confident, and inflation is under control and no one sees any real dark clouds on the horizon, the price of these metals tends to decline; whereas, if inflation is running rampant, war is imminent, or people are uncertain about the stability of their political institutions, the price of these metals tends to rise.

Gold and silver have certain economic characteristics in common, but they also are significantly different. Although they have both been money during most of human civilized history, they also have industrial uses, silver to a much greater degree than gold, so the fundamentals which determine their market value are somewhat different, and will be treated later. However, for purposes of this chapter, we will examine their "survival money" function.

Until the invention of the printing press, silver and gold coins were the only money used by major civilizations. The invention of the printing press introduced paper money, and ever since then, governments have tried to substitute it for precious metals with varying degrees of success. Paper currencies rise and fall, but gold and silver always come back—generally after the collapse.

In the uncertain future against which we are trying to prepare, what place do we give gold and silver?

There are three positions.
1. Your survival position.
2. Your break-even investment position and
3. Your aggressive get-rich position.

We will deal only with Position #1 in this chapter.

SILVER LININGS

The United States stopped minting 90% silver coins after 1964. Before that you could have gone into the bank with $1,000 in paper money and walked out with $1,000 in dimes, quarters and halves. These coins have been pretty well scrounged out of circulation by now, but are available from coin dealers by the "bag" or half bag. A bag consists of $1,000 in "face value" of the aforementioned dimes, quarters and halves, weighs about 55 lbs. and contains 715 to 725 ounces of silver. The coin industry refers to this as "junk silver."

As of our original publication date, one bag would cost around $4,200.* You are not paying the face value, you are not paying an inflated price, and you are not paying a "premium." You are merely paying the current market price of that much silver, plus 2-3% commission to the dealer. You may pay slightly more or less than the going silver price. Bags of coins are fast disappearing into vaults and safe deposit boxes, never to be seen again, and there could be a substantial premium by the time you read this. In fact, because of this, the

---

*And now it's over $13,000 a bag—and still a good buy.

price of bags could rise even if silver drops.

I recommend that you buy one-half bag* of "junk silver" for each member of the family.

Remember, if you had done so in 1964, it would have cost you $1,000. In the fall of 1979, it would have been worth $8,800, a 780% profit in 15 years, which would have kept you well ahead of the inflation rate. If I'm wrong about a monetary collapse and inflation merely continues at our present relatively moderate rates, the past indicates silver will continue to be a fine protection against inflation.

For many years the world has been mining less silver than it is using. We have been recovering and recycling silver, which has kept the price from going through the ceiling, but it has not prevented a steady price increase over the years. When economies are booming, especially near the peak of an expansion cycle when business is optimistic and expanding, industrial use of silver increases, so it also tends to do fairly well in periods of economic boom.

There are myriads of uses for silver in the electronics industry and huge quantities are used for photographic film.

But silver also does well when people become concerned about paper money, so it has outstanding market price support during times of difficulty. Such authors as Harry Browne, Robert Preston, and others, have helped to enhance silver's "inflation hedge" image, but the phenomenon is much more fundamental than that.

During periods of runaway inflation and

---
*Make that one quarter—more if you can afford it.

paper money collapse, coins of all nations tend to circulate quite freely. In China immediately after World War II, paper money was rejected almost everywhere, but despite the almost nonexistent communications and the civil war which was raging, silver coins of all nations were universally accepted by merchants as a means-of-exchange, and an invisible market consensus as to their purchasing power seemed to rise almost by magic over the entire country within a very few weeks.

One of my subscribers sent me a silver coin made in Germany in 1923. It was about three times the size of an American silver dollar and it was 100 million Deutschemarks. Prior to the inflation it was probably equivalent of 5 or 10 Deutschemarks. In terms of purchasing power relative to stable currencies, its value had hardly changed. Those who held paper money lost everything, but those who held gold or silver coins managed to preserve much of their wealth.

Our silver coins will serve several basic functions:

1. In case of a total collapse of a paper money economy you will be able to purchase goods and services at pretty much the same prices as before the collapse. A head of lettuce (if you can get it) might be $10,000—or one silver quarter!

2. They may be the only universally acceptable means of exchange for the purchase of necessities.

3. They will help preserve the purchasing power of your assets until such time as a

new universally acceptable (inevitably gold-backed) currency is established by government.

4. In a world which falls short of that kind of calamity, it will probably continue to be an excellent inflation hedge. In any event, over the last 14 years, it has done better than stocks, bonds, or anything you can mention, including real estate.

I choose coins in preference to bullion for a very simple reason: They are more easily divisible into spendable units. They weigh no more and take up no more space. They do not require an assay when you sell or spend them as bullion does. The commonly circulated "junk silver" will be accepted without question. Counterfeiting of these coins is almost non-existent.

HOW TO BUY THEM

Purchasing coins is simple. You can buy them from any coin dealer, but there are some real pitfalls to avoid.

1. Don't buy medallions from private mints. You will pay a large premium over the silver price so the mint can have its profit. The only way that will work out well for you is if the free marketplace values those medallions over and above their silver content, and I do not consider that likely. Metals will have to rise a long way before you break even.

2. Don't buy a bag of coins "on margin" and leave them with the coin dealer to store. During the previous inflation scare in 1974 and

1975, a lot of people did this, assuming they could use the principle of leverage to make more money, and those who bought early in the inflation cycle and sold out fairly early, did just that. If you could buy a bag of coins for $2,000 and only put down $400, when silver rose to $4,000 a bag, you would have a $2000 profit on your $400 investment, or a return of 500%, as opposed to those who bought their coins outright for $2000, sold them for $4000 and only doubled their money (100% profit). Those who bought early and got out were the lucky ones, however, as some of the largest firms in the business ran into some interesting problems. By selling on margin, these firms could sell four or five times as many bags, and earn four or five times as much commission on a sale. One huge dealer headquartered in Las Vegas found himself in deep trouble when an investigative reporter from the local paper discovered there were no coins in his vault. Customers thought that the coins they had bought on margin were being held safely for them. The company had taken the customer's money and was speculating in the commodities market. The exposure forced the company to cease operations and nearly everyone lost his money.

I've seen coin dealers offer incredible bargains in bags of silver well below the market price. Almost invariably this is a "margin" dealer who finds himself short of money, takes the customer's stored coins, prices them for a quick sale and sells them cheaply, hoping his fortunes will change and he will be able to repurchase them before the customer asks for his money. He is also operating under the assumption that only a few of his customers would ask for their coins. Usually he goes broke, leaving you holding no bags.

Sounds dishonest, doesn't it? And it is! But, it's no different from the way the banks handle your money, except the banker tells you he's going to use your money. And, in fact, when I asked the former president of one of these collapsed firms to tell me why he did it, he said, "We are doing no differently than the banks."

So, the most basic rule is, pay for your coins in full and take delivery at the time you pay, unless you know you are dealing with a sound and reputable firm. Keep them in a safe deposit box (for now, as long as the banks are relatively stable), or in a private vault or safe in your home. Don't speculate on margin with your survival coins. Our survival position requires that you have one bag of fully-owned coins for each member of the family.

This recommendation is second in importance only to the food recommendation. It's also a very close second in low-risk. If the price should drop out of the bottom of silver, which, of course, is possible, but not likely, you still have at least the face value of the coins. At today's prices that would mean a 75% loss, but at least it could never completely disappear, as you can always spend the coins.

Your survival coins are to be held through thick and thin, through every up-and-down in the silver market. This is not an investment position, it is a survival position. It's your insurance policy, and if at some future time you should realize some loss on them, you should look at that loss as the premium you paid for the insurance coverage you never had to use.

If you have sufficient funds, you should have an equivalent dollar amount invested in bullion gold coins. I am not talking about rare coins. I am talking about gold coins which are issued as the circulating currency of several countries, such as the South African Krugerrand, the Austrian 100 Corona and the various Mexican pesos. Their price will be related to the price of gold, plus a small premium. The premium can fluctuate up and down, depending on their scarcity. As of this writing, the premium will run from 3% to 5%, but in a time of great demand for these coins, such as we will find as the monetary chaos progresses, the premium can rise, and there is a possibility of considerable speculative profits through the increase in the premium, as well as the rise in the price of gold.

Gold coins also serve several functions in your investment program.

1. It is survival money in the same sense that silver coins are because they also can be spent, but it is the equivalent of $100 bills or $1,000 bills and does not take the place of your small denomination silver coins.

2. It's a "chaos-hedge." If inflation is the chaos we have, it's a hedge against that. If deflation is the chaos we have, it's the hedge against that. Traditionally, it is also the world's "scared money" and will be acceptable in a breakdown of paper currency.

3. It's counter-cyclical. It does well when other things are going badly. Even if my worst case does not materialize, it is a good investment when the world anticipates problems. When problems overwhelm us, it will skyrocket through the ceiling. In a real hyperinflation, it will be worth thousands of dollars per ounce.

4. It's also a "time machine." It's a method of getting your assets from today to tomorrow—from one side of the gulf to the other when things will return to normal.

5. It's also a means of aggressively accumulating assets in times of difficulty. These methods will be covered in another chapter.

For now, however, you should own some fully-paid-for gold coins, stored in the same way as your silver coins.

Gold has certain advantages over silver in that it is roughly 30 times as expensive per ounce,* so you can store more wealth in a smaller space. The advantages of gold coins over gold bullion are roughly the same as silver. Gold, however, is more directly keyed to the "fear cycle" than silver, as it does not have heavy industrial usage when times are good, as does silver, so it is much more directly a fear hedge, and more likely to decline when things get better.

The stock market and the gold price are almost exact mirror images of each other. The price of gold also tends to rise in tandem with increasing interest rates.

Your survival gold should be bought and held through any and all circumstances. This is not true of your investment gold or your

---
*That ratio will probably narrow, making silver look even better than it does now.

speculative gold, which you will want to buy and sell according to conditions, as we will explain later.

Gold coins can also be bought through coin dealers. The value of the coins generally bears no relationship to the political or economic fortunes of the country that issued them. However, if South Africa should go broke, the value of a Krugerrand would rise, as it would become a rare coin. If the supply of new coins was cut off and the demand remained steady, obviously the premium would increase over and above the gold price, but the value of a Krugerrand would never fall below the price of gold, even if South Africa ceased to exist.

You should maintain as much privacy as possible when purchasing coins. My suggestion is that if your bank says they only microfilm the front of all checks, your check to the dealer should be made out to "Cash" and endorsed to the seller on the back, and there would be no record of the purchase. This would not alert your bank as they are accustomed to clearing checks made to "Cash."

All of the warnings about dealing with coin dealers also apply to gold coins. Pay for your coins at the time you purchase them. If you wish to speculate in coins on margin, buy the coins and borrow against them, but not with your survival coins. They should be fully paid for.

If you followed all of my recommendations in Chapter 16 and have bought a good supply of storage items and have your home paid for, you will have very little need for these coins for spending purposes. I prefer to use them for their "store-of-value" function, as opposed to their "means-of-exchange" function, because, no matter how desirable coins might be, if the market place is not distributing goods efficiently for a while, you might not be able to buy what you want at any price. Later you will use these coins for both a store-of-value and a means-of-exchange as times permit.

When the monetary system is still hanging together, if you wish to cash in on your coins or sell a few, coin dealers will always buy them. If the economy has collapsed, they will be used directly as money for purchasing whatever is available.

Will the government ever call in your gold, as they did in 1933?

Probably, but only after one or two attempts to re-establish a new fiat paper currency (which no one accepts). After a decision has been made to back our currency with gold, I willingly will exchange my gold for a gold-backed currency, as I don't really care what you call money as long as someone is willing to give me something of value in exchange for it.

Investment Rarities (see Appendix) is a dependable dealer for both gold and silver coins.* They have serviced my clients efficiently by mail for several years. They do not sell on margin, they are financially stable, and they completely understand and agree with the philosophy expressed in this book. You can do business with them with confidence.

As is always the case, I receive no finan-

---

*I have also added Deak-Perera to my recommended list. See Appendix.

cial benefits from my commercial recommendations, as a matter of deliberate editorial policy so that no conscious or unconscious bias will creep into my recommendation, and people will respond to my suggestions. If you wish to shop around for prices, please do so, as there will be times when you can beat their prices slightly, but if you are dealing with any other firm, observe all of the precautions expressed in this chapter. Investment Rarities and Deak-Perera tend to resolve legitimate disputes in favor of my clients, as they value my recommendation.

SPECIAL NOTICE: As this edition goes to press, the gold and silver recommendations are still valid. However, in 1980, there were periods in which the metals markets were dangerous to your financial health. Wild fluctuations indicated our security blanket was having a nervous breakdown. My newsletter clients were advised to avoid gold and silver for a short period. When you read this, conditions may have changed again. Check THE RUFF TIMES to be sure. We'll send you the current issue free (See Appendix). The alternative strategy in Chapter 20 may be currently valid. That's why I have a newsletter.

13
PERSONAL DEBT

Ruff's Recommendation No. 3. Avoid unsound debt, while using sound leverage for safety and profit.

How can you safely take advantage of the bias towards borrowers in an inflationary spiral? Like porcupines in love. Very carefully. In theory, the best thing you could possibly do is go heavily into debt and pay it off with worthless dollars. If you do it just right, it can work out as planned, but there are some big potholes along the way. Let me list them.

1. You could get yourself so over-extended that if you find yourself out of a job because of the economic dislocations that inflation creates and are unable to make your

loan payments, you could be wiped out. This is especially true if you live in a big city.

2. The government might "index" debts so that contracts are adjusted to the rate of inflation. Several countries have done this in an attempt to deal with their inflationary spirals.

3. Being heavily in debt can be a substantial strain on the old fear bone and keep you awake at night, and even though that's not strictly an economic matter, it's important to my over-all strategy to increase your peace of mind, not jeopardize it.

So what are the basic rules for managing debt in an inflationary spiral?

1. Eliminate all "consumer borrowing." Have no outstanding obligations that you could not meet if your income were cut off due to inflationary or recessionary distortions in the economy. Cut your standard of living or get a second job, if you have to. Your personal security requires it.

2. Use borrowed money only to purchase income-producing investments, or those which are good bets to do well when people are scared, and which are basic to human needs. They should increase in value faster than the rate of inflation plus the interest charges.

3. Be sure that your loan agreement does not permit your creditor to obtain a "deficiency judgment" in the courts. For example, if he repossessed your car or your house and sold it for less than the loan balance, would he have the right to come after you for the difference, or would he have to be satisfied with the property alone?

4. Be sure you have some kind of liquid cash reserves to service your debt if your income should be cut off. In case of installment contracts, you can probably pay them off with greenbacks, even if they become worthless. If you have a contract requiring $100 a month and you have $600 in greenbacks set aside and your income is cut off for six months, you might buy sufficient time to solve your problem. But if all debts are indexed, then you would be in trouble. The better alternative would be to have gold or silver coins, which would tend to increase in value equal to the rate of inflation and a few of them could be sold to raise the cash to satisfy your obligations.

5. Do not use "leverage" in volatile markets unless you are prepared to coolly accept some losses as part of the process, and then, only with a small percentage of your money—your risk capital. I am referring to the commodities market, precious metals on margin, stocks on margin, options, or any of the volatile, rapidly fluctuating investments. You could be right about the primary long-term trend and get whip-sawed out by a temporary decline and a margin call. Use leverage for investments where the lender will not call your loan because of a quoted price in the newspaper. Your best bets are small town real estate, producing farms, diamonds, or businesses which might turn out to be counter-cyclical in difficult times.

6. If possible, pay off your residence completely, if it's in a safe place and meets all of our criteria, as described elsewhere. Your home

is really two things. It is an investment and it is the place where you live. If you intend to live in it no matter what, it doesn't matter whether the price goes up or down, because it is still just a home and it has not altered its function or its size. The property tax revolt movement has made it less likely that you might lose that home to taxes. It's your safe haven. But I repeat, if it's not paid-off in full, you should have a very large loan on it with the proceeds of the loan employed in relatively liquid counter-cyclical holdings.

7. Never be a lender, except very short-term, in the most secure ways possible. I won't lend any money to anybody for anything unless I want to help a friend in need. I will never do it for business or investment reasons until we move into a deflationary cycle, unless I can get a gold clause contract for inflation protection. As I pointed out earlier, lenders get ripped-off by inflation. Get rid of any paper as soon as you can. This is the hardest advice for most of you to follow, because you are almost all lenders—to the Savings and Loan, the insurance company, the bank, the United States government, or some city or some state. Loans are guaranteed instruments of confiscation!

It is theoretically sound to pay off your loans in rapidly dwindling dollars, but use caution and be sure that you are protected against the bumps in the road between now and the time you might want to pay off.

14
PASS ON THE OLD MAID

Ruff's Recommendation No. 4. Sell (or trade) all big city or suburban real estate and invest in small town income property. Move if possible.

Some years ago when my daughter Sharon was about ten, I was sitting in the living room reading the newspaper when I heard her asking her mother a question in the next room. Kay answered, "Gee, I don't know, honey. Why don't you ask your father?" to which Sharon replied, "I don't want to know that much about it."

We are now moving into a subject which will probably be the most complex of any covered in this book. I hope I don't tell you a lot more than you want to know about it, but real estate is the one subject that will touch the life of every reader. You don't have the option of avoiding it.

Back in Chapter 6, I touched on the future of real estate investing in the broadest of terms. Now I'd like to dig into the basic principles of real estate investment in the light of my basic investment philosophy, and I will try to strip it to the barest of essentials and keep it very simple.

Real estate can be stuffed into two pigeon holes—(1) your home, and (2) everything else. You have some very important decisions to make.

I'll try not to cover all aspects of how to make money in real estate, as there are far too many good books already written on that subject. The best by far is Dr. Albert J. Lowry's *How You Can Become Financially Independent by Investing in Real Estate* (see Appendix). The function of this chapter is to answer the real estate questions that have been raised by my advice. A lot of it will be handled in question and answer form.

FUNDAMENTALS

Let me restate the fundamentals against which we will measure our real estate decisions.

1. We are headed for an economic smash-up after an inflationary spiral.

2. Big cities will go broke and taxes, crime, racial and social frictions (both real and imagined), etc. will accelerate the trickle of middle class and prosperous whites from

the cities which will become a steady flow.

3. The chief beneficiary of this exodus of people and money will be the small towns of America as far from the large urban centers as is necessary to feel safe.

4. That means a price trend reversal in the expensive surburban real estate market on a random unpredictable basis, and a general boom in small town real estate.

5. In an inflationary spiral the long-term *lender* gets hurt and the long-term *borrower* reaps windfall profits.

6. To prepare for the depression environment it would be best to either pay off your home, if it's in a good location, or have it mortgaged to the hilt—nothing in between. If it is in a bad location and you still want or need to stay there, you can refinance it. The refinance money should be used for small town real estate, coins or diamonds.

7. There will be a general demand for rent controls (along with wages and prices).

8. Residential income property (one to four units) in small towns is an excellent hedge against inflation and depression.

So here we go. I will be using a Question and Answer format, based on the most common questions we receive in *The Ruff Times* Member Services department.

WHERE TO LIVE

Q. How can I tell whether or not the area in which I live is a good one?

A: Has your neighborhood been in a long explosive inflationary spiral (15% a year or more) lasting several years? Do you live within a few miles of a depressed racial or economic ghetto?

Do you live in an area which could suddenly become depressed because of the closing of one major plant or industry?

Has there been a substantial increase of listings of homes for sale in your area, compared to last year at this time?

Have the homes listed for sale tended to remain on the market for longer and longer periods of time during the last year?

Has crime had a sharp increase in your area recently?

Have there been articles in your local newspapers about the fiscal instability of your community?

If several of these questions are answered "yes," you're in a good place—to get out of. How far out? There probably ought to be some open country or farm land between you and the city. About 25 miles out I'd breathe a small sigh of relief, and when I got 75 miles away, I'd really feel pretty good.

Q. Wouldn't it be better to stay in close because of possible fuel shortages? If we had gas rationing, wouldn't there be an increase in the value of close-in property?
A. That will help urban home values, but not

much. You will have to balance your priorities—your personal safety and the value of your real estate holding, against the possibility of being isolated from your job. If you must work in the big city and the energy crisis worries you, I suggest you sell your home and rent.

I am not as concerned that you move from the city as I am that you should not have your money tied up in real estate equities in the city. If you rent and have some place to go to quickly in time of trouble, you will probably be all right. It's just that most people have their largest single asset in the form of equity in their home and that should be changed now, as it is so illiquid.

Protection of your assets and protection of your person are two different matters. Protection of your real estate assets requires advance action because homes are not instantly liquid and you cannot judge precisely when the market is about to peak and turn down and reversals in the market could come too fast for you to sell in time.

Your personal safety merely requires that you be mobile. If you sell your urban or suburban home, you might buy something in a small town and rent it out until you need it. My immediate concern is financial.

Q. What are the criteria for judging a small town?
A. That's pretty easy. There are hundreds of candidates.

Keep it under 100,000 population. It should not be dependent upon one industry or plant for its prosperity. It should be surrounded by a diversified agricultural economy so that if the distribution system becomes undependable, the town could be reasonably self-sufficient. By diversified agriculture I mean livestock, chickens, grains, vegetables, etc.

Some states to consider are Utah, Idaho, Arizona, New Mexico, Wyoming, Texas, Oklahoma, Missouri, Arkansas, North and South Carolina, Florida, Montana, Washington, California (in the extreme North, the Central Valley and the Sierra foothills) and Oregon. There are reasonable alternatives in almost every state in the union but I like the Sun Belt because of the low energy requirements if we should run out of oil and gas. I like the Inter-Mountain states,[*] even though they have cold winters, because there's plenty of wood and a much better chance of being self-sufficient on the land or supplementing the diet with hunting or fishing. There are lots of fine small towns. Just because I've left out a state doesn't mean it doesn't have possibilities.

I would also be concerned about the water supply. The area I chose in California had a huge underground reservoir which held up well even during the 2⅔ years of California drought.

Don't buy a farm unless you are experienced at farming or it's large enough that you can hire a competent resident manager. A lot of people intend to become self-sufficient farmers and don't know how. Most of you would be

---
[*]And how! I now live there.

better off living in a small town with most of the services you are accustomed to. My feeling is that big cities may become dangerous, but living alone in the countryside could be equally dangerous if the worst of all possibile bad cases came to pass and we had total anarchy. That's fairly low on the probability scale, but I still feel better living around others. The best compromise is small town life. Right now, your investment in a small town property could be the best thing you ever did financially. A lot of desirable towns have already had substantial price increases over the last two or three years, but they are starting from such a low base that there is still a long way to go. and I think you will be astounded at how cheaply property can be purchased. You could actually increase your standard of living with the same amount of money. (Obviously, you all differ in your ability to take this advice.) You might be making too much money with your big city job to leave, but at least consider selling and renting, or refinancing.

If you refinance, read the small print and be sure that your liability, if you had to walk away from the property or if you lost it because of financial reverses, is limited to the property itself, so the lender couldn't come after you for a "deficiency judgment." It is possible that the market price could break below the level of your total indebtedness, in which case you just might want to let the lending institutions have it. I'm not advocating that, however, as it is ethically dubious, so you will have to decide that for yourself.

IF IT'S REALLY BAD

Q. What makes you think prices will break in in the big cities? Real estate prices have done nothing but go up over the last several years.

A. Real estate prices don't always go up. Look what happened to Florida in 1974 when land and condominium prices broke badly. They are still recovering. All speculative bubbles burst, without exception, and the faster they blow up the bigger and faster the bust. Everything happens first in New York or California.

During California's building boom of the last few years, as many as 35% of the new homes were bought by speculators, leaving a dangerous overhang of properties threatening the marketplace. As of September 1978, only a small percentage of these have been dumped and no panic has developed; however, the other phenomenon that makes this overhang so dangerous is that many people have borrowed to the hilt against their equities, in effect, leveraging their paper profits, and spent the money. If you bought a house for $60,000 with a $40,000 mortgage, and it's now worth $100,000, the chances are you have borrowed another $30,000 and now you have $70,000 in mortgages. It is dangerous to borrow against paper profits, unless you do it specifically with a plan, as we have recommended, and invest the funds in relatively liquid counter-cyclical investments, or in additional well located real estate. But most people have spent their refinance money, and when real estate prices break, they could panic and dump these homes on the market, or simply walk away in default, if the market value drops below the total of their loans. Financial institutions could be forced to foreclose on many properties that are worth less than the total indebtedness. This kind of thing could trigger the panic selling by the speculators who have been playing a game of "Old Maid" and waiting for a "bigger fool" to come along and pay them a higher price.

FINANCING

Q. When I buy a home, should I put a big mortgage on it or a small mortgage?

A. The basic ground rule is to use as little cash as possible, or pay all cash for it. Nothing in between makes sense. If you take out a big mortgage, then you can use your excess funds to make the other kinds of investments we have discussed in Parts II and III. Also, the investment profits on that money, properly employed, should more than offset the increased interest payments.

The smaller the equity, the less likely your lending institution is to foreclose on you, as they would have to write off a large loan to acquire a small equity. In a general economic calamity, when everybody is in trouble, the homes on which they will foreclose will be the ones with the smallest mortgages, because they can improve their balance sheets with those properties, and a lot of foreclosures on small equities could make them insolvent.

If you can pay off the property completely, once you have decided you are in the proper area and that's where you want to live, then that's what you should do, because then you can never lose it. I learned the hard way that you have to be in debt to go broke, and if I can eliminate personal debt from my life, I feel better. In an inflationary spiral, the long-term borrower usually makes windfall profits, but ideally, I would rather not encumber my home, if I know I want to live there, all other things being equal. This decision—pay it off or have a big loan—is a matter of financial reality, temperament, and personal discretion. Either approach is O.K.

Q. What if I can't get an all-cash buyer on my big-city house, and they ask me to take back a "purchase money" second mortgage?
A. The purchase money "second" is a simple device for helping to close the gap between the amount of cash the buyer has and the amount of money he might be able to borrow. Let's say you are selling a $100,000 home and the buyer can only qualify for a $60,000 mortgage, leaving a $40,000 cash requirement. If the buyer only had $25,000 or $30,000 in cash, you would then write a second mortgage (which is a note—in some states, it's called a note and Deed of Trust). On whatever terms you can

negotiate, he agrees to pay you the additional amount over a period of time. However, if you accept my advice, you don't want to be long-term lender, and that's what you are if you accept a note on the sale of the property. There are several ways to deal with that problem.

First, the note is negotiable. Most people think that the only way you can turn a second mortgage into money is to sell it at a 20% discount to some mortgage broker, but there are better choices than that. Think of the "second" as an asset that can be used to buy another piece of property. I recently purchased a property with a combination of (1) the assumption of their existing loan, (2) some cash, (3) a note and Deed of Trust against my present home that I was going to sell. Here's how it works: Building A is available for $150,000. I want to buy it with as little cash as possible because I don't have enough money to pay for it in full, so I assume the seller's $80,000 first mortgage (take over the payments and have it transferred to me). I give him $30,000 cash, leaving a $40,000 gap. I still own Building B, which had not yet been sold. I give the seller a Second Mortgage on Building B in the amount of $40,000. It's O.K. with me to have a mortgage on the home I'm going to sell because that, in effect, means I have my money now, rather than later, and I don't have to make my new purchase contingent on the sale of my old building.

Here's another variation on that theme. I once bought a home where the amount of cash I wanted to put down was not enough to pay the real estate commission and provide the seller the money that he needed to buy a new home. (1) I assumed his loan, (2) I gave him some cash, (3) he took back a $40,000, seven-year, interest-only second on the property, and (4) I gave him a small second mortgage against the property I was living in, part of which the real estate brokers agreed to take in payment for their commission when my house was sold, because the deal couldn't be made any other way. They figured that a loaf of bread later was better than no loaf of bread at all. I then explained to the seller how the second mortgage I had given him on the property he sold me could be used in lieu of cash to help buy another home.

Intelligent real estate negotiation creates a fluid, flexible situation where the search for alternatives can break down the traditional barriers. If you are selling your property in the big city and you have to take back a purchase-money second in order to sell it, think of it as the "Old Maid" that you have to pass on to the next guy, and when you look for a new home or for an investment property in a small town, use it to help pay for your new property. The guy you are buying from would probably be willing to give you a purchase-money second on the property he is selling you. Why wouldn't he be willing to accept a "second" on an equally good property somewhere else, in lieu of some cash?

Think about it. It takes a little creativity to sell this idea, but it can be done. Be careful, however, because there are some possible adverse tax consequences.

If you have taken back a note as part of a tax-avoiding installment sale, and you use that note to purchase another property, there is a possibility that the installment sale angle could be set aside by the I.R.S. and the tax on the profits of the sale could be immediately due and payable. This is not true if you take a note on the sale of your principal residence and use it to buy another principal residence, because under Section 1034 of the Tax Code, you can invest profits on the sale of your home in another personal residence of equal or greater value, without any capital gains tax liability, if you do it within 18 months. But if you are trading for investment property, be sure to check with your tax advisor as to the tax implications. You may have to make a nasty choice between accepting the tax lumps or holding a note in inflating dollars on a property in an endangered or depreciating area, and that's not an easy decision. At least the above described technique does give you some alternatives.

If my advice requires you to sell a parcel of highly appreciated real property for cash, then you are faced with the dilemma of reporting a sizable capital gain. Tax avoidance calls for an installment sale to defer the tax bite. But then you are stuck again with a long-term promissory note secured by property with a dubious future—and that's another inflation no-no!

An alternative solution is a sale requiring "alternative security" for the installment note other than the real property sold. This is a little complicated, but the tax and inflation protection advantages make it worth puzzling out.

In this example, you sell to a buyer under a contract which requires an alternative security—gold, silver, diamonds or some other commodity—securing an installment note, which protects you from the consequences of inflation. This proposed solution, however, has the taint of "constructive receipt" which the I.R.S. often raises in such situations, and, in fact, the I.R.S. has been highly successful in disallowing installment sales and causing the taxpayer to report the entire gain in the year of the sale because of the theory that he has "constructively" received payment with the use of alternative security. This would especially be true if the taxpayer were to attempt to provide a gold inflation clause in the installment note and have the substitute security be gold bullion.

One solution is to form an Irrevocable Trust with an independent Trustee, and Trust Beneficiaries other than you or your spouse, such as your children, grandchildren or other close relatives, and sell the property to the Trustee under an installment contract. The promissory note would be structured to qualify as an installment sale, but with a gold clause or other commodity inflationary index to hedge against dollar devaluation. The security for the initial installment sale to the trust will be the property sold.

Following the receipt by the Trustee of the title to the property, the trustee would then negotiate a cash sale to a new buyer (which had already been arranged, of course) for a value equal to or higher than the purchase price, with the tax result of very little, if any, gain to be reported.

The Trustee would then invest the cash in gold, or any other inflation-hedge commodity, as a hedge against his obligation to pay gold-value dollars on the promissory note to the original seller.

Now the security for the note between the original taxpayer and the trustee will be the coins, bullion, or other assets held by the trustee.

The interest rate on the original sale to the Trustee should be 6% or more. As the coins appreciate in value, the trustee sells off enough to pay the interest on the note.

This, of course, presents an oversimplification of a very complex legal transaction, and actual documents, together with a legal summation of cases of other precedent-setting programs, should be prepared by competent counsel. If you don't have competent counsel who understand this strategy, you can call Anderson and Reiser (1924 Tice Valley Blvd., Walnut Creek, CA 94595, 415-938-2500), our law firm, and ask for B. Ray (Bill) Anderson, who has assisted me in developing this strategy.

THE OLD MAID

The desired net result when you sell your big-city property is to not be stuck with paper. Your choices are: (1) go for a cash sale, (2) use the foregoing trust technique, or (3) accept the paper and pass it on in your next real estate transaction. Remember, the people you deal with do not share our philosophy and probably won't have our bias aaginst being long-term lenders or against big-city real estate, especially if they receive the typical 10% interest rate that prevails on second mortgages as of this date. You will also be astounded at how often a seller is willing to accept a second mortgage with interest payments only. This gives you the use of the funds, and the inflation rate, in my opinion, will eventually make that a real bargain.

For clarification, let's reiterate the fundamentals, one at a time.

1. When you are a seller, either do not accept long-term paper as part of the deal, or get rid of the "Old Maid" by using it in your next real estate transaction, or sell to a newly created Trust on an installment contract, with your children as beneficiaries, on an installment con-

tract, and have the Trustee re-sell for cash and buy gold coins with the proceeds as security for the note, to hedge against dollar devaluation

2. When you are a buyer, use as much "paper" as possible, or pay cash in full. Nothing in between. Remember that the long-term lender gets ripped-off because he is paid back in dollars worth less than those he loaned. The seven-year second mortgage that I used to help pay for my property will be worth a maximum of 48 cents on the dollar, and might be close to worthless, 7 years from now, according to Table #1, so I will be paying it off with very cheap money. Actually, it could be worth much less a lot sooner than that.

TABLE #1—$40,000 2ND MORTGAGE

Inflation Loss of Principal on $40,000 2nd After 7 Years

Rate of Inflation	10%	15%	20%	25%	30%	50%
Purchasing Power Loss	20,868	27,177	31,611	34,661	36,706	39,687
Percentage of Purchasing Power Lost	52%	68%	79%	87%	92%	99%
Future Value of Mortgage Remaining after 7 Years	19,132	12,823	8,389	5,339	3,294	313

If I can avoid shelling out $30,000 or $40,000 in cash, and, instead, give a $30,000 or $40,000 note, as far as I am concerned, that's the same as having a $19,000 to $39,000 price reduction. The interest also will be paid in inflationary, diminishing dollars. Look at Tables #2 and #3. Not only does the lender pay taxes on the interest received, but it is deductible for the borrower. If I am in the 30% tax bracket, here's how it looks.

TABLE #2—INTEREST ON A $40,000 2ND MORTGAGE

Yearly Tax and Inflation Loss of Interest to Lender
(10% interest—$4,000/year—30% tax bracket)

Inflation Rate	10%	15%	20%	25%	30%	50%
year 1	$ 1,600	$ 1,800	$ 2,000	$ 2,200	$ 2,400	$ 3,200
year 2	1,960	2,310	2,640	2,950	3,240	4,200
year 3	2,284	2,743	3,152	3,512	3,828	4,700
year 4	2,576	3,112	3,562	3,934	4,240	4,950
year 5	2,838	3,425	3,889	4,251	4,528	5,075
year 6	3,074	3,691 *	4,151 *	4,488 *	4,729 *	5,137
year 7	3,287	3,917 *	4,361 *	4,666 *	4,871 *	5,169
Total of Inflation loss & Tax Cost to lender on $28,000 interest	$17,619	$20,998	$23,755	$26,001	$27,836	$32,431
% of interest Income Lost to Taxes & Inflation	63%	75%	85%	93%	99%	115%

*Cost greater than income due to fixed nature of tax cost.

BORROWING

Q. I already live in a nice town that meets your criteria, but I don't have enough money to buy gold or silver or diamonds. Should I borrow against my home?

A. Borrowing against your home would probably be the lesser of the two evils, although you don't have any real good choices. If you borrow, make sure you can meet the mortgage payments from dependable income, and be sure to borrow enough to be able to set aside some liquid reserves so you could

TABLE #3—$40,000 2ND MORTGAGE

True Interest Cost to Borrower After Inflation and Tax Benefit
(10% interest—$4,000/year—30% tax bracket)

Inflation Rate	10%	15%	20%	25%	30%	50%
year 1	$2,400	$ 2,200	$ 2,000	$ 1,800	$ 1,600	$ 800
year 2	2,040	1,690	1,360	1,050	760	*(200)
year 3	1,716	1,257	848	488	172	*(700)
year 4	1,424	888	438	66	*(240)	*(950)
year 5	1,162	575	*(111)	*(251)	*(528)	*(1,075)
year 6	926	309	*(151)	*(488)	*(729)	*(1,137)
year 7	713	82	*(361)	*(666)	*(871)	*(1,169)
Net interest Cost to Borrower after Inflation & Tax Benefit	$10,381	$ 7,001	$ 4,023	$ 1,999	$ 164	($4.431)
Average True Interest Rate Paid Per Year By Borrower	3.7%	2.5%	4.1%	7%	—	—

*Represents negative expense—or income—due to tax benefit of interest expense.

make some payments if your income was cut off. If you put some of the money into gold or silver coins, then you have an offsetting asset that could be used to make the payments, if you occasionally sell off a few. If I am right about the future, they will appreciate more than enough to make up for the extra interest, and, if a true hyper-inflation sets in, the price of the coins could possibly explode through the ceiling and enable you to pay off your whole house at some future time.

If you borrow, don't make the mistake of not borrowing enough, and don't spend the mortgage proceeds for a trip to Europe. It's only wise to mortgage if those funds are prudently invested so that they are available as a cash reserve to meet payments.

Q. What do you think of having a retreat in the mountains, either as an individual or a group, in case things get a lot worse than you think they are going to get, which, incidentally, I think is going to be the case?

A. Well, I'll have to disagree with you on what the worst case will be, because I don't believe the nation will collapse into total anarchy, at least not this time around. I'm expecting a depression, not a new "Dark Age." Other than difficulties in buying the things you want, life in the small towns should go on pretty calmly. The big cities are where the trouble will be concentrated, with a possibility of sporadic problems elsewhere. Being off by yourself in a retreat seems dangerous to me. If there is no national anarchy a retreat is unnecessary. If there is anarchy (possible, but not probable), roving bands would look for isolated homes. If people leave the cities looking for trouble or food or money, I don't think I'd want to be all by myself. Above all, I don't want to be put into a position where I would have to shoot somebody, although I have recently bought some hunting rifles so that I can become self-sufficient off the land if necessary, but the thought of using a gun on a human being is totally abhorrent. I would if my family's safety was at stake, but I'd rather not be out there by myself where this could become a necessity. The big cities will be dangerous. Being alone could be dangerous. The small town represents more safety and security because you can join with neighbors who wish to protect their safety also.

Group retreats can be a reasonable alternative as long as the developer is selling at a fair price and it also can be used as a vacation home with recreational potential. If it makes you feel good to live in a group retreat, there are several good ones around to which we refer our *Ruff Times* members through Member Services, but it doesn't particularly turn me on. The retreat concept is probably an unnecessary reaction, but if it makes you feel more comfortable, by all means do it. We don't have to agree on this.

MAKING MONEY

Q. What kind of real estate investments should I consider other than my home?
A. Stick with residential income property, preferably four-plexes on down to single-family dwellings. One of the last-ditch efforts to stop inflation will be wage, price and rent controls. Under previous rent control legislation in various parts of the country, four units or less generally were exempt. I prefer residential over industrial and commercial property because of the relative ease of finding tenants. Housing units are relatively

standard, but business or industrial requirements can be unique, and a building property that is ideal for one company may be totally unsuitable for another, and when they become vacant, they tend to stay empty longer waiting for the client who needs that kind of facility. Houses and apartments have numerous potential renters, and in a depression, home sales go belly up, and demand for rentals rises. Also, in a business recession or depression, businesses go broke and companies close branch offices and pull in their horns. I realize that during that kind of a depression, renters could also be financially in trouble, and find it difficult to pay their rent, but safety lies in the fact that everybody has to eat and have a place to live and those are the first things they will pay for. They will give up a lot of other things before they give up the roof over their heads. Also, if we reach the point where everybody is in trouble, the number of properties in default to the financial institutions could reach epidemic proportions. When that happens, if they foreclose on all of them, the lending institutions will be in terrible trouble because they would be faced with writing off such huge loan losses that they could quickly become legally insolvent. If you have sufficient cash reserves, or other assets that can be quickly turned into cash, such as gold or silver coins, sufficient to help you ride things out for six months to a year, by then lenders very likely will be making deals because they can't foreclose on everybody. This happened during the 30's. There was a rash of foreclosures on farms and homes and the lending institutions found themselves with properties which were empty, deteriorating, sometimes being vandalized by squatters, and the write-offs were so huge the institutions made deals so that people of good character could retain their properties and pick up their payments when things got better.

All in all, I'd stick with residential properties.

SPECULATION VS. INVESTMENT

Q. What about buying raw land and speculating on price inflation?

A. You need to understand the difference between speculation and investment. There are elements of both in most real estate purchases, but basically, you can draw the line between them by defining an investment as something that returns sufficient income to meet all of the expenses and give you a spendable return. A speculation generally does not produce income and you are betting solely on the rise in price, either through a general inflation, the building of a new freeway or industrial plant, or some external event that you have forecast, to give you a profit upon resale. If you have forecast properly, your speculation will pay off. If it takes longer than you expected, expenses, interest, and time can reduce your profits and your return on investment.

The investor is generally looking for income, and he expects to be able to increase the resale value and income of his property through his own predictable actions. That's why I like the Lowry-Nickerson concept of real-estate investment, which involves finding undervalued income properties which have "valuable deficiencies" that turn off other prospective buyers. If you are able to detect the swan under the ugly duckling, you buy it at a distressed price, improve it, receive income and tax shelter from it in the meantime and market it at a profit. That way you are not betting on the general inflation rate. You are betting on improving its intrinsic worth—more specifically, its income-earning potential—through your own predictable action.

The details of Lowry's approach are thoroughly explored in his book, which at the risk of repetition, I must say is the best book on real estate investment ever written. It's clear, precise, fun to read and gives you some of the darndest creative concepts for financing and negotiating that I've ever seen in print.

I recently looked at a home in my town which had been allowed to be run down terribly, and yet it had incredible potential. The carpets were in horrible shape. It was desperately in need of paint. It had a beautiful circular driveway with big pot-holes all over it. The shrubs were overgrown, and the lawn was dead. The trees hung down so low over the driveway that you couldn't drive into it, yet it was basically sound, had a wonderful floor plan and a beautiful swimming pool, and could be bought for $40,000 to $50,000 below its potential quick-sale price. $10,000 to $15,000 would put this into ideal condition. And it is currently being rented. I'm probably going to buy it, partly because I can't stand to see orphans neglected and I take in strays, but mostly because there is $20,000 to $30,000 to be made quickly in this property. In the meantime, it can be rented so that my mortgage payments are covered, and I won't have to pay operating expenses out of my pocket. Because it has been sitting on the market for so long, turning off all the buyers who could not see below the surface, the seller is anxious and I'll probably be able to get it with a very small down payment and a lot of paper and fix it up with a property improvement loan. When I sell it I should realize a 100% to 300% return on the actual invested money in the next six months, even if real estate prices soften (which they won't in my town), because there is such a margin of safety built into the transaction.

That's what you should be doing. This will be the safest kind of real estate investment in this wildly unpredictable market we are facing. Over the long haul, if you select the small towns where the boom is in its first 10% to 15%, inflation will still bail you out of your mistakes. The first three principles on real estate investment are: (1) location, (2) location, and (3) location. And the big city with its expensive suburbs will be a bad location, and small towns generally will be outstanding.

Q. What degree of self-sufficiency is desirable?
A. The more the better. By all means you should have food storage, and/or a garden. If you can have some chickens, rabbits, or geese that's even better. If you live in town, the neighbors might not want crowing roosters, but rabbits are pretty quiet. You should have a well and an auxiliary generator so you can always pump water. Have a good, modern wood stove and a nearby source of firewood. I would like to have an underground gas storage tank and, of course, a safe place for my emergency supply of food. I would want a safe concealed under carpeting and sunk into a concrete slab floor, if possible. I would like a bicycle, a Mo-ped, or a V.W. Diesel Rabbit or its equivalent, so that I could always get someplace in a fuel shortage. There should be good hunting and fishing nearby so I could supplement my diet. But I also want to be able to live comfortably in the world as it is now, so I'd like to be relatively near stores and schools and job opportunities and all the other things that I consider important in my family's life. So what's the best compromise? A small town—but I think you've heard that before.

TAXES

Q. I attended a meeting held by some noted tax rebels and they recommended that if I sold a piece of property, to avoid taxes I should demand payment in silver coins. I didn't understand what they meant. Can you explain it to me?

A. At publication time, a bag of American silver coins with a face value of $1,000 is worth almost $4,000.* The theory is that if I sold a property for $40,000, which I bought for $25,000, I have a potential $15,000 taxable capital gain. I should demand $10,000 face value worth of junk silver coins from the seller (which have a market value of about $40,000). As money is defined in the Constitution as gold and silver coins, I would only have received $10,000—the face value. Consequently, I would not have had a taxable profit on that home, because I have sold it for $10,000 of legal tender, so I have turned a potential $15,000 capital gain into a $15,000 capital loss.

The theory is great, and constitutionally sound; however, the I.R.S. has already issued a ruling saying that they would value the sale of the property at the fair market value of the coins. However, Deak and Company reported an interview with Forest D. Montgomery, an attorney in the Office of the Mint. He said that if there was an exchange or barter of property for property (house for coins) as long as properties of

---
*One bag now costs over $12,000.

equal market value were exchanged, there would be no capital gains tax on the difference between the silver dollar's face value and the property's market value. There still will be a capital-gains tax if the new property (the coins) is sold for a sum greater than the original purchase price of the house. You might then be liable to pay taxes on the difference between the stated value of the coins at the time of the initial exchange of properties, and the sale price. But if you hung on to the coins, you would get the inflation protection potential of the coins, and pay no taxes until you sold them for cash.

If that sounds confusing it's because it is. Government positions on this are inconsistent, so be careful.

Q. I now own an apartment house in a big city. Because I have depreciated it so far I will take a tax beating when I sell it. Should I just take my tax lumps and sell out?

A. There is more than one way to skin a cat. I would suggest a tax-free exchange. Perhaps the best kept open secret in the real estate world is the nation-wide network of Real Estate Exchange Counselors who help people exchange properties. I recently spoke at an exchange meeting in Phoenix where 40 or 50 Exchange Counselors were gathered from all over the country to exchange properties. If you want to exchange your big city real estate for small town real estate, somewhere there is somebody in a small town

(Mr. Smith) who has placed on the market the distressed property you are looking for. He may not want your property and needs cash, but there might be a third party in your town (Mr. Jones) who does want your beautiful, improved property. You would have Jones buy Smith's building, and then exchange buildings with you. Now Smith has cash, Jones has your building, which he wants, and you have Smith's building and a tax-free exchange under Sec. 1031 of the tax code. That's a relatively simple exchange. It usually gets more complicated than that.

At the exchange meeting which I attended, millions of dollars of transactions were cemented together. If you trade your equity in your property for the equity in another property, it is not a taxable event, and you legally deny Uncle Sam his chunk; whereas if you sold the property for cash, Uncle Sam would take his bite and then you could only invest what's left. Of course, the gains taxes will ultimately have to be paid when you eventually sell for cash, but you will have had the use of Uncle Sam's money and its earning power all this time, and the taxes can be postponed year after year. If you would like help with this, we refer our *Ruff Times* members to the exchange counselor network and they will refer you to the local person with whom you should list your property.

Don't conclude that your property cannot be exchanged. These people are incredibly creative and a lot of things can be thrown in to make deals, including miscellaneous lots and the second mortgages we talked about earlier. And they can solve such problems as unequal equities, tax implications, etc. Sometimes even the sales commissions are taken back in paper or properties, as a lot of these counselors get involved in these transactions to build their own estate through commissions.

Another way to deal with the tax problem is not to sell at all but to refinance the property and use that tax-free money to buy other properties, then later on you can trade your relatively small equity for something else when the right deal comes along. The property with a big assumable loan on it will be easier to unload anyway.

Q. You haven't said anything about tax shelters. Can you still get some protection from taxes by owning buildings?
A. Yes. Real estate is one of the few remaining shelters that really works. Most tax shelters loopholes have been plugged by recent tax "reform"; however, a properly structured real estate deal will produce paper losses through depreciation deductions which are in excess of the income received from the property, and you can use that excess to offset your ordinary income and reduce your total tax bill, while enjoying additional spendable income.

In summary, if you do this right, you will find an undervalued property, buy it cheaply with a lot of paper, fix it up physically and financially and enjoy the income and appreciation while you are preparing to trade your newly created equity for another property, or refinance it. Sooner or later you will want to stop this pyramiding process and get off, either by a sale, a trade of all your equities for one paid-for building, or a trade for silver coins, as described above. And you will have used Uncle Sam's share of the money all along. All debt pyramids eventually collapse and so will the real estate debt pyramid. The trick is knowing when to get off and that's where we will help you with our *Ruff Times* timing reports.

Q. What do you think of land as an investment?
A. My basic principle of real estate is to buy those properties which can be improved in such a way that their intrinsic value is increased. Land that can be subdivided falls in that category. However, personally I prefer not to speculate in land because (1) it takes more time and marketing attention than I am prepared to spend, (2) it does not earn income, so the ongoing expenses, including debt service, come out of your pocket and tend to increase your investment and eventually lower your rate of return, and (3) it usually takes a lot longer than you anticipated to get a parcel subdivided and zoned, so much of the profit can be drained off in expenses. When you sit down and figure what happens with most land acquisitions, by the time you have paid as-

sessments, taxes, interest and development costs, plus taxes on the resulting profit, the rate of return for an awful lot of work is lower than you would have had if you had gone into a more passive investment like gold or diamonds. And there is little or no tax shelter.

If you stick with improvable residential income properties, you get tax shelter, income from rentals, and capital appreciation. And the payments don't come out of your pocket. The resulting profit is generally greater. And if you stick to small towns, you will have your mistakes covered by continued price inflation, which is much less likely in the big cities.

Q. Why should I have a big loan on my city house if I decide to keep it?

A. When I recommend having a small equity in your home in the big city, I am trying to free up your funds in advance of a selling panic so you can use it now. Also, the smaller the investment the smaller your potential loss if you should find yourself unable to make the payments, and you lose the property or are forced to sell. The smaller the equity, the smaller the loss. It's as simple as that. Chop up your money into smaller pieces and spread your risks among as many investments as possible.

Q. Do you have any ideas on negotiation? I always seem to get skinned.

A. I won't go into that in detail, as that is covered so beautifully in Al Lowry's book, but you do not buy a home until you know exactly what it's worth now, based on comparable sales, and, in the case of an income property, its current net income. You also can determine what it will be worth when you fix it up and increase the net income. After you determine what you want to pay, each step of the negotiating process is aimed at arriving at your predetermined price. Most people simply try to get the cheapest possible price, whatever that is. The successful negotiator knows where he wants to arrive and choreographs his every move to get there. You need to have a narrow range. The low end in the price you are shooting for and the high end is the most you are willing to pay. If you have to pay the higher price, you demand better terms for more leverage.

I have sometimes deliberately paid "too much" for a piece of property because I was able to buy it on such great terms, and the return on my investment was acceptable. The old adage, "My terms, his money. His terms, my money" is one of the most important lessons you can learn in real estate.

I recently negotiated the purchase of a home. The seller had made a counter offer that, in his mind, was the lowest offer he could make, but it was $10,000 above the maximum I was prepared to pay. I solved that problem by making two offers at the same time, one $10,000 lower than his counter offer, and one $20,000 lower than the counter offer. Those two offers were structured so that there was $15,000 more cash down payment with the smaller offer than there was with the larger offer. I didn't care which one he accepted, because I was willing to pay $10,000 more for the property if I could put down $15,000 less cash. I knew that over the next two or three years I could earn enough with that money to compensate for the increased purchase price. In fact, that's the way I preferred it. By presenting the two offers and informing the broker that I was firm and would negotiate only between those two prices by raising or lowering the down payment and relaxing or tightening the terms, I gave him a range with some constructive opportunities to negotiate, rather than an ultimatum which could only offend and stiffen his resistence. The end result was that he accepted the higher price of the two offers and we ended up friends with a transaction at a fair price, and he's now a subscriber to my newsletter.

Q. How can you think about buying real estate with today's high interest rates?
A. The nature of the residential income property business is that the costs are passed on to your tenants. The market is competitive, but you can price the rent to cover your expenses if you have chosen your areas properly. Also, if you improve the property and make it a more pleasant place

to live, your tenants probably will not move when you raise the rent. The interest is tax deductible, which provides you some tax shelter, and if you think interest rates are high now, you just wait. We may see short-term dips, but the long-term trend of interest rates is up. Sure, I wish we had lower rates. Everybody does. But I still consider it worthwhile to use leverage to get a higher rate of return on my money. It cuts into the profit somewhat, but not a heck of a lot, really.

Q. What if I build this investment pyramid by fixing up properties, trading them and selling them and acquiring more, and all of a sudden I get stuck when the big crunch comes?

A. I have a couple of alternate suggestions:

1. As we get close, when the signal goes out in the *Ruff Times*, either sell off enough properties to realize sufficient profit to pay off the rest and have them free and clear, or trade all your equities for one large, paid-for building. I think we still have at least a couple of years to go in the small town market.* That's enough time to make some money.

2. Keep your buildings, and maintain some cash reserves so you can make the payments for a while if the tenants can't. If you spread your risk among several properties in three or four communities, the likelihood that you will need to do so diminishes. Then you think of your property as

---
*I now see five good years ahead.

a time machine to get your assets from this side of the gulf to the next. I am convinced that if you can hang on for a few months, the financial institutions will have to start making deals to prevent their own collapse and you should make it through. If you take the long view, value for essential human needs tend to be quickly reestablished after economic collapses, and housing is certainly an essential.

FOR FARMERS

Q. What about farm land as an investment? It seems so high in relation to the return, considering today's low crop prices.

A. I agree, but I still think it represents a good buy because commodity prices are going to rise again. In fact, as this is written we are in the beginning of a strong bull market in grains, and that means that the spiral in farm land prices will resume.*

If you want a farm, be sure it's either small enough so you could live on it and farm it for self-sufficiency, or big enough that the earnings could profitably support a resident manager. Nothing in between makes economic sense. If it has potential for residential subdividing and is in the path of the growth of the town you have selected, so much the better. However, the disadvantage is that you may have some negative cash flow until commodity prices strengthen.

This problem is behind today's farm re-

---
*Still valid.

bellion. Many farmers paid too much for their land, kept no cash reserves, and are suffering negative cash flows due to depressed crop prices. And they are hurting because of this imprudence.

Don't buy farm land unless you know farming and have enough land to farm efficiently. The farmers who are making it today are good businessmen, not just good farmers.

Q. Will the time come when we will want to go back and buy property in the cities?
A. Not for years in the central cities, but I would love to go back into the lovely suburban community I moved from, after everything settles down, and pick up some beautiful properties there at the depressed prices that we will see later on. Remember, in 1929, those who prepared themselves for the crash were in an excellent position to buy a lot of things very cheaply in 1934, including stocks, farm land, income properties, businesses, etc. It is a valid alternative to keep your money liquid, or in diamonds, gold and silver and wait to buy real estate later on. However, there is still great profit potential now in real estate.

Q. How about hotels, motels and transient trailer parks and campgrounds?
A. Well, they are obviously a form of real estate, but they are really businesses, requiring advertising and a constant search for new customers. They also are a heck of a lot more

work, and the rate of failure in these businesses is far higher than the rate of failure among those who simply buy residential income property where people live, rather than depending on transient customers. Money can be made in those businesses but it's a lot harder and the returns are not as sure, and depression means less business and recreational travel. Stick with buildings where people make their homes.

Q. How much cash reserve should I keep on hand?

A. I obviously can't give you a dollar amount, but I would like you to have at least six months of mortgage and other installment payments in demand deposits, Treasury bills, Capital Preservation Fund, or in gold and silver coins, as a safety margin so you could keep your investment alive in times of difficulty. Even if you get paid in worthless money for your rentals, your mortgage contract is also written in worthless money, and you simply pass the "Old Maid" on to the Savings and Loan. The objective is to keep the property until such time as proper values are reestablished. It's a method of preserving your wealth and getting you from here to there across the gulf of depression.

Q. What is the future for the real estate salesman?

A. If you are in the big cities, you may starve. If you are in a small town serving the people who will move in, you could have some glory years.

LOANS—FIXED AND VARIABLE

Q. What do you think of fixed-rate mortgages as opposed to the new variable-rate mortgages?

A. Each has its advantages and disadvantages. Obviously, in a period of rising interest rates, you would wish you had a fixed rate; however, rates must move sharply before the lender is able to increase the interest rate on a variable-rate loan, and when rates fall, he is forced to reduce his rates rather quickly. Generally, a "variable" is assumable, and you can sell your property more easily. Also, if your interest rate has been increased, you can pay off the loan within 90 days without a prepayment penalty. Most variable-rate mortgages have a ceiling beyond which rates cannot be raised, regardless of how high interest rates go generally. On balance, I think I'd probably rather have a fixed-rate mortgage on the home I know I am going to keep, and would probably lean towards the variable on the property I knew I was going to fix up and unload.

At any given time, some institutions are loaded with loan money and you can often negotiate better terms. Don't think that when you walk into the savings and loan that the terms they present to you are the ones you must take. It does pay to shop.

Sometimes you can save yourself from a quarter of a point to a half a point in interest. Sometimes you can get them to waive the prepayment penalty or the loan fee. It depends on whether they are tight at that moment or not, and you won't know unless you shop.

Q. Why is it that the man at the bank who approves the loans isn't the same one who wrote the ads? I've found it awfully hard to get loans to buy investment property and my credit is pretty good.

That's one area where Lowry's book and his weekend course can be so helpful. He shows you how to go to a lender with a loan presentation that will have him conclude that you are a good businessman who knows exactly what he's doing, and that the bank will have a fine customer. Prepare your presentation so the loan officer knows exactly where the money will come from to fix up the property, precisely what the market value of the property will be based on the comparable sales in the area, and what the income will be from the completed improved property. Loan officers will often approve or disapprove loans based on the degree of professionalism that they can read into the loan presentation. Often the loan is considered by a committee which has not met you, so your devastating charm won't work. The loan presentation is everything. Most people who try to buy an apartment house have no plan, no program, and find trouble getting the funds they need.

Also, there are several creative ways to get as much as 100% financing. Again—Lowry's book. His chapters on creative finance are worth a thousand times the price of the book. But remember the key. Have a plan set down on paper, in a cogent, systematic manner, so the banker concludes he is dealing with a professional who knows where he is going.

Q. When I buy or sell a property, should I use a broker?
A. Yes, most of the time. A good broker is immensely helpful in arranging financing, negotiating as a third party (which can prevent emotional confrontations which break down negotiations), and helping with all the details in setting up an escrow and getting it completed. If you make an exchange as recommended in this report, the exchange counselor will perform all those functions. The only circumstance under which you might not want to use a broker is when you are the seller, if you are extremely experienced in all aspects of real estate transaction and know how to open an escrow and handle the entire transaction yourself. And then you will need an attorney. Also, you would need to be positive that you can find your own prospects. If you wish to handle the deal yourself, then you should read one of the better books on the subject called

For Sale, by Owner by Gerald M. Steiner (see Appendix) and *Sell Your Own Home "By Owner"* by Ron Jensen. Remember, a broker has prospects when you don't and of course, he has access to the Multiple Listing Service or the Exchange Network.

Never go in to negotiate and buy a listed property without using a broker on your end. The commission will be paid out of the sale price anyway. Usually the listing broker divides it with the selling broker.

Before you select a broker, ask him for some references from satisfied customers for the same kind of property you are buying. Don't engage a broker who has done nothing but sell tract houses to help you to find an apartment house.

You will have to guide the broker in all your transactions, because he probably does not understand the principles in this chapter, and probably knows nothing about creative fiance, but you still need him because he understands the mechanics of closing a deal that you could probably not handle.

My last piece of advice is: get an education! Read everything you can on the subject. Thoroughly digest the real estate sections of your Sunday paper and that of the small town you're considering. Buy and read every book you can find, including Nickerson's *How I Turned a Thousand Into a Million in Real Estate in my Spare Time*. Same subject as Lowry's book, only Lowry's is better! In this business, knowledge is power and the person who understands certain key principles has great mental leverage in dealing with others. Most buyers are unsophisticated, have no plan or program, and, in fact, don't know what the heck they are doing, and that's even more true of sellers. The average guy buys premium property at premium prices with no room for improvement. He still does fairly well, but nowhere near as well as the guy who knows that most property is mismanaged and the world is bristling with bargains if you know how to find the "uncut gem."

But don't go into it deaf, dumb and blind just because of some vague feeling that real estate is a "good deal." Everything you read will have to be evaluated in the light of the principles in this book—that is, if you accept them.

15
PREPARING FOR THE BLACK MARKET

Ruff's Recommendation No. 5. Prepare for price controls and a black market inflationary economy.

I advise the following steps:

1. Commit a fixed portion of your after-tax income each month to a program of buying mass produced consumer goods.

2. Try to find a similarly inclined, diversified group of people in your area who are interested in barter. A church or RUFF TIMES Discussion Group would be likely places to start organizing.

3. Start improving your survival education by subscribing to such publications as *Mother Earth News* (see Appendix) and *Organic Gardening and Farming* (see Appendix).

What kinds of items should you now buy? That depends on how much capital you have, and what kind of skills you have. You will need to store up durable goods in the following categories:

1. Storage food. In a truly serious crisis, this is the ultimate currency. You need extra quantities beyond your own consumption needs for barter.

2. Seeds for growing food, preferably non-hybird seeds (which are more resistant to disease).

3. Tools for self-sufficiency. The most comprehensive list I have seen is found in the Appendices of Joel Skousen's book, *Survival Homes* (see Appendix).

4. Tools connected with your during-the-controls business. Repairs of all kinds will be in high demand. Buy and stockpile spare parts.

5. Barter items, especially ammunition of all kinds.

6. Books and other educational materials connected with self-sufficiency (see Appendix).

7. Durable clothing, especially warm clothing, shoes, boots.

Obviously, these items could consume a big chunk of your capital. You may not be able to afford everything you want, so you have to do the best you can and make choices. In the early stages of the controls, or even before the controls are officially declared, buy the items that the government is most likely to ban, ration, or otherwise control. Stay two jumps ahead of each shortage.

Which items are most likely to disappear

first? We can never be sure just how the public will respond, but manufacturers will tend to shift production to those luxury goods that are not mass produced that command a high profit margin per sale, and they will not be in short supply. Cadillacs will be more available than Chevrolets. The waiting lists to buy a Rolls Royce will be shorter still. Levi's will be scarcer than Guccis.

Start accumulating cases of soap, toilet paper, motor oil, and light bulbs when they are on sale. Buy (or order) a case of the item at the sale price.

If you belong to a church or other group of people who understand what is coming, start a co-op buying group and buy in bulk. It is a lot of work, but it can save you a bundle. For more information, write to the Cooperative League of America, Suite 1100, 1828 L St., Washington, D.C. 20036.

CONTROLS: STAGE ONE

You should already have stocked your home and business with emergency goods by this stage to avoid the charge of "hoarding." "Hoarding" is a nasty term for "saving." It really means "buying more than your share of scarce goods in competition with others." Buying in advance of shortages is not "hoarding."

If necessary—and it probably will be—go into debt only to buy large equipment, like a 4,500-watt gasoline-power generator, or a set of power tools, or other big-ticket items. Be sure that your liability is limited to the purchase item. Personal debt should be strategic and limited.

Your top priority is dehydrated food. You should have a bit of land to grow more food. You need extra supplies to help friends and for barter. In the great inflations of this century, without exception, the most important single investment was food. In second place was fuel. Finally, you need clothing. But food is primary.

You need to buy what you want, when you think you need to store it, at the price you are willing to pay, and at the price your supplier is willing to sell it for, which means, do it now. If not, you might be forced to find a black market supplier later on. You must avoid dealing on the black market as a buyer of absolute necessities.

Buy replacement parts for your cars: spark plugs, fan belts, water pumps, hoses, and so forth. Read the chapter on "Auto Maintenance and Price Controls" in Dr. North's book, *How You Can Profit from the Coming Price Controls* (see Appendix). In World War II they rationed gasoline, not because gasoline was in short supply, but because rubber was scarce, and the bureaucrats wanted to reduce the consumption of tires, so buy a complete set of new tires, plus a spare, the day price controls are announced.

Buy up what you can well in advance of starting a major building or re-modeling project, so that last-minute trips to the hardware store (or wherever) are not mini-disasters. In 1974, housing projects were shut down just prior to completion because the supply of toilets shrank almost overnight. Developers were paying interest on millions of dollars worth of construction loans, and there they sat (or didn't sit). Something like it will happen again. It will be a way of life.

If you have a tendency toward ulcers, buy now.

CONTROLS: STAGE TWO

How can you legally pay more than the controlled price of an item you need, if that's the only way you can obtain it?

Here is one strategy. When you offer to pay the controlled (sub-free market) price, pay for some of it with pre-1965 American silver coinage. You have kept within the law, and so has he. After all, these coins are legal tender, at face value, although they are worth more. The Constitution says so.

The whole idea in the second stage of price controls is to find ways to transfer extra purchasing power, preferably legally, to the seller of whatever you really want.

CONTROLS: STAGE THREE

At this point, the government starts rationing necessities. You are stuck with ration coupons. Start bartering. Trade "equals for equals," as far as any bureaucrat can determine.

Buy used goods today—which are very difficult to control and won't be rationed—at swap meets. Used goods can command a price premium over new goods on the legal markets, since used goods are here, and new goods are "on order." A junk yard will be a good business.

Frequent the Goodwill stores, and Salvation Army stores, and all the other volunteer stores. These are fantastic bargains, if you have in mind 1982. You can buy cheap, store for a few years, and barter for what you need then.

The rationing stage is miserable. It breaks down the economy and makes barter necessary. A broad, flexible market requires a universally acceptable monetary unit. Rationing destroys the usefulness of the monetary unit and shrinks the market. The highly specialized worker is now too specialized. The jack of all trades, especially in the repair industry, becomes king.

This is an especially dangerous stage for large-scale producers of necessities. This is the period when large-scale farms (over 100 acres) might be visited by government "buyers" of grains or cattle. These "buyers" will present farmers with a check for their crop—the fixed price set by the government—and haul it to the rationing center in the nearest large city. Large-scale agri-business becomes large-scale agri-bureaucracy. Agri-bureaucracy universally produces food shortages.

The small farmer will be king if he is not big enough to be policed carefully, or is not producing a controlled crop that has a daily market on a commodities exchange. There is greater safety in produce: fruits, vegetables, and possibly corn or other grain.

CONTROLS: STAGE FOUR

If controls have not been abandoned or broken down by now, this is when panic hits. Crimes against property soar. The government either breaks down locally, or else it tightens its grip so much in the cities that something like martial law prevails. Money becomes worthless. Ration coupons mean little. Barter is everything. Starvation, freezing, strikes, a breakdown of municipal services—power, water, sewers, trash collection—and universal misery are normal. You cannot afford to be dependent on Social Security checks, pension checks, salaries, or government services. To be an urban dweller is to be totally dependent upon the competence of a disintegrating government, disintegrating money, and a disintegrating culture. Your best bet is a small town. This moral and economic decay in the urban centers in an inflationary economy is described in Adam Fergusson's *When Money Dies* (London: William Kimber Co., 1975). In Austria, Hungary, and Germany from 1921-23, those who got by best were the peasants. The diamonds, silver sets, pianos, and heirlooms that had belonged to the upper classes steadily were transferred to the peasants for sacks of potatoes.

CURRENCY REFORM

Eventually, it must come. When people refuse to give up resources for the old paper money, the government must shrink the currency, erase several zeroes, back the currency with confiscated gold, and start over. Controls cannot stay on forever. No one knows how long. But when the currency finally collapses, investing must be geared to the eventual coming of deflation.

At this stage, the best assets are debt-free, small-scale agricultural properties, single-family dwellings, gold and silver coins, and simple tools. Diamonds, jewelry, and similar luxury goods do survive, and they can save your life, but in stage three some might be better liquidated for sufficient paper money to pay off all real estate debt. The idea is to come out of the crisis of inflation with zero debt and fully-owned assets. Eventually, the successful speculator must get off the debt pyramid. Productive real estate is still the best visible capital asset "for all seasons," but only if it is debt-free when currency reform finally is imposed. Debt-encumbered real estate is suitable only between now and stage three. The best invisible capital assets "for all seasons" are now, and presumably ever shall be, the gold or silver coin, or a high quality diamond. You should never sell all of your land or your gold except to save your life, simply because the idea of zero gold coins is sensible only in an era of fully trustworthy government. But it would be sensible to sell off a portion of your coins when inflation forces up their price to such an extent that you could pay off all your debts (and taxes).

The deflation has one wonderful side-effect. It lowers your monetary income, dropping you and everyone else back into lower tax brackets. This means that a real estate pyramid drops in nominal value, and it can be passed on to heirs at far lower inheritance tax rates. Meanwhile, the real estate tax benefits can keep you in a low tax bracket. You pay bankers instead of tax collectors. Debt-free real estate is a "real" estate in a time of deflation.

But deflation is a long way off. We have hell to go through first.

Neither I nor anyone else knows for sure whether all four stages will be experienced. My opinion is that the odds favor a breakdown in the price control system fairly early in the game. My testing of the public attitude is that lawbreaking and black markets will be so widespread that price controls will be no more effective than prohibition, and control-induced shortages will fuel a raging "real market" inflation, much worse than we would have had without controls. Your job is to plan ahead to be ready for a combination of shortages and runaway inflation.

16
PANIC-PROOF

And now, here comes *Ruff's Recommendation No. 1*. Store enough food for one year. Survival starts here!

In June, 1978, I was one of several speakers at a monetary conference in the Bahamas, sponsored by The National Committee for Monetary Reform.

The speakers included Harry Browne, Harry Schultz, Richard Russell, etc., all of whom I respect greatly, because they are nearly all of the same "Hard Money" economic persuasion. One after another they trotted out their scenarios of serious economic problems. Some felt that we were headed for a hyperinflation, and others felt that we were headed for a deflationary depression similar to the 1930's. (By now, you know where I stand on that issue.) All of them predicted some kind of monetary collapse, and they all made investment recommendations. Not one attempted to deal with the practical problems that we will all have to face if these scenarios come true. I stood in front of that group of 800 people and asked a simple question:

"How many of you believe that we're headed for some kind of monetary chaos?" Nearly every hand in the room went up. I then followed up with one more question:

"Do you honestly believe that in a period of monetary collapse that you will be able to safely drive down to your supermarket in your gas-guzzling car, make a selection from a dazzling variety of goods on the shelf, pay them with your personal check, walk safely out the door to your car, drive home and put them in your dependable, electric-operated refrigerator?"

That's the first time I ever got an ovation for a question—after a moment of reflective silence.

I simply cannot for the life of me understand how people can recognize our potential problems and somehow believe that the marketplace will still function normally.

The marketplace is a hardy weed and it's pretty hard to kill off. It's not that there will be no marketplace. I'm saying that it will not function dependably and it is likely there will be some periods of disruption. There may be times when there is some food available, but not what you would prefer to eat. You might have to stand in line for scarce goods. There is a distinct possibility of labor troubles upsetting transportation; in fact, I think it is a probability. Historically during periods of runaway inflation, organized labor fights hard to keep up their spending power, and their only weapon is the strike. There will also be rumors which will panic people into running for any food they can get their hands on.

Back in 1962, I was driving through the eastern Colorado prairies on a business trip when I turned on my radio and heard President Kennedy announcing the Cuban Missile Crisis. When he told us that he had put the Strategic Air Command on alert, my stomach turned over, and an actual physical chill spread through my body.

I stopped at the first service station and called my wife and asked her if we had any food in the house. That's a rather embarrassing question for a Mormon to ask, as we're supposed to have a year's supply of food. But back in those days, we just didn't feel we had the money to do it. When she said we didn't have very much, I told her to go down to the supermarket and buy everything she could with whatever money she had.

When I got home, I found that the stores were jammed with people buying everything in sight. Many supermarkets in Denver were literally stripped of anything edible, while newspapers reported fights and some minor rioting as everyone translated that frightening news into personal action to provide some security. Food was their first instinctive response.

I had another example of the "fear syndrome" when we had a meat shortage in California in the early 70's. There was the darndest panic buying you ever saw. One day I stopped at the supermarket to pick up some groceries for my wife and I was walking by the meat tray, which was an empty, glistening chrome wasteland. Suddenly one of the clerks came up with a cart full of plastic wrapped packages of hamburger and dumped them in the tray in front of me. There must have been an announcement made over the store P.A. system that I didn't hear, because as I reached for some to take home, I found myself literally swarmed under by a crowd of pushing, gouging, elbowing women, who were all grabbing for hamburger. Being caught up in the general hysteria, I began grabbing for all I could get (doing my share of pushing and shoving) and charged off to the check counter with my arms full. After I paid for the ten packages of hamburger that I had managed to corner, I suddenly realized that I didn't even like that store's hamburger that much. I had been caught up in a small panic and I didn't like what had happened to me.

Perception is as bad as reality in its effect on the marketplace. There's an old adage in the stock market that says, "Buy on rumor, sell on news." Johnny Carson created a toilet paper shortage that lasted for over a month when he told a joke about such a shortage on his T.V. show.

Gustave LeBon wrote a book on manias and the madness of crowds, in which he described the mob psychology, and it could be very instructive reading today. In my opinion, the American people swing between total apathy on the one hand, with a lack of perception of any of these problems (or at least an unwillingness to admit them), and overreaction on the other hand.

My whole problem is designed to panic-proof your life. I think we should start where we and the system are most vulnerable, and that happens to be food. You're vulnerable because you can't do without it. It would only take two days to be very uncomfortable, and three or four days to create real suffering, and a week or ten days to produce severe health problems. Food is perishable, and the distribution system is the most sensitive to disruption.

I don't believe we will ever have an African or Asian-type famine in this country, with people dropping dead in the streets. We will always produce enough food in the vast agricultural areas of California and the Mid-West to feed our people. We could have a 60% failure of our wheat and corn crops and still feed ourselves, as we export that much. But if such an event occurred, prices would go sky high and you might be reduced to a bare subsistence diet because of skyrocketing prices. However, it is the disruption of the monetary system that represents the largest threat.

In recent years we have been subjected to pitiful wirephoto newspaper pictures of small children with matchstick arms and legs and distended bellies in places with such strange names as Biafra, the Sahel and the Ogaden. It seems that in this world of incredible abundance and surpluses, people are starving. In Ethiopia, untold tens of thousands of people have died and children have had their physical and mental growth permanently stunted from lack of protein and sufficient calories in their diet. And strangely enough, this happened in the face of the fact that the world generally is producing more food than it can consume, and could produce several times more. The United States and other prosperous nations were willing to send more than enough food to Africa, and did so. It arrived safely in the port cities, but the people still starved. African politics and distribution systems weren't prepared to deal with such problems, and political intrigue made pawns of dying people.

This is a simple, tragic example of how famines are generally political, social and economic in nature rather than related to natural disasters. The creeping desert in North Central Africa is largely a result of the way man has treated the land, by overgrazing and poor farming techniques, but there's still no need for anyone in this world to be hungry, based on the amount of food that is available.

The problem is distribution and money.

We prosperous Americans, surrounded by wasteful abundance, never question the assumption that "it could never happen here," but if our economy is disrupted, those mountains of surplus wheat in the silos of the Mid-West could be just as far away from us as the grain rotting in warehouses in Addis Ababa is from those children who need it desperately.

Bear with me while I make a point in a rather circuitous manner.

In 1964, I bought an airplane for business use and learned to fly. Later, someone convinced me I'd be a lot safer if I had two engines instead of one, so we went out and bought a very expensive twin-engine Beechcraft Baron, under the assumption that if one engine quit, I could always fly home on the good engine. Great idea, but after I bought the aircraft I made an interesting discovery.

When you have two engines, you have more than doubled the complexity. Complexity increases vulnerability, so there is several times the chance of something going wrong. Surprisingly, the rate of fatal accidents is higher in twin-engine aircraft than it is with singles (if you exclude student-pilot training accidents, which is the only fair comparison). Twin-engine aircraft don't fly very well on one engine, and when one engine quits, your problems have only begun, because the skill required to deal with the emergency is often beyond that of the businessman/pilot, unless he constantly practices and prepares for engine-out emergencies. And engine failures are most likely at the most critical times—take-off, for example, when engines are under maximum stress, and a split second of indecision or a small error can kill you.

Our nation has developed a distribution and marketing system of incredible complexity that functions beautifully as long as our economic aircraft is not bounced around too vigorously by financial turbulence. But the chance of malfunction increases as economic stresses and complexities multiply.

253

The analogy is almost perfect. Consider the miracle of food on the supermarket shelf. Every day shoppers spend millions of dollars in all the supermarkets of America, and the next day, as if by magic, these shelves are full again and ready for more hordes of shoppers. How does it happen? It is the end result of a complex system that gets food from the ground into your home.

The process depends on an efficient transportation system (which, in the U.S.A. depends upon profits to reward the trucker) and labor peace. It also depends upon normal credit and a sound banking system so the farmer is willing to deliver his wheat on credit to the elevator operator who delivers it on credit to the barge operator, who takes it down the Mississippi, and so on up the chain, until the supermarket trusts you and the banking system enough to accept your check for a loaf of bread. Imagine what would happen to that system if the banks were in trouble and everyone's ability to pay was in doubt. Would they accept your check at the check-out counter? Would credit be routinely extended at every point in that complex chain? What if the inflationary spiral triggered labor troubles (as inflation always does) with a gauntlet of picket lines to be crossed by union truck drivers (if they aren't on strike) between the farmer and you at any one of the crucial transfer points in the chain of transaction? Remember the inflation losses faced by lenders under inflation? If the credit system became unworkable, we would have to totally reorganize the system by which people are paid for their product or services, and the changes would be monumental, disruptive, and would take time.

What if the rising spiral of inflation, rising interest rates and a collapsing bond market and deepening recession causes heavy unemployment in the cities, forcing cities into bankruptcy by draining the public treasuries, exhausting all the unemployment funds and causing civil disorders as angry people realize that government promises are going to be broken. Would food move into your local supermarket, and could you safely walk in with your money and walk out with your food?

What would be the effect of an Arab oil boycott on transportation? And what if this process continued for several months with the farmer not knowing whether he would ever be paid for his product, or whether or not the money he would receive would be worth anything, and he just decided not to risk planting this year, or he didn't have the seed or the fuel?

I've carefully studied the 1974-75 recession, and we came within a gnat's eyelash of losing our banking system or, at the very least, having it shut down for a while. How do you buy food if the banks are closed, or aren't trusted enough for the supermarket to accept your check? The banks will go into the next recession weaker than the last one.

We will recover, of course, after a lot of pain, but the big question is: Will you get through with your health intact?

STORED FOOD

I've talked to hundreds of clients who say, "I agree with your philosophy and I would like to ask you a question," and then they ask my advice about money. When I routinely check to see if they have a food storage plan, they say, "Well, no, I haven't done that yet. But I have some silver coins. I'll always be able to buy food with silver coins, even if the currency collapses." But, brother, you can't buy it if it isn't being transported. You can't buy it if there's panic at the supermarkets and there's a crowd standing around waiting to storm the delivery truck.

The delivery chain can even be upset by the weather as indicated by this article from the *Indianapolis Star*, January 30, 1978, during the big storm that hit the Mid-West.

MY KINGDOM: FOR A LOAF OF BREAD

When a Pepperidge Farms delivery truck carrying bread to Fort Benjamin Harrison Saturday night broke down near the Marsh Delicatessen at 62nd Street and Allisonville Road, the store's enterprising assistant manager saw a golden opportunity and negotiated for the bread.

But when some 50 persons shopping at the store realized what was going on, Dan Dudley was almost sorry he had. The shoppers rushed the truck in an every-man-for-himself frenzy to get the bread. Two men even got into a fist-fight over a loaf, Dudley said.

"I didn't think the guy was going to make it into the store alive," he said.

On February 2, also in Indianapolis, another article reported the following:

> Grocery store cash registers continued to ring madly Wednesday and truck delivery men scurried around the city trying to keep up with the demands of customers flocking to stores in fear that a winter-storm watch might develop into a blizzard.
>
> "They're buying everything they can get their hands on," the manager of the Kroger store at 4100 South East Street said.
>
> The grocery store rush began Tuesday night after the forecast of more snow was made. Customers evidently were recalling what it was like when they opened their refrigerators and found empty shelves when the worst blizzard in the city's history raged outside last week.
>
> A Kroger manager at 2620 West Michigan Street said persons were buying ridiculous amounts of milk, bread and eggs. "We can't keep bread in the store," he added.

The significance of those two stories is that panic buying could occur even if there isn't a real problem, but if people anticipate one.

There are all kinds of other reasons for having an emergency supply of food on hand. Let me give you a few.

Back in 1968 when my business went down the tubes, fortunately my wife had finally accumulated a substantial supply of stored food. That food helped sustain us during the next several months until I could establish a new income and get on my feet. If we had not had it, perhaps we would not have been able to use what money I could earn or borrow to continue to make the payments on our home and maintain some semblance of stability through that very difficult period. There was no generalized famine in this country but there sure would have been one at our address without that stored food.

In the next economic downturn, a lot of you will lose your jobs or find your businesses in trouble. The peace of mind and security that comes from an emergency food supply in a period of vulnerability makes it worthwhile, even if you never have to eat it. Just being able to stay home if there is any kind of civil disruption is important to your personal safety and peace of mind.

As this book is written, the nation faces a serious balance of payments problem and the dollar is sinking into both oceans because we are sending more money abroad for imports than is coming into this country to buy our exports. We cannot allow the dollar to sink much further without the international monetary system coming unglued. One major factor keeping our balance of payments deficit from being worse than it is, is the billions of dollars worth of food we export. The Government would be in an interesting position if the crops failed. They would have to decide whether to allow some real domestic shortages in order to export food to save the dollar and allow food prices to soar, or keep it all home and allow the world to come unglued, as it is American food and capital that is the glue that holds civilization together.

With all these pressures, plus continued monetary inflation, food prices will continue to soar. A food storage program purchased now will give you an outstanding return on your investment—tax free—as your profit consists of the money you don't spend later to buy expensive food when prices explode. They can't raise prices on food you bought last year.

I'm also deeply concerned about the financial status of America's farmers. The farming industry has been in trouble for years from a combination of problems. There has been a lot of bad business management. Many farmers over-extended themselves by buying a lot of high-priced land during the commodity price peaks in 1973 and 1974 without keeping sufficient cash reserves to cushion them for a bad year or two. Now they are confronted with depressed commodity prices which pay them less than the cost of production. If general price inflation continues to rise and commodity prices lag behind, we could have a rash of bankruptcies in the farm belt.

THE WEATHER

In two out of the last three years[*] we have been faced with severe drought in the Mid-West and the crops have been saved at the last minute with adequate rain in late summer. If it had been delayed more than a few more days, we could have been faced with a disaster, but as it was, we got through and even built up large surpluses. Before we get too excited about that, bear in mind that those surpluses are only

---
[*]1976-78.

about 40% greater than the total surpluses we had in 1972, and that was wiped out by one Russian grain deal which created shortages that sent food prices through the roof.

Add to this the fact that many climatologists are taking the position that the world's climate is changing just enough to bring us potentially serious problems in the great food growing areas of the world.

It is the opinion of such men as Reed Bryson, Iben Browning, and others, that we have just gone through a 40-year period of remarkable stability in the world's weather—a benign period of temperate, relatively mild winters and warm, relatively damp summers. Three or four years ago that pattern began to change. Many scientists believe that it is merely the earth's climate "returning to normal," and that means shorter growing seasons, much wider extremes of temperature and moisture and an increasing probability of wet springs delaying planting, and early frosts destroying crops when they are the most vulnerable.

The 1975-77 drought in California was of epic proportions and was broken dramatically in the winter of 1977-78; however, during the 1930's California was also in the grip of a drought that lasted approximately seven years and there was one abnormally wet year in the middle of it and then things went dry again for three more years. There is a better-than-even chance of a repeat, with perhaps two wet years in the middle. California reservoirs were down to rock bottom until, mercifully, the rains came. Most everyone has forgotten the drought now and they are returning to their old profligate water-wasting ways.

Many experts have claimed that a temperature change of 1 to 2 degrees in the northern hemisphere could shift growing and farming patterns enough to be immensely disruptive, with the implication being hunger for a lot of people.

OIL TO FOOD

The American farming system, urged on by the proponents of the "Green Revolution," has become almost entirely dependent upon large scale application of fertilizers, pesticides, herbicides, etc., made from petroleum and natural gas. It can truly be said that the food chain begins in the sands of Saudi Arabia or in the bowels of the earth below the Gulf Coast of Louisiana. Government policies and controls have locked into place those factors which will create inevitable growing energy shortages. At the present time, we are importing more than 50% of our oil from the OPEC nations, about two-thirds of that from the Persian Gulf. If OPEC should ever squeeze us again with an oil boycott, and the odds are that they will during the next Middle-East war, we could find our food chain cut off at the first link.

This is also why I am concerned about the Russian drive for control of Africa. They are expanding their influence in the "Horn" (Ethiopia, Somalia, etc.). They are squeezing Southern Africa through pressure on Rhodesia, and eventually South Africa. They already control Angola and Mozambique on both the east and west coasts and when I look at a map, it looks to me very much like control of the sea lanes by which about half of the world's petroleum is transported. Approximately 35% of the oil consumed in this country travels these routes, and the Russians are almost in a position to cut us off on an international dispute. They can destroy our agricultural production and our economy with means short of war.

If farmers cannot continue to apply the petroleum-based pesticides and fungicides to protect the Green Revolution plants that were bred for yield, not resistance to insect infestation and disease, and if we cannot run the pumps to pump the water to irrigate those crops which were bred for yield and not for hardiness or drought-resistance, or if we cannot continue to literally and figuratively pour back into the soil eleven calories of energy, mostly in the form of petroleum or its derivatives, for every calorie of food we take out of it, the nation's food production could be crippled.

It doesn't need to be that way. There are modern eco-science natural methods of farming utilized by a few big farmers in the Mid-West and elsewhere who are growing crops, such as corn and wheat, without dependence upon chemicals, and are producing yields which in most instances are better than their chemical neighbors at costs which are comparable or below. And they are more drought and pest resistant. This is a far cry from the backyard organic gardener, but the philosophy is the same. Rather than depleting the soil, in effect, "mining" it of its nutrients and having to replace them with ever-increasing amounts of chemical fertilizers for the ground to be productive, they actually improve the soil every year, and crops grown in it have inherent resistance to disease and fungus, and massive application of chemicals is unnecessary. There is an interesting publication called *Acres U.S.A.* (see Appendix) which speaks for this point of view, and is a must for any farmer considering switching to these methods.

I must admit to a certain pessimism as to whether or not we will ever voluntarily convert to these methods, so it is safe to say that, as of now, 98% of the food you eat is dependent upon petroleum and natural gas, and a cut-off of these commodities at a crucial time could be disastrous. We will one day be forced to try these new/old methods, but because it takes a few years to recondition the land for large scale farming, there could be great food shortages in the meantime. The change-over would be painful, but ultimately beneficial.

ODDS

I consider one or more of these problems to be likely. The odds favor it. I don't know when, but if I had to identify the most urgent threat, it would be the inflation-caused disruption of the nation's marketplace.

That brings us back to a previous concept, which is that some of your inflating greenbacks should be exchanged now for those things without which your life would be difficult or uncomfortable if you couldn't buy them any time you wanted. Start with food.

The storage, or, as the popular press likes to call it somewhat derisively, "hoarding," of food sounds a bit paranoid to a lot of people, because it implies that there will be a need for it, and most people simply can't make that mental leap. In fact, I would bet that two-thirds of the subscribers to my newsletter who think they have wholeheartedly accepted my opinions of the effect of inflation on their lives, have not been emotionally able to make the logical move of storing food, and that is so sad, because it is the one piece of advice in this book in which there is no risk whatsoever. It is an essential part of your financial planning and if you are not willing to do that, you probably didn't believe the rest of this book. If I'm wrong, the worst thing that would ever happen to you is that you would eat it and save your money. If I'm right you will eat it and save your life. Modern storage foods are a long cry from the old K-rations. Dehydrated and freeze-dried foods are almost indistinguishable from the fresh product. We often use our food storage program when we are too lazy to go down to the grocery store to buy something we just ran out of. It's very economical because there is no waste. What comes out of the can is 100% edible.

If you are still not convinced, *Parade* magazine recently featured a devastating report on the Russian civil defense program. It seems that the Russians have stockpiled enough food underground to feed their entire population for a year, much of which we sold or gave them.

80% of their population also would be safe from nuclear attack, so the next time someone derides you for storing food and criticizes your "bomb shelter mentality," I suggest that you point out to them the Russians think it's a pretty smart thing to do.

You spend hundreds of dollars every year to insure your cars against the accident you fully expect not to have, and you can't eat the cancelled checks. Your money is wasted unless you're "lucky" enough to have an accident. Food storage is the insurance you can eat. And just to give you one more perspective, if inflation disrupted the system, wouldn't you wish your neighbor had a food storage program?

A discussion of this subject usually raises so many moral and technical questions, I'd like to raise some of these questions and answer them.

Q. Isn't it likely that if I store food and we should have a famine that hungry people might try to take it away from me and I might have to defend myself with guns?

A. I hear that question all the time and it's based on the following rather shaky assumptions, which at one time I accepted, but no longer do.

    1. There will be no food anywhere and hordes of people will cast aside all civilized restraint, and

    2. You can outgun a mob.

The history of famines is that hungry people are lethargic. Even in Europe after World War II when it was known that many of the Mormons still had some food left from their storage programs, there was no generalized mob-looting in the countryside and in the small towns. There was some theft from the fields, of course, but the picture of you sitting on your pile of dehydrated food, holding off a mob of neighbors with guns simply doesn't square with any of the lessons of history. It just doesn't happen that way.

Also, my worst case says that this kind of civil disorder will mostly be limited to the core of the cities, with some problems spilling over into the suburbs, and that period will be brief. The odds are you won't be in any personal danger if you stay home during the worst of it, especially if you live in a small agricultural town. I expect brief periods of panic if the food distribution chain is disrupted, and a lengthy period where food process will be terribly high and rising and many commodities will be in short supply. I don't envision people dropping dead of starvation in the streets in the United States.

Small towns are more likely to have a tradition of law and order, and this kind of lawlessness is not likely. They also tend to be self-sufficient. If you select one that has a diversified agricultural economy, you can still get along all right if long-range transport is disrupted.

I expect to use my food storage program to tide me over brief periods of severe shortages, and the lengthy period where the variety and quality of food that I need to maintain good health may not be available. I can supplement that which is available by dipping into my food storage over a period of months, or perhaps years. This is not a preparation for the end of the world. That's impossible. It is a preparation for a period of personal hardship, possible loss of job or failure of your business, temporary disruptions in food supplies and a prolonged period of national convalescence where you may not be able to buy what you want, when you want it, in the quantity and quality you want.

Just as a rudimentary caution, I also would not have a neon sign in front of my home that said, FOOD HERE. I also would like my neighbors to have a food storage plan And I have stored some extra food to help others. The best way I know to persuade them to prepare themselves is to put this book in their hands. It will probably be a better persuader than you, so loan this to them or give them one for their own library. Then they represent no threat to you, even in the most extreme of circumstances.

But back to the hard question. Would I shoot someone if he threatened my life or well-being in a period of lawlessness?

Of course I would and probably so would you. If anyone came to hurt me or take my property by force I would do whatever was necessary to protect my family, but I prefer to plan my life so that eventuality is the lowest possible on the probability scale. We should never lose our feeling for the sanctity of human life. The one thing that must survive all these difficulties is the collective values that make nations governable and societies peaceful. The decision to injure another or to take a human life should be made with great reluctance and only after taking every possible precaution to avoid being placed in the position where that decision would have to be made. But, yes, I am ready if necessary.

Q. Is it moral to store food when people are starving? If everybody took your advice, wouldn't it create shortages?

A. There is enough surplus grain now to provide between 100 and 150 pounds for every man, woman and child in America and wheat is one of the basics of our food storage program. There is no question that a massive food storage movement would strengthen food prices, but it might also save the farming industry, which is sick, and I'm willing to pay some higher prices if it will accomplish that.

It is moral to take my advice in times of surplus. If you wait until there are shortages and scramble to grab more than your share of the limited available supply, that's "hoarding" and that's immoral, and the government may even make it illegal by rationing.

When people store food in times of

plenty, that means they will not be competing for scarce foods, and there is more for everyone else, including the poor and the profligate. I'm sure that the people in my home town will be glad not to have me standing in the food line ahead of them with my wife and nine children. I won't have to because I will have taken care of myself with my choice of food at much lower prices long before the problem occurs. The storage of food is good for you and good for America.

Q. Where can you store food, and how much space does it take?

A. The new concentrated dehydrated foods only need approximately 1/4 to 1/7 of the space of an equivalent amount of fresh food. If you use the proper mix of grains, beans, supplements and dehydrated and freeze-dried foods for a balanced and interesting diet, a year's supply for one person could be put under 1½ card tables. That can easily be stored in the bottom 2 or 3 feet of your closet. Properly prepared, it requires no specialized storage facilities and it doesn't take up a lot of room.

Q. How long will it last?

A. Nitrogen-packed dehydrated food has a nutritional shelf life of from 4 to 7 years, which means it will not start losing nutritional value for at least 4 years, depending on the temperature at which it is stored. Wheat, if kept dry and protected from rodents and insects, will last for two or three thousand years. Some that was found in the tomb of King Tut was still edible, and it even germinated.

Q. How much does a good food storage program cost?
A. If you prepare a complete do-it-yourself program, like some Mormons have done (you can contact your local L.D.S. Ward and ask for the President of the women's organization. The Relief Society, and they are very happy to help), you could set aside a year's supply of food for as little as $350 (as of July 1978).* If you want an interesting varied diet which falls somewhat short of gourmet fare, but by any reasonable measurement is attractive, using some dehydrated and freeze-dried foods, you could obtain a one-year supply for one person for $600 to $950.† Price-wise, that is very close to the cost of feeding one person for a year, shopping at your local supermarket. In fact, it's a little bit less. The Department of Commerce says the average American is now spending $90 per month per person on food, or $1,080 per year (1977).**

If you want a real luxurious gourmet food program based entirely on freeze-dried foods, complete with beef stroganoff, shrimp creole and sirloin steak, you can pay as much as $1,500 to $2,000. It all depends on your pocketbook and your in-

---
*Now $450.
†Now $750–$1200.
**Now $115 per month, or $1380 per year.

clinations, but in any event, it isn't a heck of a lot compared with what you are now spending on food. And you can buy your program a bit at a time.

Q. When should I buy this food?
A. You already know the answer to that question. Buy it now! I'd rather be a year too early than a few days too late. Until you have done it, you shouldn't be following any of my other advice. If your money is limited, then do what you can. It's your surest investment from a strictly dollars and cents point of view, and it's the one indispensable piece of advice that applies to everyone. Disruptions in the marketplace can come with stunning swiftness, and labor troubles, international warfare, gas rationing—any number of things—could create problems overnight as things deteriorate. You might not need it for a year or two, or three. But then again, you might need it next week.

NUTS AND BOLTS

I hope I've made my point as to why you need an emergency supply of food. If I haven't persuaded you, you might as well skip the rest of this chapter because I'm now going to tell you how to do it. You need a carefully reasoned advance response to the potential problems that make good sense for these times—an insurance policy against hunger and inconvenience. You can't get insurance when the barn's on fire. The best insurance is to become food self-sufficient.

There are three basic ways to do it.

1. Nineteenth-Century Style. If you live on a farm or have an acre or two, you can become self-sufficient by using intensive methods of organic gardening and by raising chickens and rabbits. You would then have relatively little need for a food storage plan, although you might want to have some commercially prepared food-stuffs set aside for the winter and spring when supplies might run low, or as a protection against crop failure. If there is good hunting or fishing nearby, so much the better. If you have the land, the skills, and the inclination, that's a great way to go.

2. A Do-It-Yourself Food Storage Plan—the approach which has been adopted by many Mormons. Most of you can't be self-sufficient in food production, although most everyone can grow something, even if it's only a window box or a sprouter. You buy certain bulk basics, such as wheat, powdered milk, honey, salt, beans, etc., and you purchase containers and prepare them for long term storage. This approach to storage is a lot of work, but it can be a real moneysaver.

There are several outstanding books on this subject that have treated it far better than I can in these pages, which you should add to your library. *Making the Best of Basics* (see Appendix) by James Talmage Stevens and *Passport to Survival* (see Appendix) by Esther Dicky are classics.

I believe that those who depend on these programs, however, are ignoring some potential health dangers and they need to add a few things, which I'll discuss later, but it's a good way for the penny-saver to start. You can prepare a rather austere and boring one-year supply of food for one person, which would keep you reasonably healthy for less than $350, and at a little less than $30 a month,* that's a pretty good bargain.

3. The Commercial Dehydrated or Freeze-Dried Food Storage Plan. These programs are prepared by firms which are in the business of preparing food storage. They consist primarily of dehydrated and freeze-dried foods with some grains and food supplements. They range in price from $2,000 or more for a one-year supply of luxurious gourmet freeze-dried meals, which are indistinguishable from that which you would consume in an upper-middle quality restaurant, on down to somewhat less spectacular programs, which offer good variety and taste in the $700 to $1,000† range. There is a tremendous variety for your pocketbook and palate. The problem is that most of these programs are poorly planned and have some serious nutritional problems.

Back in 1973, when I became concerned about the state of the nation and began thinking through the implications for my family, my instinctive response was to look at the commercial food storage programs, because I am not a farmer, nor do I have time to do a heck of a lot of do-it-yourself stuff. I have a deep interest in health and nutrition, and I was in the

---
*Now $450 and $37.50 a month.
†Now $800–$1200.

food supplement business at that time. I am an obsessive reader of nutritional literature, ranging from the far-out natural food freaks to the mainstream scientific and professional journals, so I felt reasonably qualified to choose a sound program. I found to my horror that the commercial plans I looked at were totally at odds with the healthy nutrition lifestyle I had chosen for myself and my family. There wasn't one that I would buy as a "unit," which was the way they were being sold. I would have to design my own unit. When I began delving into the food storage industry, I found that not only were many of the programs nutritionally unsound, but most of the companies were unstable. One of the largest had just gone broke and there were lengthy delays in delivery—as much as six months. It was a growth industry undergoing a typical shake-out.

The food storage business is literally "feast or famine." When people are scared and we're sliding into a recession, the companies can't meet the demand. They then expand capacity, and just about the time they are ready to handle the increased volume, the panic is over, business falls off to zilch and they find themselves in financial trouble. They are victims of a wildly swinging business cycle.

Let's look at the do's and don'ts of food storage.

First, the don'ts:

1. Don't rush out and buy a lot of canned and frozen goods. They both have problems for storage.

The most significant measurement of the quality of food is the calorie, which is a measurement of the amount of food energy that will be derived from it. Canned goods are expensive, relative to the "cost-per-calorie." Canned goods consist of part water and part product. Not only is it expensive to ship water back and forth across the country but the taste and color are generally inferior to the dehydrated or frozen product, particularly in vegetables.

The shelf life of canned goods is somewhat in doubt despite the protestations of the industry. I published in my newsletter a study from the University of Idaho Agricultural Extension Service by Don Huber, Plant Pathologist, and Esther H. Wilson, Extension Nutrition Specialist, entitled *Store a Year's Supply of Food and Household Items*. It triggered a rather irate letter from an old friend who was a Washington lobbyist for the canning industry, but I have not yet seen a refutation of the data. What interested me most were the tables on shelf life of foods.

Not only is the nutritional value of canned goods lower because of the heat used in canning but the "nutritional shelf life" is brief at best. By "nutritional shelf life" I mean the length of time you can count on the food having the same value that it had when it was canned. The nutritional value deteriorates long before the food begins to deteriorate enough to become unpalatable or dangerous.

STORAGE LIFE OF CANNED GOODS

Canned Goods	Storage Life
DAIRY PRODUCTS	
Milk	1 Year
MEAT PRODUCTS	
Beef	18 Months
Chicken	18 Months
Fish	1 Year
Ham	18 Months
Lunch Meat	18 Months
Pork	18 Months
Turkey	18 Months
CANNED VEGETABLES	
All	18 Months
FRUITS	
Applesauce	12-18 Months
Apricots	12-18 Months
Berries	6 Months
Citrus Juice	6-8 Months
Citrus Slices	12-18 Months
Cherries	6-12 Months
Peaches	12-18 Months
Pears	12-18 Months
Pineapple	12-18 Months
Plums	12-18 Months
MISCELLANEOUS	
Peanut Butter	12-18 Months
Shelled Nuts	1 Year

If you do store some canned goods, use them regularly and replace them well within the storage life figures from the above table. Also, you need to compensate for the nutritional losses with a good natural multi-vitamin supplement and extra Vitamin C.

Don't use any cans that are bulging, leaking or rusted. "If in doubt, throw it out."

Frozen food has an even shorter shelf life, to say nothing of the vulnerability to power outages, and in a period of real financial or economic chaos, I would not want to have to depend upon a steady flow of electricity to my home. If you do store frozen food, make sure you have a smoker unit so that any meat or fish could have its shelf life extended by smoking if the power went out for long. Canned and frozen foods can be part of a short-term storage program, but for long-term storage there are much better alternatives. If my forecasts were right over the long haul, but my timetable was off by a year or two, you want to be sure you can safely eat your stored food with good nutritional results, several years after its acquisition.

2. Don't just buy any "food unit" from any food storage dealer without following the guidelines in this chapter. Many of the "units" are based on economic considerations rather than sound nutritional principles and even those companies that have made an effort to be nutritionally sound that generally relied upon government nutritional tables, which have very little relevance to reality. I haven't seen anything yet the government has not been able to foul up. And in my opinion, the Food and Drug Administration is the most biased, industry-influenced regulatory agency of them all and I would not depend on any data produced by the F.D.A. They are captives of the food processing and sugar industries and that bias is reflected in their conclusions, their studies and their press releases.

3. Be very wary of "bargains." Whenever you see a food storage company clearing out a lot of inventory at a cheap price, it is probably reaching the end of its shelf life, or the company is suffering from slow sales and cash difficulties, which means the food may have been

sitting around for a long time. It is not likely to be fresh. Shelf life is one of your most important considerations. "Shelf life" means how long it will be of high nutritional value and edibility from the time you buy it, not from the time it was canned. I know of some companies that have had storage food sitting around for more than two years, still for sale. If you see such a bargain, demand documentation on when it was canned. Each can must be coded.

4. As I said, I wouldn't put up a neon sign in my home saying, "Food Here." It would be best to be a bit discreet. You don't have to be paranoid or extreme about it. Just don't go shouting to the world that you have an emergency food storage program.

5. Don't just let your food sit there. Rotate it. By that I mean use it and replace it on a regular basis. There are several good reasons for this.

First, it will have a higher nutritional value when you use it if you are constantly replacing it with fresher products, and, second, if the time should ever come that you should need to rely on it for your family, the transition will go a lot smoother if you are accustomed to it. A change of diet to unfamiliar foods can be stressful. If our family had to switch to our food storage program it would take relatively little change in our eating habits. We are accustomed to using these foods. Get used to using whole wheat, beans, protein powders, etc. It's a healthy diet, and you will also find it a fine way to save money, as foods bought in bulk are a lot cheaper than those bought on a weekly basis at your supermarket.

6. Don't accept exaggerated shelf life claims of storage foods. A lot of sincere, enthusiastic food storage dealers are claiming that their product will be good for 15 to 20 years. Don't you believe it. I know of too many people who have had to throw out food storage programs after 7 to 10 years and I've got a good group from which to take that sampling in my Mormon friends.

Shelf life has to be measured in two ways. Our first concern is nutritional shelf life, which is the length of time over which you can count on the food having the same nutritional value that it had when it was canned, particularly in reference to the volatile or water-soluble vitamins (the B-complex and C), and many of the minerals which will gradually oxidize and break down. That shelf life for most properly packed dehydrated or freeze-dried foods is 4 to 7 years, depending on temperature. The lower the temperature at which the food is stored, the longer the shelf life. There might also be a significant loss in color and flavor after seven years.

7. Don't pay for the food before it is delivered, unless you know the firm and can depend on them. Too many people have paid for food and not had it delivered because of the financial instabilty of the industry. You can count on our recommended firms as we monitor their finances and their business on a regular basis and they are all dependable. The best way to handle it is either to order C.O.D.,

or to pay a deposit with the order and the balance upon delivery. A legitimate food storage dealer who doesn't know you might object to this, as he will have just as much concern about your ability and willingness to pay as you would have about his willingness to fulfill the order. The resolution of the stalemate is to know your dealer and trust him if he is dependable.

Now, let's review some of the do's.

1. Buy a one year supply of food. I'm not sure a year is enough but it certainly isn't too much, not because I think the nation would be without food for a year, but because there is a distinct possibility of intermittent disruption of the marketplace—possibly days or weeks at a time—for several years. It doesn't take very long to get hungry. I would also be able to draw from my emergency food supplies over a period of several years of depression to replace those foods which may not be available in the quantity, quality or variety of choices to which I am accustomed. I also feel I should have enough to share with those I love who do not believe my message. I also want some available for barter, so a year's supply for each member of my family makes pretty good sense.

You will obviously have to work within your own financial limitations, but food is your number one priority and comes ahead of any of my investment recommendations. I wouldn't want to be the richest hungry man on my block.

2. Be sure your program is nutritionally sound. Nutrition may bore some of you, but if

you don't want to take the trouble to plow through this nutritional stuff, maybe there is someone in your family who will, so delegate that responsibility. Your choice is to either take my advice about our recommended dealers and trust them to sell you what you should have, or get an education on the subject through this chapter.

Here are the fundamentals of nutrition as it relates to food storage.

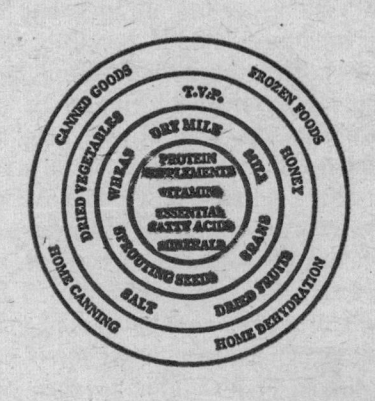

(Diagram: concentric circles target. Bull's-eye: PROTEIN SUPPLEMENTS, VITAMINS, ESSENTIAL FATTY ACIDS, MINERALS. Next ring: T.V.P., DRY MILK, MILK, HONEY, GRAINS, DRIED FRUITS, SALT, SPROUTING SEEDS, WHEAT. Outer ring: CANNED GOODS, FROZEN FOODS, HOME DEHYDRATION, HOME CANNING, DRIED VEGETABLES.)

Think of your food storage program as though it were a target. The most points are in the bull's-eye and you receive lesser points as you move to the outside of the target. The ideal food storage program will be arranged in that manner.

In the bull's-eye I have put food supplements. If you have met all of your nutritional requirements for the elements that your body is known to need, you could probably live on edible weeds and roots if you had to. (There are several good books on that subject available in paperback, including *Field Guide to Edible Wild Plants* [see Appendix] by Bradford Angier.) After your nutritional requirements are assured from supplements, the quality of the rest of your food storage program, although still very important, is not as critical. You can gain sufficient bulk and calories from almost anything.

This is exactly the reverse of what your present eating habits should be. You are generally better off getting all of your nutrients from the food you eat, if possible, and using supplements for just that—supplementation, which my family does routinely. In an emergency situation, your problem is exactly reversed. Even the best of food storage programs come up short nutritionally, because your nutritional needs increase under stress, and obviously we are talking about a time of potentially great stress. Also, the processing of foods for long-term storage, under the best of conditions, will result in some nutritional losses, plus the aforementioned losses under storage.

The major reason for supplementing, however, is that you cannot afford to get sick. If there's anything that I learned from a study of the Arab oil embargo of 1973, it is that many critical medications, such as penicillin, depend on petrochemicals in their manufacturing process. If the Arab embargo had not been lifted when it was, we could have had a serious shortage of certain medications. We almost had a severe shortage of penicillin and several other antibiotics because the government petroleum allocation program did not provide enough for those industries to meet their manufacturing needs. Staying well becomes a matter of something more than convenience. Sickness that is now routinely handled by a trip to the doctor for a shot could become life-threatening. In addition, there might not be the fuel for you to get to a doctor, and the doctor might not have all of the high technology electronic and chemical tools at his disposal to help you. Your best bet is to stay well, and the greater the stress, the more difficult that is.

When you look at the nutritional claims of the food storage programs, keep in mind the nutritional loss factors in storage foods.

All of the major storage companies buy from a handful of major processors, and can the product themselves. Despite their claims, no one knows the actual nutritional value of the food by the time you get it on your shelf.

A technical bulletin issued by California Vegetable Concentrates (C.V.C.), a Division of General Foods that makes dehydrated foods for the storage food industry, is very candid about it.

> There is no truly reliable representative nutritional information pertaining to commercially processed dehydrated vegetables. What work has been done on processed vegetables has been fragmentary, difficult to correlate for many reasons, and of only indicative value in determining food values.
>
> . . . values shown for dehydrated vegetables have been calculated based on concentration ratios with no assumed processing losses.

That means that nutritional tables for dried foods are an approximation, at best, based on government tables of food values which assume the product is fresh.

C.V.C. says further,

> We know of no data indicating retention of nutritional values after prolonged storage. C.V.C. vegetables do retain good color and flavor for periods in excess of one year and in several instances, for considerably longer periods when held at 70 degrees F. or below.

The answer to that uncertainty is simple. Store food supplements, to be sure that you are consuming sufficient nutrients to compensate for that great unknown.

Another reason for supplementation is that, in the interests of profit margins, processing difficulties, or shelf life considerations, a lot of foods you are accustomed to are not included in storage programs. Fresh meat, eggs, fish, and dairy products, which presently provide most of your protein and a substantial amount of your vitamins A and B, are either missing, in short supply, over processed, or terribly expensive in most food storage programs. The major protein substitutes (beans, rice, etc.) are both lower protein percentage and much lower protein quality, although that level can be improved somewhat when they are combined in the same meal.

For a discussion of how to improve the protein value of vegetable proteins, I heartily recommend the book *Diet for a Small Planet* by Frances Moore Lappe. She points out how, for example, you can combine wheat (low in lysine, an essential amino acid) with rice (high in lysine) and you improve the quality of both proteins. That doesn't solve the whole problem, however, as I still believe you still need some of the higher quality animal proteins under stress conditions, but it can sure help.

Stress is not just emotional or mental trauma. Stress is really measured by the degree and rapidity of change in your life. According to those who study stress, even a vacation, Christmas, or a change of diet can trigger the body's stress responses. Under stress, your body produces additional adrenal hormones, which bring about great changes in the body. This is generally some level of response to the "fight or run" syndrome. God created us so that when stress occurs, the body marshals all of its resources to either fight or run. The severest stress is the death of a spouse. Next to it is a divorce. Even a promotion or change of job is stressful. When you react this way, you cannibalize your muscle and bone tissues to get high quality protein to use as raw components for hormones, enzymes, antibodies, white blood cells, etc. This internal cannibalism makes you more susceptible to disease. In children it can stunt both physical growth and the growth of brain tissue.

Under stress conditions you need more well-balanced animal protein. The vegetarian societies that flourish in good health, like the Hunzas of Central Asia, tend to be low-stress societies. Under stress conditions your body consumes large amounts of vitamin C and the B complex, and minerals such as calcium. One researcher has indicated that a half an hour of severe stress or fear can deplete all of the vitamin C in your blood, and a day of intense worry can destroy all of the vitamin C stored in your adrenal cortex. As vitamin C is a vital component of white blood cells and is a potent viruscide, your resistance to virus and bacterial infections is reduced. Under severe stress conditions the vitamin C recommended daily allowance published by the FDA is woefully inadequate, to say nothing of the fact that vitamin C is the most susceptible of all the vitamins to food processing losses.

Going back to that C.V.C. technical bulletin, the following table illustrates the vitamin losses from the use of sulfites in the storage process. These chemicals are dusted on the food prior to canning to make sure that the rate of oxidation is reduced. They float free of the product and dissipate into the air when it is reconstituted in water so they represent no health threat in and of themselves, but look what happens to the vitamins.

VITAMIN LOSSES FROM SULFITES

Vitamin	Percentage of Loss
Thiamine	10% to 40%
Riboflavin	0% to 15%
Niacin	0% to 21%
Pantothenic Acid	0% to 28%
Vitamin C	50%

By now you should understand the need for supplements in the storage program, but now you need to know some of the guidelines by which you select these products.

Let's start with protein powders.

Protein powders have been the recent whipping boy of the Federal Trade Commission (F.T.C.) which has been holding hearings to determine whether or not they represent a health threat. As I told you, the F.D.A. is the captive of processing industries and they have never liked food supplement industry running around saying things like, "Our foods are overprocessed and depleted of their vitamins; therefore, you need food supplementation." The F.D.A. had run up against some legislative limitations in their assault on the supplement industry so they conceived the strategy of having the F.T.C. work under their direction to attack the supplement industry under the very broad, vague umbrella of "fraudulent sales practices." The hearings began in 1976 and were held for almost a year and a half. The F.T.C. alleged that protein powders could be dangerous to children under three because excess protein in infants can cause severe dehydration and it is also allegedly dangerous for people with liver or kidney problems.

That's absurd! The allegations were based strictly on theoretical assumptions and a year of hearings did not produce any children who had suffered any of those problems from consumption of protein supplements. Not one example was introduced into evidence! But the preordained guilty verdict was published anyway. Remember, regulatory agencies are judge, prosecuting attorney and jury, and they lay down the rules for the defense. Oddly enough, they rarely lose a case.

Bear in mind that a high-quality protein supplement is merely a concentrated food that in our food storage program is designed to replace those high-quality proteins which are generally omitted because of expense or other factors.

It is also designed to supplement the low-quality vegetable proteins, when consumed in the same meal. For example, if one protein food is high in lysine, a "limiting" amino acid, and another is low in lysine, all your body knows, if you ate them in the same meal at the same time, is that your protein intake is sufficient in lysine. If any of the 8 essential amino acids is missing or in short supply, the body's use of it is limited, and your ability to fight infection or to rebuild tissue is impaired.

Your protein powder should have the following characteristics:

1. It should taste good. There are many protein powders that would gag a maggot. They taste like ground-up coal miners' boots. That's neither desirable nor necessary. There are some very good tasting protein powders around. Unfortunately, some of them are not of high nutritional value, but it is possible to get both factors in one protein powder.

2. It should have a high Protein Efficiency Ratio (P.E.R.). P.E.R. is determined by feeding immature rats a protein product as their only source of protein and then weighing them

to measure their growth. If they show no growth, it has a P.E.R. of 1, meaning they stayed the same as they are and the protein has no growth-promoting capability. If they increased in weight 2½ times during the test period, it has a P.E.R. of 2.5. Most animal proteins are in excess of 2, with the exception of gelatin, which is a lousy quality protein, because it is almost totally lacking in tryptophan, one of the essential amino acids. An egg is the highest, generally around 2.8. Most meat is in the 2.2 to 2.5 range, as is fish and fowl. A protein powder's P.E.R. should be in excess of 2, and the can should say so. If it doesn't, the manufacturer should be consulted.

3. Mixability. There should be little or no grit-factor and it should blend with a spoon. Its solubility in water or milk is somewhat of an indicator of its solubility in the body.

4. It should be high in lysine and tryptophan. In fact, its lysine level should exceed the ideal amino acid profile of the World Health Organization so that there is extra lysine available with the product to complement the protein value of the grains included in your storage program. Thus when grains and the right protein supplement are eaten in the same meal, the protein quality of the grain is enhanced.

The label can help you to determine the value of a protein powder. Generally speaking, if soya is the first ingredient, the product will not have the same value as a product which has casein as the first ingredient, as the products are listed in descending order of quantity, and casein is a high-quality animal protein. In fact, it is used as the basic standard for measuring proteins.

The label should also indicate a variety of protein sources, such as lactalbumin, and b-lactoglobulin (the protein fractions from milk), soya, brewers yeast, etc.

5. Don't pay for protein powder that lists milk powder as one of the first two ingredients. If that's what you want, you can buy milk powder a lot cheaper without paying health food store prices for it. Besides, powdered milk has some possible problems in terms of the availability of amino acids, as explained in *Famine and Survival in America* (see Appendix). Even though it may test as having adequate lysine, there is some evidence that under conditions of drying, even low-temperature spray drying, the lysine locks up with the milk sugar and becomes unavailable to the body. That case is not completely proven, but I've seen enough information on it to not want to depend upon powdered milk as my sole protein supplement.

6. It should probably be sweetened with *fructose*. Fructose is the scientific name for the so-called "fruit sugar." It has several advantages over other sugars.

First, it is twice as sweet as table sugar (sucrose), which means you get the same sweetening for half of the sugar intake.

Second, your body does not use insulin to metabolize it, consequently, it's generally safe for the person who is afflicted with either diabetes or hypoglycemia. Although this is a matter of some scientific dispute, the preponderance of the evidence seems to support those conclusions, and the sweetness level is indisputable.

Third, it also has a "protein sparing action," which means that when protein is taken with various sugars, your body does not have to convert protein into sugar for energy, but can use protein for the things that only protein can do. Fructose has the highest protein sparing action of all the sugars.

If the supplement is sweetened with glucose, much more sugar is required because glucose is the least sweet of the commonly used sugars.

Some nutrition writers, including Dr. Carleton Fredericks, a man whom I admire very much, have taken the position that fructose or fruit sugar is not safe for diabetics or hypoglycemics, based on the fact that many of them cannot tolerate fruit. Dr. Fredericks is ignoring the fact that most fruits are rich in sugars other than fructose, and it's my opinion that they are reacting to the other sugars, not the fructose.

Fourth, the fructose-sweetened supplement, because of the lesser amount of sugar required, will also have the highest possible percentage of protein in the can, consistent with tasting good. Remember, one problem with a protein supplement is not just its health benefits but its palatability, that is, if you want the kids to accept it. High quality, predigested (with enzymes) protein supplements, sweetened with fructose, can be a delicious addition to your diet and do not take much getting used to.

Our recommended dealer, Marten's Health & Survival Products, Inc., carries the protein powder that my family uses in our storage program. It's called Super Ease, and is made by the Neo Life Company of America.

VITAMINS AND MINERALS

There's probably no subject on which there is more violent scientfic controversy than vitamins and minerals. At issue is whether we need them in supplemental form at all, as well as what form is best.

I'd better admit to some bias right here so you can decide whether or not to take my advice. I am convinced that natural vitamins are superior. I would like to expend a little effort making that case.

The F.D.A. says that anyone who claims there's any difference between natural and synthetic vitamins is a "quack." Well, that makes me a Mallard.

Here's why I disagree.

Chromatography is an analysis method used to literally photograph molecules of both organic and inorganic substances. Chromatographs show a distinct difference between the synthetic and the natural vitamin C molecule. Synthetic ascorbic acid and natural vitamin C are chemically identical, except that the chromatographs of the natural vitamin show "impurities" which have been determined to be enzymes—protein factors that apparently assist the absorption and utilization of the vitamin on a cellular level. The visual difference between the natural and synthetic of these two is significant. That doesn't necessarily prove that natural is better than synthetic, but it certainly does prove they are different, and I believe it is better.

Writing in the August 27, 1973, issue of the *Journal of the American Medical Association*, Dr. Samuel Ayers, Jr., an M.D. from Los Angeles, disputed a contention of Marguerita Magy, M.S., of the A.M.A. Department of Foods and Nutrition.

She had made the statement (*Journal of the American Medical Association*, July 2, 1973) that bio-chemically, a vitamin has a single molecular structure and it didn't make any difference if it was natural or synthetic because the body couldn't tell the difference.

"That may be true of some vitamins," Dr. Ayers wrote, "but it is definitely not true of Vitamin E (tocopherol), in which the alpha fraction contains virtually all the therapeutically active principle. d-Alpha-Tocopheryl acetate is derived from natural sources, such as wheat germ oil, whereas dl-Alpha Tocopheryl acetate is the synthetic form.

"While they may appear identical chemically, they affect polarized light differently and in animal experiences the d or natural form is considerably more active than the dl, or synthetic form," he wrote.

Dr. Ayers cited several sources, including Roels, who said, "The Animal Research Council subcommittee for Vitamin E standards has shown that the relative potency of d-Alpha Tocopheryl acetate is 1.2 times (20%) greater than the dl form (Nutrition Reviews, 24:33-37, 1967).

"In order to obtain the maximum therapeutic effect from Vitamin E," Dr. Ayers concluded, "the physician should specify d-Alpha-Tocopheryl acetate."

British researcher, Isabel W. Jennings of the University College of the University of Cambridge, speaks of the comparison between synthetic and natural vitamins in her book, *Vitamins in Endocrine Metabolism* (Charles C. Thomas, 1970).

"The close relations, although useful in many ways, pose some problems in that they may have only a fraction, whether large or small, of the biological activity of the natural product." She points out that while vitamin C, for example, is chemically identical to the natural vitamin and an equally effective antioxidant, it does not have the same value in promoting the health of the capillaries.

For all of these reasons, I prefer the natural form of the vitamins, but I have one more argument that I think is even more significant.

A synthetic multi-vitamin-mineral product contains a pinch of this, and a dash of that, pulled from the shelf, based on the chemist's current opinion of which nutrients the body needs and in what ratios.

A natural vitamin is generally a concentrate of a food which is rich in that vitamin.

For example, a good B Complex formula will generally be a concentrate of yeast. There are unknown nutritional factors, or even factors such as choline and inisotol about which the scientific community is not yet agreed, which will tend to occur naturally in such a product. Even though it's not on the label and its value is not yet determined, it's there. The body does not wait until the F.D.A. has made a decision before it decides to use a nutrient. I'd rather be sure I'm getting it.

"I'm also convinced that scientific opinion on this subject is growing increasingly biased in favor of the synthetic forms simply because those who take other positions are officially labeled "quacks" and ostracized in the scientific community, which could tend to dampen your enthusiasm if you are a researcher with a contrary opinion.

I consider the F.D.A. to be dangerous and another example of bureaucracy run wild. I can't remember the last thing they said that I agreed with.

So when you buy vitamins for your food storage program, they should meet the following criteria:

1. It should be an all-natural formula.

2. It should be in a soft gelatin capsule, as that substantially improves the shelf life.

3. It should have vitamins, minerals, and essential fatty acids (lipids and sterols).

4. It should also be canned for long-term storage.

Your vitamin C should be separate from

your multi-vitamin as it is bulky and when consumed in the necessary quantities would never fit into a capsule with other vitamins.

It has been assumed by most scientists that the shelf life of vitamin C is quite limited, but I have in my hands a technical bulletin from Roche Chemical Division of Hoffman-LaRoche, Inc., the largest manufacturer of vitamin C in the world, which says,

> We have made extensive studies of a variety of formulations of ascorbic acid tablets under a variety of conditions, including various temperatures and humidities, and found little or no loss of potency in periods up to five years.

That is true of the hard-pressed tablet form of the vitamin but not necessarily true of the powder.

Also, the *Journal of Pharmaceutical Services*, Volume 59, pp. 229-232 (1970), had the following to say about vitamin C:

> Sodium ascorbate, a common synthetic form of the vitamin, was the most susceptible to loss of potency from moisture.

I recommend that you use a natural form, which should probably be a concentrate of citrus fruit, or a combination of citrus fruit, rose hips and acerola cherries. You need from 200 to 500 mgs. per day for every member of the family, plus some extra for large therapeutic doses if you share the opinions of Linus Pauling and other vitamin C advocates regarding mega-doses of vitamin C.

Calcium tablets also need to be added to your supplement program. A diet which is high in grains, such as most food storage programs are, will increase your requirement for calcium, as there are factors in grains that tie up the calcium in your body. A good calcium tablet with hydrochloric acid added can make a big difference in your health. Calcium is nature's natural tranquilizer and is essential to the functioning of every muscle in your body, including your heart. Calcium deficiency can lead to leg cramps, nervousness, heart irregularity, and even psychological problems, as your whole nervous system is affected by this essential mineral. It isn't just used for bones and teeth.

Natural vitamins generally are more expensive than the synthetic but they are worth it because of the increased potency. Besides, one or two years into a famine is no time to find out that your diet has been lacking in some undiscovered essential nutrient and, as I said before, those nutrients will tend to be associated with natural vitamins as "naturally occurring factors."

THE STAPLES

The first ring of your target consists of wheat, dry milk, beans, and sprouting seeds. You could theoretically live in good health with your bull's-eye and first ring, although you might die of taste fatigue.

Wheat is an ideal storage food because it keeps forever and is one of the most versatile and best balanced foods found in nature. It only needs to be kept safe from moisture, rodents and insects. You can buy it in bulk at

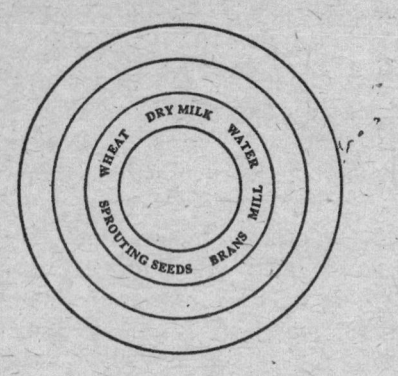

(Diagram: concentric circles labeled WHEAT, DRY MILK, WATER, MILK, BRANS, SPROUTING SEEDS)

your local feed store, or you can buy it already canned in one gallon tins from your food storage dealer. It's a lot cheaper to buy it in bulk; however, it does need to be treated. This is best done by adding some dry ice to the container of wheat, putting the lid on loosely until all the dry ice has dissipated, forming gaseous carbon dioxide, which, being heavier than air, will stay in the container. Then seal the container. If you seal it too early, the build-up of pressure could give you a bad case of wheat shrapnel. Carbon dioxide prevents the development of any weevil eggs which might be in the wheat. It could be kind of disturbing to open up your can of wheat in the middle of a famine and find it seething with little weevil worms, even if weevils are high in protein. That has happened to us, so you need to be very careful. The one-gallon sealed cans of wheat bought from your storage dealer are a lot safer, but cost more. But wheat is still pretty cheap anyway. Our personal storage program wheat is about half bulk and half canned.

Your local Mormon Church may have a co-op buying arrangement which it is happy to share with non-Mormon friends which would enable you to buy wheat in bulk. It should be very low in moisture and of the hard red winter wheat variety. It can be ground into flour for various bakery products. It can be cracked and used as a delicious hot cereal, or it can be soaked in water and sprouted and prepared without any cooking whatsoever. We enjoy it often in our family. It doesn't take a lot of getting used to.

The best books on how to use wheat are *Making the Best of Basics* (see Appendix) and Esther Dickey's book, *Passport to Survival* (see Appendix).

I have also included beans in this target ring because it is a complementary protein to wheat, and they should be eaten in the same meal. A piece of bread and a pot of chili gives you fairly good protein quality (especially when accompanied by a glass of your favorite protein drink). They both also provide some high-quality carbohydrate, some essential fatty acids and a fairly good spectrum of the B-Complex.

Dry milk is included, despite my reservations about its nutritional value, because it is so useful in cooking and food preparation and it does provide substantial protein value and some high quality carbohydrate as well as calories.

The sprouting seeds are not for the purpose of growing a garden but for growing edible sprouts in your kitchen. When sprouted seeds are served in salads or casseroles, the nutritional value is enhanced. It's another method of preparing food without having to cook if you have a real energy shortage.

It obviously would be a good idea to have a mill which could be used to grind wheat. We have one which works either by hand or by electricity. However, they are fairly expensive, —generally in the $250 range although there are some which are less expensive than that. Reliance Products (see Appendix) carries several fine brands.

There are also small hand grinders. You have to run the wheat through them several times which can be hard work, but they are available for under $30.

THE SECOND RING

The second ring of the target includes dehydrated or freeze-dried vegetables and fruits, along with some soy bean meat analogues (imitations) called T.V.P., and various condiments and seasonings.

This is where the pitfalls arise in storage programs. This is where most of the commercial food storage programs begin and end. Dehydrated food can be a major source of calories, bulk and variety. You could live in fairly good health on the bull's-eye and the first ring, but it is especially important for children to have enough variety in the diet that their food is palatable to them and they will eat it. Some children have actually starved to death in famines because they would not eat unfamilair

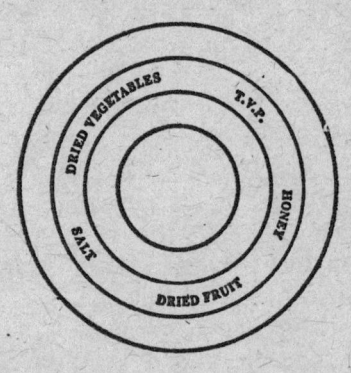

DRIED VEGETABLES — T.V.P. — HONEY — DRIED FRUIT — SALT

food. Although we are not contemplating that kind of famine, the principle is still valid. The typical food storage program attempts to solve the protein and cost problems by using T.V.P. (Textured Vegetable Protein) which is a meat imitation made from soy beans. My opinion is that it is dangerous health-wise to rely on these as your principal protein source. They are loaded with chemicals. The ingredient list of some pork-imitating T.V.P. from a large manufacturer reads like this (in descending order): "Soy flour, salt, hydrolyzed vegetable protein, whey solids, flavorings, monosodium glutamate, spice, hydrogenated vegetable oil, disodium inosinate, disodium guanylate and U.S. Certified Color."

Doesn't that sound tasty? What that means is that you are eating a product which had to have a heck of a lot done to it to change it from a soy bean into a pork chop. Monosodium glutamate, for example, is now banned from commercially prepared baby foods because studies have determined that it probably causes brain damage in young animals. It's the same product used as the principal ingredient in such flavor enhancers as Accent. It is suspected as the cause of the "Chinese restaurant syndrome" where people who have had a Chinese dinner suffer from severe migraine-like headaches a few hours later. Foods treated with large quantities of M.S.G. should be taken sparingly and should not be fed to infants or toddlers.

The hydrogenated vegetable oil may be the most dangerous part of the product. Liquid fats (vegetable oils) are highly unsaturated with the exception of coconut oil and olive oil. Polyunsaturated oils are generally thought by cardiologists and nutritionists to lower cholesterol and triglyceride levels in the blood. When a food processor wishes to harden a polyunsaturated oil to get a different consistency (such as making margarine out of corn oil or safflower oil), or to prolong its shelf life, he "hydrogenates" it. It is heated under pressure, and hydrogen is bubbled through it in the presence of a metal catalyst (nickel or platinum). The hydrogen atoms combine with the carbon atoms and the product becomes "saturated" and hardens.

Dr. Bicknell describes it as follows:

The abnormal fatty acids produced by "hardening" (hydrogenation) are the real worry. The atoms of the molecule of an essential fatty acid (EFA) are arranged in space in a particular manner ... but hardening may produce a different spatial arrangement, so that a completely abnormal ... essential fatty acid is produced. The same mistakes are made by the body when presented ... with the abnormal EFA. Not only does it fail to benefit by them, but it is deluded by their similarity to normal EFA and so attempts to use them. It starts incorporating them in biochemical reactions and then finds they are the wrong shape: but the reaction has gone too far to jettison them and begin again with normal EFA, so they are not only useless but actually prevent the use of normal EFA. They are in fact anti-EFA. They accentuate in man and animals a deficiency of EFA. An analogy is jamming the wrong key in a lock: not only is the lock not turned but the right key also is rendered valueless. [Franklin Bicknell, M.D. *Chemicals in Food and Farm Produce: Their Harmful Effects* (London: Faber and Faber, 1960 pp. 69-70).]

The super-saturated fat may be a major factor in heart disease. Ironically, some processors and sellers of T.V.P. tout its low-fat content and lack of cholesterol, implying it helps to prevent heart disease. The experts are not agreed on that but I believe it is harmful and is a far greater health danger than natural saturated fats, and I include margarine and vegetable shortenings.

My principal concern is that, however

much T.V.P. looks like meat and tastes like meat, it is not a good substitute for meat as your protein source. And that's true in spades when you are under severe stress conditions.

A small amount of T.V.P. in a food storage program as a condiment for flavoring stews or vegetable dishes is not objectionable. We can't give up everything that might hurt us or we wouldn't be able to eat anything. But to use it as a one-for-one substitute for meat is, in my opinion, most undesirable. When you use such products, there is some evidence to indicate that vitamin C taken at the same time and at the same meal is a protective factor. It has been clearly established that vitamin C can prevent the formation of nitrosamines in the stomach when sodium nitrate and sodium nitrite are eaten. Nitrosamines are among the most potent cancer-causing agents known to man and are routinely used to cause cancer in laboratory rats. Vitamin C in the stomach at the same time blocks the conversion of nitrates and nitrites into nitrosamines. These chemicals are found in wieners, lunch meat, ham, bacon, all canned or processed meats—and often T.V.P.

SUGAR

Another thing to watch for in the typical food storage program is excess sugar (sucrose, glucose, corn syrup, dextrose). Many programs rely on gelatin for protein and calories. Most commercial gelatins are half sugar and half very low-quality animal protein, along with food dyes which are presently under investigation for their cancer-causing properties.

Sugar is a negative nutrient, not just a bad nutrient. You require substantial amounts of the B Complex to metabolize it in each cell. Sugar contains none of these vitamins, so your body must rob its tissues and it actually creates an excessive need for those nutrients.

Sugar is also a stress factor because it is so rapidly absorbed that the body sends out alarm signals and produces insulin in excess amounts in order to reduce the blood sugar levels. Not only does this result in a rapid conversion of sugar to stored fat rather than energy, but it is a stress to the body. Stress, as I said before, comes in many different guises, and I see no merit in adding nutritional stresses, when we will already be beset with other stresses. Your storage program should be as low in sugar as possible, and the program that I have designed which is sold by our recommended dealers is as close to sugar-free as we could get, with what was available in the marketplace.

HONEY

Honey in five-gallon containers belongs in your food storage plan in place of sugar. It has a lot of advantages.

Common table sugar (sucrose) is a compound sugar consisting of approximately 50% glucose and 50% fructose. As we explained earlier, fructose is at least twice as sweet as sucrose and provides most of the sweetness of common table sugar. The sugars found in honey have a much higher ratio of fructose. Consequently, you can do the same sweetening job with less sugar intake, and that's beneficial. Honey is not basically a food but a relatively-healthful condiment.

Honey contains traces of minerals and B vitamins which are used in its metabolism, eliminating much of the "negative nutrient" aspect that plagues sugar.

Once you have used it for a while you will probably prefer its taste over that of sugar. It is the only sweetener we use in our home.

Honey keeps virtually forever. For reasons I don't understand, bacteria cannot exist in honey. It does crystallize and become solid, however, but this is readily solved by putting the container in a large pot of water and heating it until the honey liquefies. In the summer you can get the same job done just by putting the container in the sun for a couple of days.

We like to transfer a five-gallon container of honey into smaller containers, as a thirty-pound can is pretty hard to handle when it has gone solid and you are trying to pour it.

BRAIN SUGAR

As we said before, when you are under stress the water-soluble vitamins (C and the B Complex) are destroyed rapidly, and these vitamins, particularly the B Complex, are involved in the process by which your nervous system, including your brain, is fueled and powered. Your brain cells can only use blood sugar for energy and this requires the B Complex for metabolism. There is much evidence now that shortages of these vitamins can produce states of anxiety, fear and even paranoia and schizophrenia.

One team of researchers, when visiting the pellagra wards of African hospitals, found that most of the patients were exhibiting mental and emotional disorders that were indistinguishable from paranoid-schizophrenia, and pellagra is a B vitamin deficiency disease.

SUMMING UP

To sum up my advice on food storage:

1. Store a year's supply of food.
2. Make sure it's nutritionally balanced as an anti-stress program.
3. Don't rely on canned or frozen foods.
4. Rotate your food supply and replace as needed.
5. Don't buy a "junk food" storage program. Your health requires that you eat soundly as you don't dare become ill in the uncertain world ahead of us.
6. Buy it now. Transportation problems can come with stunning suddenness and the food distribution chain is most vulnerable to labor problems. If you acted today, it would possibly be a few weeks before it was delivered. It wasn't raining when Noah built the Ark. Buy your food before it is "hoarding," at a time when it is readily and freely available and the marketplace is functioning properly.

And if it should turn out that I am wrong

about our future, the worst thing that will happen to you is you will eat your food storage program and you will be amazed to find that it is indistinguishable from the food which is served in a lot of good restaurants.

FOOD STORAGE QUESTIONS

Now, let's look at my most commonly asked questions.

Q. Which is better, freeze-dried or dehydrated food?
A. Dehydrated food is generally less expensive and occupies less space. It also takes longer to reconstitute, generally requiring some cooking or overnight soaking. There are no commercially available dehydrated meats, eggs, fish or fowl. Dehydrated food is the cheapest way to build a very palatable, acceptable food storage program.

Freeze-dried food offers more variety, and freeze-dried meats, shrimp, fish, eggs, etc., are delightful, although quite expensive. The freeze-dried storage program will be considerably more expensive than the dehydrated program, but the ease of reconstitution makes it very attractive. To reconstitute freeze-dried shrimp, all you have to do is soak it in water for a few minutes. The freeze-dried casseroles and combination dishes are ready to eat when mixed for sixty seconds or so in boiling hot water.

The elegant combination dishes, however, such as shrimp creole, beef Stroganoff, etc. are loaded with chemical additives and flavor enhancers. Although they are delicious, I don't like them in my food storage program except as an occasional treat. If you don't share my biases in this area and have sufficient funds, then by all means buy a few packages, as they are delicious.

A well-balanced, inexpensive food storage program will consist of supplements, grains and mostly dehydrated foods with some freeze-dried products. Then you add a few luxury items such as freeze-dried meat, fish and combination casserole dishes as "reward foods." A more luxurious program would substitute all freeze-dried foods for dehydrated.

As for taste, I give a slight edge to freeze-dried, but not much.

Q. Are there any standards of packaging that would help me select good quality?
A. Yes, there are. Any food storage program should be "nitrogen-packed" in cans. The food is put in cans which are not completely sealed, which are placed in a vacuum chamber. All the air is removed and then the chamber is flooded with nitrogen under positive pressure, which replaces the evacuated oxygen in the can. The can is then sealed. Nitrogen is an inert gas and it reduces the chance of oxidation and rancidity. The label should guarantee less than 2% residual oxygen. If the label does not specifically brag about the nitrogen-

pack process, it is not nitrogen-packed.

I also prefer to have the smaller size cans. Many food storage programs use only No. 10 (one gallon) cans. That's fine for grains, powdered milk or freeze-dried foods (because of their bulk, which is about the same as fresh food). However, I prefer to have my dehydrated foods in No. 2½ (one quart) cans, unless you have a very large family. The minute the can is opened the dried product begins to absorb moisture from the air like a sponge and the oxygen in that moisture can accelerate the oxidation, and you could have a fairly rapid nutritional loss. One No. 10 can of dried apples will make several times its volume in reconstituted apples. With the smaller cans you can use several products at once without exceeding your kitchen storage capacity, and the product gets used up before substantial nutritional losses can occur.

Q. What if someone is allergic to wheat and milk? They are the most common food allergies.

A. It makes your problem a little more difficult but not impossible. You can buy dried corn, corn meal, oats and rice from any food storage dealer. They don't have the long-term storage capabilities of wheat, but can be stored for up to three years. Powdered milk is not an essential in your program and can safely be eliminated. This will cause some inconveniences but you can get along without it. Incidentally, it is true that more people are allergic to the dried milk products than are allergic to the pasteurized whole milk. Raw milk is best of all, but obviously you can't store it.

Q. Are there ways of preparing your own dehydrated food?

A. You bet there are! There are several excellent dehydrators on the market. You buy fruits, vegetables—in fact, almost any food product—and slice it thin, dip the slices in an ascorbic acid (vitamin C) solution or diluted lemon juice and dry them for twenty-four hours or so. There are several good books on the subject, the best of which are: *The ABC's of Home Food Dehydration* (see Appendix) by Barbara Densley and *Home Food Dehydration* (see Appendix) by Emma Wheeler. My recommended brands of dehydrators can be obtained from Reliance Products (see Appendix) and they are in the same catalog where the wheat grinders are listed. The home-dehydrated product will not have the same shelf life as the commercially nitrogen packed product, but it's good for 6 months to a year in zip-lock plastic bags, or glass or plastic jars, and if the food is properly rotated, it can be an excellent low-cost way of stretching your food budget. It is less expensive than home canning, less work, and occupies a fraction of the storage space. In the late summer and fall our dehydrator is going around the clock. You can even dehydrate leftovers and store them unrefrigerated in any reasonably cool environment. An immensely helpful piece of machinery to have around the house! It can pay for itself in a year or two, despite a price tag of about $150.

Q. How much food do I really need for a year?
A. The calorie count is a determining factor. The average person could safely rely on the following table.

AVERAGE CALORIES REQUIRED DAILY

(depending on size and physical activity)

Adult Male	2000-3500
Adult Female	1800-2500
Teen-Agers	2000-3000
Children under 12	1000-2000

I figure that if the storage program averages two thousand to twenty-five hundred calories a day that it will average out reasonably well over a family, with the small children needing less and a hard-working father needing more.

Q. Is it really moral to store food when other people are starving in India and Africa? Won't your advice create shortages?
A. No, because not that many people are going to listen and act. Besides, we have huge surpluses overhanging the marketplace.

If we have a real shortage, would you really want the Ruff family standing in line ahead of you trying to get their share of scarce food supplies? If you store food, that means that there will be more for those who could not or would not, and you are not competing for those scarce supplies.

If enough people like the Ruffs were to store food and other basic commodities, it would mean they collectively would not be part of the panic that would occur if it became evident that financial collapse is imminent or that the food was not going to be delivered to the supermarkets. That means that there would be a segment of our society who are relatively secure and who would represent stability in a very difficult world. And that's good for America and the world.

MISCELLANEOUS SELF-SUFFICIENCY

On my TV show, Gary North told me a story of a company that bought a five million dollar computer that went out of commission because of a failure of a $5 part. It seems that particular part was price-controlled, and as a result, the manufacturer stopped making it. The computer owners were the proud possessors of a five million dollar pile of junk—a rather expensive spare parts depot.

We can't store everything in the world but we can look about us and determine those miscellaneous items that are crucial to our comfort and well-being and our ability to function in a disrupted society.

There are a lot of miscellaneous items that should be included in your survival program if you are going to realistically prepare for hard time. At the risk of being repetitious, let me remind you that when inflation rages past the 20% level, the marketplace is in danger of being disrupted and a lot of things you take for granted may not be there to buy, or are priced out of sight. I have a few fundamental recommendations.

ENERGY SELF-SUFFICIENCY

There are so many ways that our gas and electricity and heating oil supplies can be cut off that I think it is simple prudence in a cold climate to have a modern wood-burning stove and a supply of fire wood.

Modern wood-burning stoves are a far cry from the old Franklin stove. They are air-tight and the rate of burn is controlled by regulating the amount of air that enters, which is an extremely sophisticated form of draft. You can heat with them and cook on them, and one load of wood will last for many hours.

I started recommending this about two years ago before the weird winters of 1976 through 1978 caused a lot of discomfort. I received a letter from one subscriber in Pennsylvania who described what happened when the big winter blizzards hit. He said,

> When the big storm hit, the natural gas pipeline pumps froze as did the water lines, but having taken your advice we had enough emergency water supply to last for two weeks and we simply dusted off our new Gibraltar stove and lived off our food storage. The freeways were blocked for several days, and the trucks

were not able to get into our town and the stores were bare. Besides, we're two miles out of town and don't have a snowmobile. But we're getting one.

For our family, it was merely a relatively minor inconvenience as we were warm and fed. I cannot thank you enough.

If you live in a moderate climate in the sun-belt, you could probably get along without one for heating, but at the very least, you should have a good charcoal grill and a substantial supply of charcoal. (But don't use it indoors without adequate ventilation. That's dangerous!)

There are heating units that can be installed in your existing fireplace to avoid the loss of heat. Most people don't realize that you can't heat a house with the typical fireplace. It generally creates a negative flow of warm air. When the fire is lit, the hot air rises up the chimney drawing air out of the room. Cold air is drawn into the house through cracks and openings and the net effect is that the rooms away from the immediate vicinity of the fireplace get colder. There is more heat lost up the chimney than is gained through radiation into the room. There are attachments that can be installed in your fireplace which will recirculate hot air back into the home. You can actually heat a pretty good-sized home with a fireplace.

I personally own a Gibraltar stove, as it seems to meet my family's needs, but there are several good ones available in the marketplace.

WATER STORAGE

If you are storing dehydrated food, it takes a lot of water to reconstitute and prepare it, and there are any number of things that could disrupt your water supply. If the pumping stations were put out of action by terrorists or urban guerrillas, or simply a major power failure, you could have problems. During the New York City blackout, most buildings were not able to get water from the faucets above the third or fourth floor. If this happens for just a few hours, it's a minor inconvenience with a little discomfort, but if it lasts more than a day in the hot summer, it could be a serious problem. Emergency water storage is another of those harmless ideas that cost you nothing but could be lifesaving.

You should store at least two weeks of cooking and drinking water, more if possible. Before we bought a home with a swimming pool, we used every spare container to store water. We added a couple of drops of chlorine and bought some inexpensive portable emergency water filters. The unit I like best is a simple, portable unit called The Water Washer made by American Water Purification (see Appendix) that takes up about the same amount of room as a quart bottle. You simply pour the water through it and it removes the chlorine and kills and traps any bacteria. The active element is silver-impregnated activated charcoal and it's good for about 1,000 gallons. The last I looked, they cost about $22.95. I take one with me whenever I go to areas where Montezuma's Revenge is a problem and drink the water with impunity. I simply run it through my Water Washer. There are other good units, but I like this one best.

I also equipped our entire family with waterbeds. Each king-size bed holds about 250 gallons of water and the copper sulphate algicide that is used to inhibit the growth of algae can be removed by pouring the water through the same type of filter.

ODDS AND ENDS

Go through your house, room by room, drawer by drawer, cupboard by cupboard, and take a look at all of those items that would make life difficult or uncomfortable if you couldn't buy them on a regular recurring basis and stockpile them. Where you would ordinarily buy one, buy three. Buy spare parts for your car, such as fan belts, hoses, points, spark plugs, etc. A few spare tires on hand wouldn't hurt. It will be an excellent investment as they are going to cost a great deal more in the future.

TRANSPORTATION SELF-SUFFICIENCY

In addition to my VW diesel Rabbit, we have two mo-peds. These little gadgets are the greatest inventions since sliced bread. We bought Velosolex mo-peds which have a motor mounted on the front fender which runs the front wheel by friction. I can either pedal it like a bicycle or run it like a little mini-powered motorcycle. It only goes 18 to 20 miles per hour and I have to pedal to help the engine when I go up a hill, but it's good exercise and it gets about 150 miles to the gallon when I'm not pedaling.

HUNTING AND FISHING

I'm so often asked if you should store guns. No, I don't think you should store guns. You should use guns. Anyone who wants to be self-sufficient should become a reasonably effective hunter. I have never hunted before, being a fisherman by inclination and temperament, but I will be out during the appropriate seasons getting good at it, as I think it will be important to the supplementation of my diet. Also, it doesn't hurt to have the security of knowing that I could protect my family if necessary, even though I consider that necessity a low probability in my neighborhood. With the aid of my cousin who is a gun manufacturer and knows a lot about them, I selected a 20-gauge shotgun, a 12-gauge shotgun, a 30.06, and a .22, as well as a 9-shot .22 pistol. I also bought as much ammo as I could afford. I doubt if there will be a better barter item in a period of currency breakdown than standard ammo, and it may be the best possible investment you could make, not just for barter purposes but for price appreciation in an inflating monetary system.

MEDICATIONS

If you have a medical problem, consult your doctor and stock plenty of the appropriate medication and check the literature or consult with the manufacturer about the shelf life so you can rotate it at appropriate intervals.

PART III
STRATEGY

INTRODUCTION

Up to this point I have concerned myself with those things which are fundamental to preserving life, limb and homestead during a period of great social and financial difficulty. Now it's time to talk about what to do with whatever money you have left over. Many of my survival recommendations will also be good money-making strategies in the environment that I foresee. For example, your gold and silver coins would do very well in a relatively orderly inflationary world, as well as in a chaotic coming-down-around-your-ears financial and social collapse. In Part III, I may use the same investments for either conservative break-even approaches or more aggressive, somewhat speculative, win-the-game-big strategies involving somewhat higher risks.

The investment recommendations in the preceding section are for you to hang onto as long as the very long-term broad trends are inflationary, while ignoring the possible short-term and intermediate (up to 3 years) corrections in the trends. If, however, I am wrong about the severity or the imminence of the inflationary spiral, you have to be ready to catch the economy going both ways. If we should have a recovery from the next recession, you would still hang onto your survival silver and gold coins, your food storage plan, etc., because they are your chaos insurance. But if you have any funds left over after taking my survival advice, you can adopt a much more flexible strategy with those funds to maximize your financial benefits from the trends. That's what Part III is about.

In a sense, this section is the climax of the book. I hope the rest of the book has laid a foundation for these stretegies.

Don't take a shortcut past the survival steps. If you contacted me for advice on how to implement the strategies in Part III, and had not taken the steps in Part II, I wouldn't be very interested in talking to you, because it could be dangerous—financially and personally.

17
THE BREAK-EVEN-OR-BETTER STRATEGY

Our basic strategy is very simple. All you need to know are two things: are interest rates rising or falling, and is the rate of inflation rising or falling? Fortunately, for our decision-making process, we live in an era of broad waves where intermediate trends, once determined, can be counted on to last for one to three years. For example, we began moving into a recession late in 1973. It didn't bottom until the end of 1974 or early 1975 and the recovery continued well into 1978. When interest rates were rising early in that cycle, you would have made a great deal of money by selling your bonds and loading up on gold and silver. When interest rates were falling during the recovery, you could have made a fortune by moving out of gold and into bonds. This basic strategy is what we will use to keep ahead of inflation.

There are several methods you can use.

At a conference in the Bahamas recently, Harry Browne made a rather interesting observation when he said that, technically, gold was not an inflation hedge, but the Swiss franc was. By that he did not mean that gold would not rise in an inflationary period, but that it had no direct connection to the rate of inflation. In abstract theory, he's right, despite the fact that in the real world, gold does tend to rise with the rate of inflation. In fact, it is much more than a "hedge." The Swiss franc is the classic inflation hedge during a relatively orderly inflation. The Swiss have zero inflation. The United States has double-digit inflation. The Swiss franc will tend to rise in relation to the dollar at roughly the rate of American price inflation, as long as the Swiss maintain their zero inflation rate.

The disadvantage of owning Swiss francs is that in a genuine international monetary crisis, they might be worthless in this country. And if you are here and your Swiss francs are in Switzerland, they won't do you any good either. A genuine international financial holocaust will sweep all paper currencies ahead of it, even the gold-backed ones. But in between now and then, perhaps some Swiss francs could be held as a hedge. You can buy traveler's checks denominated in Swiss francs, from Deak and Co., which has offices in most major cities, and just hold onto them. You can open a Swiss franc account in a Swiss bank, but if it looks like we are headed for real international chaos, get out of Swiss francs. For now, it may not be such a bad idea to own some as long as our inflation rate stays in the low double-digit range and the Swiss inflation rate is near zero. I heartily recommend Harry Browne's book, *Harry Browne's Complete Guide to Swiss Banks* (see Appendix), for more on that subject.

There are two likely scenarios: (1) The inflation rate will continue to rise until it goes through the ceiling and breaks the economy, in which case I will not get out of gold until after everything else has collapsed totally, or (2) the next down-turn will merely be another recession and somewhere near the bottom of it I will get rid of all my gold, with the exception of my survival coins, and buy bonds on margin.

I will probably hang onto my diamonds through almost anything.

The average person doesn't realize the incredible potential profits in bonds in a falling-interest-rate marketplace. We have already described in detail in Chapter 3 why that is the case, but I'll repeat the rule just to refresh your memory. When interest rates are rising, the price of bonds is falling; when interest rates are falling, the price of bonds is rising. It is possible to safely leverage your purchases of bonds so that the potential profits are several times the investment.

Most people think of bonds as very conservative holdings which you buy at par, hold for thirty years, then redeem at par. Nothing could be further from the truth. When interest rates are rising, all bonds fall. You don't have the problem you have with the stock market in selecting a rising stock in a rising market. Even in a long bull market, individual stocks can move in the exact opposite direction of the general trend, and sometimes those moves seem to defy logic. That is not true of bonds. Unless the company that has issued them is in trouble, all bonds will rise across the board when interest rates are falling. The risk you might have with the fortunes of an individual issuing company can be eliminated entirely by simply buying United States government bonds. If you want to buy a U.S. Treasury bond that matures in 1999 that was issued to yield 6%, and interest rates have risen to 12%, the price at which you could buy it could be as low as $500, even though it has a redemption value at maturity of $1,000. That means you could buy that bond at a price cheap enough to yield 12%, if that was the prevailing long-term interest rate, and you don't have to pay $500 cash for it. You can buy it on margin, or you can pay the full price for it and go to your banker and borrow approximately 80% of the purchase price at the prevailing interest rate. This means you would only have $100 cash tied up in your $500 bond. The interest earned on your bond will probably cover the interest paid to the lender, so you have a break-even situation as far as income is concerned. When interest rates fall, however, the market value of the bond will rise. If interest rates fell clear back to 6%, the bond would probably rise back to par ($1,000). On your $100 cash investment, you could have a $500 profit.

This is obviously the reverse of the situation where an investor paid $1,000 for the bond and then had to sell it after interest rates had risen from 6% to 12% and found that he could only get $500 for it in the marketplace.

The advantage of this simple strategy is that you don't have to worry about which bond to buy, although there are even more profits to be made in "junk bonds." These are bonds issued by companies or cities that for some reason have developed lousy credit ratings since the bonds were issued and their fall in value is not just caused by rising interest rates, but by concern on the part of the investment community as to whether the principal will be repaid.

In relatively normal times, even times as bad as the recession of 1974-75, less than 1% of these "deep discount" bonds will default on their principal. The company's fortunes will improve, and when the credit rating is restored, these bonds will rise to the market value of equivalent securities. That means the B-rated bonds offer the greatest potential profit opportunities, with a reasonable level of risk, relative to other bonds, provided you spread your risk among several junk bond issues. The potential profits are great enough that you are still way ahead if one goes bust. Whether or not you reach for that extra profit in junk bonds depends on your temperament. Most people probably should stay with the government securities, but if you go for junk bonds, be sure the issuer is current on interest payments, and spread the risk over at least 10 to 20 issues.

This strategy only works as long as the economy is in a recovery phase. We are obviously not going to buy bonds before the market has bottomed out, but only after the economy is showing unmistakable signs of recovery, and then we might wait a couple of months just to be sure, because otherwise we might commit ourselves near a false bottom.

I've always contended that all you really need to know to get rich is which way interest rates are going. You don't try to guess the short-term squiggles. Just watch the long-term structural factors. As long as the rate of inflation is increasing, I know that the general trend of interest rates will be up.

Sometimes the price of gold is a good barometer in and of itself. Sometimes the futures market and interest rates will forecast the future. This is as much of an art as it is a science, and that's the kind of thing I try to forecast for my clients. With this strategy there's no need to mess around with the stock market. The risks are too high relative to the potential profit. You simply play the government securities game, moving back and forth from gold to 30-year bonds, and the odds favor you.

Actually, it is quite possible that the next recession will go right through the bottom and will never give us an opportunity to apply the strategy.* We will then stay with our gold, our diamonds, our small town real estate and let it

---

*We got our chance on April 1, 1980. My subscribers got a mailgram stating, "Bonds are virtually riskless. Throw caution to the wind . . ." We made a bundle!

go at that. But at least you now know what to do if that prognosis is incorrect.

If you really have courage, you might just decide to hang onto all your gold through all of its ups and downs as many people did after buying at prices over $180 in 1975. Prices in the summer of 1978 eventually vindicated them as gold went to all-time highs. But in the meantime there were a lot of sick portfolios. You will probably be better off switching, but that is a matter of personal temperament.

I'll repeat again the basic rule. When interest rates are rising along with the rate of inflation, buy gold, silver and diamonds. When interest rates and the rate of inflation are falling, buy bonds on margin.

Most margin buying is dangerous because it's generally applied to rapidly fluctuating commodities to give more "bounce for the buck" and it does substantially increase volatility. When, however, you are dealing with an investment whose day to day movements are small, where long-term trends are more easily discernible, such as bonds, real estate, etc., and where there are no margin calls, then leverage makes sense because the risks are lower.

NOTE: Just as this book was being released to the printers, the Carter administration bombed the gold market with Carter's "Save-the-Dollar" plan. Gold slid from a peak of close to $250 an ounce to under $210. By publication date, gold could be well below $200, for all I know. If that does happen, it does not mean that the basic fundamentals have changed, nor that the long-term bullish trend is over. Carter's move has only temporarily distorted the normal action of the marketplace. However, even the United States government is not bigger than the basic hunger for gold in the international marketplace. Gold will re-assert its fundamentals, and the long-term trend is toward much higher ground. This move has given us an unexpected chance to buy again at very low prices.

In any event, with the much higher prices that I see ahead, based on the fundamentals of rising inflation and rising interest rates, a difference of $20 or $30 will be a matter of great irrelevance in the long haul.

Note to the Above Note (December 1980): May I beat my breast a little bit? Gold is now over $600 and silver over $18. I was right. And what's more, you will see gold over $2,500 and silver over $100—probably before December 1983—possibly in 1982.

18
THE GOLDEN CALF

After you have your survival coins, there are lots of ways to invest in gold, ranging from very conservative to very speculative. Gold is an appropriate investment for inflationary times, particularly when the rate of inflation is accelerating. I will list all of the gold investment strategies in order of risk and profit potential, as the two go together.

    1. You can buy gold coins or bullion, paying 100 cents on the dollar for them and conceal them in a private vault or safe-deposit box. I prefer coins to bullion because of their ready marketability. Bullion needs to be assayed before it is sold, which is expensive and inconvenient, unless you leave it with the dealer, which I advise against. By far the most conserva-

tive approach to gold investment is 100% ownership of bullion coins.

2. You can buy gold, take it to your bank and borrow against it; in effect, giving you a "margin" buy. You may have to shop around a little bit until you find a bank who will loan against gold coins, but remember, the smaller your margin (equity), the greater your profit potential and your risk, as both profit potential and risk rise in direct proportion to your degree of leverage.

3. You can buy the paper equivalent of gold by purchasing gold futures contracts.

The futures market, or commodities market, deals with the basic raw materials of our economy: such things as wool, wheat, sugar, soy beans, silver, copper, cattle, coffee and, of course, gold. They are traded on major exchanges, such as the Chicago Board of Trade.

Commodity trading is a process of contracting between a buyer and seller. Here is a simple analogy. If I had a painting to sell you, we would haggle and at some price you would give me money and I would give you the painting. But let's say, for example, you wanted to buy a painting by Degas for delivery in March of the following year but you think fine art prices will rise by then and want to only pay today's price of $9,000. If I believed that prices would be cheaper in March of next year, I would say, "OK, I will take your $9,000 and deliver you a Degas in March." I am betting that sometime prior to March I will be able to obtain a Degas for less than $9,000 because I think paintings will fall in price, and I will pocket the difference. You and I have contracted for a specific item at a specific point in time at a specific price. If I guess wrong on future prices, I lose money.

The futures market works the same way. I want to buy 5,000 ounces of silver in December, and you agree to sell it for December delivery. We now have a future contract. The price I pay you for that contract is determined by whatever the market says it is worth on the day we enter into our agreement. Let's say December silver is at $5.55 an ounce. One 5,000 ounce contract costs $27,750, but I only put up about $1,000 "margin money." Of course, we never see each other. It's done through a trader on the floor of one of the exchanges. Whether or not you own the item is really immaterial but as the day approaches in December for the actual delivery of that silver, you either assign the contract to somebody else or you have to buy the silver and deliver it. If I buy a December contract for 5,000 ounces at $5.55, I am hoping that the price of silver will go up so that sometime between now and December I can sell that contract for a profit. If it moves from $5.55 to $5.65, a ten cent move, and I sell out, I will have realized a profit of $500 on my purchase, at ten cents an ounce for the 5,000 ounces of my contract.

If you sell a contract at $5.55 instead of buying, that's known as "going short." If prices moved up to $5.65, and you were "short" at $5.55, you would have suffered a loss of $500. If it goes down to $5.45, you make $500. It's sometimes difficult for novice traders to understand that you can sell something you don't have, and if the price goes down, you can buy it back at a lower price, or "cover" and make a profit, but that's what going short means. You are betting the price will fall.

Buying gold and silver futures contracts is the most volatile, risky way to speculate on the price of precious metals, but it is also the most potentially profitable.

The danger lies in the fact that you could be right about the long-term trend and yet suffer a temporary down-turn and lose all your margin money. Remember, when you buy a futures contract, you generally put up only about 5% of the actual price of the contract. If the market price of gold moved down 5%, your entire margin would be wiped out. Your broker would call you for more margin (a "margin call") and you would have to decide whether to put up more money to protect the broker or sell out. A margin call is about the most traumatic experience an investor can have, because you don't know whether it's just a temporary move or a fairly long slide. The problem with commodities is that even in prolonged bull markets they do suffer down-turns and if that down-turn occurs somewhere near the price you paid, the margin call can whip-saw you out of the market and your losses can be substantial.

There are several ways for the unsophisticated commodities trader to reduce his risk.

One is to put up more margin, which gives you less leverage, less risk, and less chance of being forced into a bad decision, or you can limit your investment to a relatively small percentage of your liquid assets so that you can afford a loss.

You can also use "stops" to get you out with limited losses when the market turns against you. Once you get a good rise and your profits begin to run, you are more protected against minor down-turns. If you have the guts to stay with a basic trend, you can make an awful lot of money. Gold and silver are just about the best commodity "plays" in an inflationary spiral.

And last of all, you need a real good broker with a grasp of timing, so you don't jump into a technically weak market.

4. Another way to benefit from rising gold prices is to buy the shares of gold mining companies, but now we've added considerable complexity to what started out as a relatively simple recommendation: buy gold.

Gold mining companies obviously make more money as the price of gold rises. If it costs a company $200 an ounce to mine gold, obviously every dollar that it moves above $200 can add to profits. If a mine is profitable at $100 an ounce and gold is selling at $200 an ounce, every time gold moves up one dollar it adds 1% to its profitability. But if it costs a mine $190 to mine one ounce and gold is at $200 an ounce, when gold moves up one dollar, it adds 10% to that mine's profitability. As gold rises, you can switch to shares of companies that have just become profitable as the price of gold rises above their profit threshold. This gives you leverage, as a 5% move in gold could mean a 100% increase in mining profits, and a big move in the stock.

Generally, the leaders, such as Homestake, Campbell Red Lake and Rosario Resources will tend to move first in response to a price rise. However, gold mining shares are not always the royal road to wealth. For example, the best, most profitable gold mines in the world are in South Africa, but as this is written, South Africa is under political assault, both internally and externally, which casts doubt upon the future profitability of those mines. Some South African gold mines pay dividends in the 15% to 25% range, but I believe that the Soviets would love to put South African gold mines out of commission, and much of their African policy is aimed towards this, as the Soviet Union is the world's second largest gold producer. If they can reduce the flow of South Africa's gold into the world market place, it could drive the price sharply upward and benefit them as the world's principal source. The Soviets are in desperate need of foreign exchange.

For that reason, I prefer to steer clear of the South African shares and stick with the North American mines if I wish to speculate in gold mining shares.

I consider them volatile speculatons and not good long-term holdings as their fortunes vary dramatically with the price of gold, but if you can catch them when gold is swinging wildly higher some money can be made. I prefer to avoid the political risks of the South African situation, however, which has not made me very popular with a lot of the specialists in gold shares as they make their livings from the sale of those shares, but I still think it's good advice.

So you can see that there are lots of ways to invest in gold. Which method you select depends upon your money, your temperament and your willingness to accept risk. Most of you should probably just buy the metal outright and pay for it. You probably won't get as rich but you will beat inflation and chaos. That's your break-even strategy. If you go into the futures market highly leveraged at the right time and have the guts to stay with it and don't get whip-sawed out by a margin call, you can get rich with a relatively small amount of money. If you bought ten gold contracts of 100 ounces each, every time gold moved up a dollar you would make $1,000. These ten contracts might cost you $7,000 to $10,000 in margin money and if gold went to $300 an ounce from the approximate $200 an ounce as of this writing, you would make $100,000, provided that you had the courage to stay with it during the intervening corrections, and if you had the nerve to parlay your profits into more contracts, you could make millions. But I cannot emphasize too much that this is a game only for those with nerves of steel and it's basically a gambler's arena. For most of you it should be off limits. If you choose to try it, you need good advice from the people listed at the end of the book.

Trading in the commodities market takes real skill. It is not just a gambler's marketplace. Your key requirements are temperament and good advisors, because your timing in entering or leaving the market determines your degree of success.

As gold rose from $103 an ounce to over $200, it had some temporary retreats of as much as $20 along the way. Each time that happened, my subscribers would write terribly worried letters as to whether or not they should bail out of their coins. My advice to them all during that rise was, "Use those corrections as an opportunity to buy more at a lower price. The upward trend is still intact." It is axiomatic that unless you are terribly lucky, any investment you purchase will be selling for a cheaper price than you paid for it at some time after you have bought it, because no one ever catches anything at the absolute bottom except by sheer luck. You probably should feed your investment funds into the market over a period of several days, perhaps a third at a time, so you don't get caught on a "spike"—a temporary one-day rise in price. You then hang on as long as the trend is intact.

As long as interest rates are rising along with the inflation rate, gold will do well, although there will be many days when it will move contrary to its trend. Stay cool and don't panic. When gold makes a big correction of $20 or $30 an ounce, if the fundamentals are still right, I am thrilled, as it gives me a chance to increase my profits.

At this point there are still some of you saying, "But I can't buy gold coins. You don't understand my problem. I need the income from my bonds (or my blue chip stocks)."

If you are still asking that, you must have missed Chapter 3. Go back and read it again.

There have probably been more investment atrocities, during inflationary periods, committed in the name of "income" than in any othar cause, except perhaps "tax shelter." Reaching for income through fixed-return investments is a sure way of destroying yourself financially in an inflationary spiral.

About the only income-producing strategy that really works in that kind of environment is to buy gold or silver coins and sell some occasionally when you need income. If my whole basic premise is right, the remaining coins will increase in value faster than you are liquidating. You will also pay taxes based on the capital gains rates, which are more favorable than ordinary income tax rates.

If you sell off coins representing 7% or 8% of your value each year, you will have the equivalent of interest, and the appreciation in the value of the remaining coins will probably keep the purchasing power of your capital intact, and then some.

When will you sell your gold? Well, we've already discussed one basic strategy. If it looks as if a recession is bottoming out and interest rates are beginning to fall, we will want to jump into bonds as I've explained earlier. However, if we go right through the bottom into a major depression and a total collapse of the currency, you won't want to bail out of gold until you can use it to buy property, stocks, businesses, etc., at distressed market prices. You may want to sell some of your gold during a wild inflationary spiral as Gary North suggests, and use it to pay off all your debts. If I had invested $50,000 in gold and it went to wild heights as a result of the depreciation of my paper money, as soon as I reached the point where I could sell off half of it and pay off my mortgages, I would do so, or I would simply hand the gold to someone in return for debt relief.

I'm often asked how far gold will go in price. If we have a real runaway inflation it will sell for thousands of dollars an ounce and perhaps even millions of dollars an ounce, and the same will be true of silver. Remember that silver coin I have from Germany that was worth a million marks? When the inflation began, it was worth five marks. The same thing will happen to us, when and if our currency collapses. If we don't have that collapse, then the trick is to find the right time to bail out. You shouldn't fall in love with anything. As the very astute Harry Schultz has said, "There is no investment for all seasons, but there is a season for all investments." And this is the season for gold.

REALM OF THE COIN

No dissertation on coins would be complete without a discussion of rare or "numismatic" coins. There is a persuasive case to be made for buying collectible items during a period of inflation. As traditional investments are ravaged by inflation, and especially as interest rates in the market place generally rise above that which can be legally offered by financial institutions, people look for various kinds of inflation hedges and shelters, and collectible items are the traditional beneficiary of these conditions. During the inflationary boom of 1973 and 1974, every kind of collectible from antique stamps and gold coins on down to old bottles had amazing increases in price.

Some of these came crashing down when inflation eased, but rare coins held their own better than most investments, and they offer marvelous opportunities for the astute investor.

Numismatic coins are basically coins that are no longer being minted and so have acquired scarcity value. With some exceptions, the best numismatic investments are those which have been around for some time. We are not talking about the commonly circulated bullion type coins we've discussed earlier in this chapter, nor the junk silver. You can, of course, buy numismatic coins that also have a high bullion value such as, for example, Morgan silver dollars and the U.S. twenty dollar gold Double Eagle. But there are a lot of coins which have very little bullion value at all which can cost as much as $100,000 for a single coin.

The market value of a numismatic coin is based on demand, availability and quality. There is a broad-based market for numismatics with a published "bid-and-asked" price.

Unless you intend to be an "international man" with travel outside the country and financial holdings in other nations, you would probably be better off sticking with the U.S. coins, because price quotes for these are available daily in this country.

If you wish to become such an investor, you need considerable expertise, but there are three ways to get around that problem. One is to buy and read all the best books on the subject, and there are several. The other is to find a coin dealer with integrity and depend upon him to supply you with the proper coins. Number three is best of all. Do both.

Five hundred dollars can get you off to a pretty good start, although, the more money you have, obviously, the better buying opportunities you have. For example, a bag of Morgan silver dollars is around $12,000 to $15,000 as of now.

If you had $500 or $1,000 to invest now, at the time this book is written, I suggest U.S. gold coins—the $20, $10, $5, $2.50, $1, and $3 coins.

The price of rare coins will vary according to their condition and you should concentrate on the highest quality coins, again using a dependable dealer. Put your money with the best merchandise, even if it costs a bit more. Resale is such a strong factor that you should avoid anything that is not high quality material.

If you have a coin with bullion value, then you have a floor on the price, represented by the market price of gold or silver. With a good coin you may pay a premium of 100% to 300% above the bullion value, but don't make light of collector demand. It is the same factor that makes a Rembrandt worth several million dollars. Most coin dealers will mark their products up from 10 to 15%, so you have even more incentive to select coins which have great liquidity and will tend to appreciate rapidly. It's not uncommon for numismatic coins to move up 30% annually year-in and year-out for as much as a decade. For example, in 1968, a $20 gold "high relief" struck in 1907 was selling for $500. Now it is close to $5,000.

SAMPLE PORTFOLIO

If you have $10,000 to invest, and you're starting a numismatic investment program, I'd put 20% of it in silver dollars, 30% of it into U.S. gold coins and the other 50% spread through U.S. "proof sets," U.S. commemorative coins and rare single coins all in choice condition.

"Proof sets" are U.S. coins which were minted for investors and collectors in 1936 through 1942 and again through the 50's and early 60's using a highly polished die. They are sharper than circulated coins and have a mirror-like highly reflective surface.

You might want to buy rolls of silver coins, such as the "Walking Liberty" half dollars, Franklin half dollars, Mercury dimes, and silver Washington quarters. You will pay between $300 and $500 for certain low-mintage coins that have excellent potential, but of course, any price I quote here is subject to change depending on when you read this book.

The only real source of such coins is dealers. The chances of an individual stumbling across a rare coin in his change from a candy counter is virtually nonexistent. The minute a coin becomes circulated it loses a substantial amount of its value anyway, so even if you found some old coins tucked away in the attic of an old house, the likelihood of their having great value is remote. Only the choice, uncirculated coins have significant value.

All U.S. numismatic coins are listed each week in the "Gray Sheets" along with the bid and asked prices in the wholesale market for coin dealers. They are similar to the New York Stock Exchange quotes in your morning paper.

If my basic premise is correct about inflation on the prowl, the continued appreciation of numismatic coins could be tremendous. With some numismatic coins you can get the benefits of bullion coins and also the benefits of the scarcity value.

The line between numismatic and bullion coins may be blurring, simply because many of the bullion-type coins are being hoarded by people who subscribe to newsletters like mine and may never ever see the light of day and may become scarce. But the supply of real numismatic coins of high quality is also rather thin. That's why the price can explode so dramatically when inflation takes off.

If you are concerned about the price of gold being too high or think the gold market is peaking, you might be happier buying numismatic coins without as much gold content. If you think the price of gold will continue rising, then you would want to buy numismatic coins with a lot of gold content. If you have sufficient funds, you probably should balance your investment program between those two kinds of coins.

COMMEMORATIVE MEDALLIONS

Commemorative medallions from private mints are generally very poor investments. The mints sell as many as they can and they have no scarcity value and you are generally paying a substantial premium over and above the silver content. If you like them, buy them from some poor guy who has to liquidate his holdings for some reason. You'll get them a lot cheaper than buying them from the mint.

CHARLATANS

One real problem you must face is that there is a fair number of charlatans in this business. Several of my friends lost money because they bought "whizzed" coins. For example, a dealer will buy a 1941 Walking Liberty for $2, and buff it up with a little jeweler's rouge and sell it for $40, $80, or even $100.

A dealer might even deliberately sell you counterfeit coins, or he might just be sloppy in his screening procedures, and there are numerous counterfeits in the U.S. gold coins. You can send them away to the American Numismatic Association headquarters to verify the coin. The fears of counterfeits can be somewhat exaggerated but it is a legitimate concern and something to be aware of.

Also, a dealer can over-grade a coin. A coin which has a little rub or wear on it is really a circulated coin and the novice investor, and even some experts, cannot readily determine that. That can make the difference between a $40 coin and a $400 coin. A dealer can do pretty well buying coins for $40 and selling them for $400.

Like all marketplaces with great profit potential, this can be treacherous. And so we come back again to our suggestion that you be scrupulously careful about your dealer. For this reason, we have a recommended dealer listed toward the end of this book. It is possible that even a good dealer could inadvertently pass on such a coin to a customer, so whoever you deal with has to be prepared to take it back if that should be the case.

In summary, numismatic coins have great potential if you follow the general guidelines that we have just outlined. I realize I didn't tell you enough to make you an expert, but armed with this information, 2 or 3 good books on the subject, and a good coin dealer, your potential for profit and inflationary protection is outstanding.

19
"... A GIRL'S BEST FRIEND"

Since 1975, I had been intrigued with diamonds as a hedge against inflation/depression. (Did you ever see what happens when you give one to a depressed lady? But I digress.) I began recommending them in June of 1977 and since then, as of the date of this writing, they have risen 125% at the wholesale level,[*] which is the only level at which they should be bought.

After you have bought your emergency food supplies, reorganized your personal indebtedness, and bought your basic gold and silver coins, if you still have liquid assets, diamonds may very well be added to your portfolio, along with real estate.

There hasn't been a significant down-tick

---
[*]Over 200% by December, 1980.

in diamond prices since 1934. They have provided price stability over the years despite inflation, devaluation of currencies, war, depression, etc. They have helped refugees covertly move their wealth from one country to another. The Israelis treat the diamond industry as almost a religion as diamonds bought many of them their freedom during times of persecution and chaos. Despite uncertainty in the world, diamonds have continued to appreciate consistently over the years. It's just that simple.

Diamonds are a controlled market. The price is set by the DeBeers-controlled Central Selling Organization (CSO) in London. They control approximately 85% of the world's diamond market. Even the Soviet Union, the world's second largest producer, has come to them to market their diamonds exclusively. (Most of the Russian diamonds are industrial grade. They produce less than 2% of the world's investment grade diamonds.) When there are a lot of sellers around, the CSO simply restricts the supply of new diamonds. If prices look like they are getting completely out of hand, they release diamonds into the market, but they always are allowed to appreciate faster than the inflation rate. They have several billion dollars in liquid assets with which to support the market as they did in the latter parts of the Great Depression.

Ordinarily, I like to avoid controlled markets, but I don't mind one where I know that the self-interest of the people who control it is to maintain stable prices in relation to inflation —to my advantage. Even when the inflation rate was 1% to 2% in the 50's, wholesale diamond prices rose at 5% to 6%.

When I say that there has never been a "down-tick," I am referring to wholesale prices. The retail market can and will fluctuate. For example, small diamonds of one-half carat or less will fluctuate downward as the economy slows down in a recession or depression. These are the engagement ring diamonds bought by young couples, and they don't feel they can afford them when they are worried about their jobs in a recession. However, I am recommending investment grade diamonds of one carat or more. At the wholesale price, there have been no down-turns, but steady appreciation instead.

Diamonds occupy a slot on the liquidity scale somewhere between gold coins and real estate. They are more liquid than real estate but less liquid than gold coins. Only invest money in diamonds that you are prepared to keep invested for a long time. They are not a speculator's vehicle. They are for the long-term investor. They are truly a "time machine" to get your assets from this side of the financial gulf ahead of us to the other with purchasing power basically intact.

Here are the guidelines for purchasing diamonds.

1. Don't plan to liquidate the stone within two years, because that is not the nature of the market. It's a long-term-hold type of investment that should appreciate at least 50% better than the bond interest rate or the worldwide inflation rate.

2. Buy stones from 1 to 3 carats. They

should be accompanied by a Gemological Institute of America (GIA) certificate which evaluates the grade. They should be VSI (Very slightly imperfect) or better. They should be "H" or better in color. They should be cut to ideal proportions, because two stones of the same weight, the same color and the same clarity can vary 40% in price, depending on cut. For $50 or thereabouts, the GIA will certify any stone that you send them, or you can go to a well-equipped gemologist, preferably one who doesn't sell stones.

3. You should invest no more than 30% of your investable assets in diamonds. The minimum is somewhere around $6,000* at today's prices.

4. Be sure you are paying close to the genuine wholesale price. The word "wholesale" is bandied about by investment dealers but the real wholesale price is that which a jeweler is willing to pay for the diamond. The degree of risk you assume is in direct proportion to the price you pay, because liquidity is really a question of whether or not you can sell it quickly at the price you want—assuming you're reasonable. If you have to pay retail, then wait until the wholesale price appreciates to the retail price you paid before you can get your money out, you are only half liquid, and you have made a bad buy.

5. Beware of the "low-ball." Many jewelers, seeing someone coming in with an unset investment diamond for appraisal, deliberately quote a very low value to discredit the invest-

---

*Now $15,000.

ment diamond business. I have seen numerous such instances. The jewelry industry has declared war on the investment diamond dealers as they depend upon a controlled marketplace to be able to sell diamonds at mark-ups around 100%. When investment dealers start selling to the public at close to the price a jeweler can pay for it, it's a threat to their business.

During the 1978 dramatic rise in diamonds, Tiffany's, the most famous jeweler in the world, took a full page ad in the *New York Times* to tell the world that diamond prices were too high and not to buy them because diamonds were a very poor investment. Tiffany's problem was that, because of investment and speculative buying, wholesale prices had risen so dramatically that they were caught in a price squeeze. They were afraid to raise prices at the retail level and their profit margins were disappearing, so they tried to reduce buying pressure and talk diamonds down as an investment. It didn't work but it scared a lot of people off from buying diamonds that might otherwise have bought them.

The pricing of diamonds is not as much guesswork as you might think. Once it has a GIA certificate testifying to its weight, color clarity and cut, the price is pretty well determined, using charts and copyrighted tables published by the GIA.

Diamonds also are good vehicles for leverage because they don't fluctuate on a day-to-day basis and you will never get a margin call. If you can get a banker to loan you 70% to

90% of the purchase price, I think you can rest assured that they will appreciate at a rate faster than the interest you have to pay on the loan. In fact, if you buy them wholesale, sometimes it's possible to borrow substantially more than you paid for it, which could give you some extra funds to buy some more diamonds, gold, etc.

To sum up, diamonds are for the person with substantial assets who wants to buy a tremendous amount of concentrated wealth that occupies a very small space. You can hold a million dollars in the palm of your hand. It requires less nerve than gold as you don't have your breakfast ruined by fluctuating price quotes appearing in the paper every day. In times of uncertainty, diamonds will hold their value. You obviously can't spend them to buy a loaf of bread, as what would they give you for change? Your food storage, silver coins, gold coins and barter items take care of that. They are a time machine for the preservation of assets from one side of a depression to the next, and they are part of your "break even with inflation" strategy.

Our recommended dealer is Reliance Diamonds (see Appendix).

20
"DO THY PATIENT NO HARM"

I have followed the admonition of Hippocrates to the new physician, to only give you advice that will not hurt you if either my forecast or my timetable is wrong. You also know now how to switch strategies if the tide should change for a while.

It's now time to put all this advice together in one easy summation so that you can come up with a personal program that fits your life and personal perspective.

First, I'd like to deal with one important principle we have not tackled thus far. It's important in the over-all scheme of things.

Most of you cannot go completely into gold, silver and diamonds now because you have a requirement for liquid cash. Your survival efforts (Part II) should be completed now, but we all need to have some liquid funds to maintain an orderly financial life while things are relatively normal.

In my company, we have exactly the same question to answer: what do we do with those liquid funds when we are nervous about the banking system?

There are two acceptable alternatives. You can invest in either Treasury bills or in Money Market Funds.

Treasury bills are the shortest-term obligations of the U.S. government with maturities generally between 90 and 120 days. They are "discount instruments" which means they sell at a discount from their face value and are cashed in at their face value at maturity, and the difference between the price when issued and the face value at maturity represents your interest return. T-bills generally are in $10,000 denominations, so you can't play that game unless you can buy in big chunks. In fact, a "round lot" in the T-bill market is $1 million, and you don't get the best price unless you buy them in round lots. The longer the maturity, the larger the market risk.

The advantage of Treasury bills is that their maturities are so short that if interest rates rise, you don't suffer a market loss. You merely wait three or four months until they mature and cash in at the face value. If interest rates were to rise abruptly and you had to liquidate suddenly, they might drop a little in market value.

In a period of rising interest rates, smart money managers "go short," which in the money market means they convert all of their holdings into the shortest term securities, and Treasury bills fill that need.

You can buy the shares of Money Market Funds which invest in Treasury bills or other money-market instruments, especially if you don't have enough money to buy Treasury bills in $10,000 increments.

A Money Market Fund is a no-load mutual fund. For example, the Capital Preservation Fund (see Appendix), which we use, invests strictly in U.S. short-term securities. You buy their shares, on which no commission is charged (no-load), as you deal directly with Capital Preservation and no salesman is involved, and they invest the fund in Treasury bills. The earned profit is passed onto you, although the management does extract a fee of one-fourth of 1% of the total assets. But because they buy in $1 million round lots, they are able to buy the T-bills for less money than you could, and that generally covers the management fees. The rate of return on the fund should be very close to that of the prevailing T-bill rate. You can take your money out at any time. Even better, they issue you blank checks drawn on their bank and you can write checks against your T-bill account as though it were an interest-bearing checking account, as long as each check is over $500.

The Money Market Fund checkwriting privilege is used by many corporate financial managers. It's a parking place for funds which are waiting to be deployed otherwise, or which are necessary for business or personal liquidity.

There are other funds, such as the Dreyfus Liquid Assets Fund (see Appendix), which utilized the same principle but earn higher yields because they are invested in commercial paper, bank paper and other short-term debt obligations, which earn more than T-bills.

It does not offer the same range of security as a T-bill fund, but the higher yield makes it seriously worth your consideration. They also offer check-writing privileges.

One reason I am quite enamored of Treasury bills is that in a real financial panic there is an instinctive flow of money in two directions: (1) towards gold and silver, and (2) towards Uncle Sam. During the depression of the 30's when banks were going broke, government securities were the hot item and they were actually bid up so high that they delivered negative yields. When everything is coming down around your ears, you want your liquid money in the thing that is likely to come down last so you have a chance to make a move. The T-bill is your hedge against being caught without sufficient time to act. There is a huge market for Treasury bills and they can be bought and sold at any time. The Presidents of the Dreyfus Fund (see Appendix), Jerome Hardy, and Capital Preservation Fund (see Appendix), James Benham, have assured me that their entire funds could be liquidated in an afternoon. This liquidity advantage, plus interest, plus check-writing privileges, make them the ideal parking place for unemployed money.

I like to have liquid cash equal to six months of installment obligations. Having them in Treasury bills or a money fund is the equivalent of keeping them in cash.

FOR INSTANCE

Now, after you have met all of your liquidity requirements, let's take a look at some sample portfolios for a family of three, each with $10,000, $50,000 or $100,000 to invest during a period of rising inflation and interest rates (Table #4).*

Table #4—SAMPLE PORTFOLIO (FAMILY OF THREE)†

Rising Inflation and Interest Rates

	$10,000	$50,000	$100,000
Food Storage	2,500	2,500	2,500
Silver Coins	5,500	11,100	11,100
(pre-1965 U.S.)	(1½ bags)	(3 bags)	(3 bags)
Cash (Demand deposits, concealed cash, T-bills or Money Fund)	2,000	4,400	10,600
Gold Coins (survival)	-0-	15,000	15,000
Diamonds, Gold, Silver, Rare Coins, Real Estate, Antiques, Stamps, Swiss Francs, etc.	-0-	12,000	50,800
Speculative Funds (Future contracts, gold shares, etc.)	-0-	5,000	10,000
	$10,000	$50,000	$100,000

You might include the other suggestions in the chapters on price controls, especially stan-

---
*See end of chapter for updated portfolio.
†This is the table which appeared in the original hardback edition in the fall of 1978.

357

dard ammunition, from .22 through 30.06, if you have a place to store it.

You must understand the present, accurately perceive the future, and have a plan that doesn't violate the principles of this book, and be willing to move in whatever direction the intermediate changes in our economic course should indicate, while maintaining your stable always-in-place survival position. Prepare for inflation, but be ready to catch any major interruption in the inflationary trend with the break-even-or-better strategy, moving between bonds and gold.

You might buy and read this book at some time in the future when we have moved from an inflationary upward trend into a temporary deflationary correction with falling interest rates. In that case, you could substitute bonds and stocks for your optional investments in gold and silver. What is important is that you understand the principles so the answers come naturally when the tide changes (Table #5).

My biggest problem in setting guidelines for you is to teach you how to recognize the signals of the changing tide. It's pretty easy in the abstract to say, "Interest rates are falling, buy bonds," or, "Interest rates are going up, buy gold." How do you tell the difference between a short-term move and a long-term trend? Basically you can't unless you spend a lot of time watching as I do. And there I guess *The Ruff Times* (see Appendix) can be helpful. In all honesty, it's not absolutely necessary to your well-being to be a *Ruff Times* subscriber if you really have mastered the principles of this book, but it could be pretty helpful.

There are some things developing in the world that might shoot down all my options. For example, if the Russians continue building their aggressive civil defense program and their war

Table #5—SAMPLE PORTFOLIO (FAMILY OF THREE)*

Falling Inflation and Interest Rates

	$10,000	$50,000	$100,000
Food Storage	2,500	2,500	2,500
Silver Coins	5,500	11,100	11,100
(pre-1965 U.S.)	(1½ bags)	(3 bags)	(3 bags)
Cash (Demand deposits, concealed cash, T-bills or Money Fund)	2,000	4,400	10,600
Gold Coins (survival)	-0-	15,000	15,000
Bonds	-0-	12,000	50,800
Speculative Funds (Stocks, "Junk bonds" on margin, etc.)	-0-	5,000	10,000
	$10,000	$50,000	$100,000

machine and move against Western Europe, or if nuclear war breaks out between the Soviet Union and the Chinese, then we face a confused economic environment which no one can really understand. In that case, you go for the ultimate chaos-hedge with the best odds, and that's gold and food. Go all out with everything you can scrape together.

In Paul Erdman's book, *The Crash of '79* (see Appendix), his hero was an ex-American banker working as a financial advisor to the King of Saudi Arabia. As soon as he saw that

---

*This is the table which appeared in the original hardback edition in the fall of 1978. See updated portfolio on page 367.

war was about to break out in the Mid-East, he immediately liquidated all of his paper holdings and bought nothing but gold, and that is precisely what you should do under those same conditions. My general attitude is to err on the side of the defensive position, and not be too anxious to catch each trend at its exact turning point. Unless it is a sudden calamity, like war, wait until a trend has established itself.

SEND ME A MAN WHO READS

The International Paper Company once ran a great advertising campaign which said, "Send me a man who reads." A man or woman who is not willing to read could lose everything he has when the economy moves contrary to his basic premises. I'd like to give you a list of publications I read for information and education.

THE WALL STREET JOURNAL

Everyone should read *The Wall Street Journal*. Its editorials are the best to be found anywhere. The statistical information regarding money supply, and markets, and some of the "think pieces" on the front and back pages are invaluable. It should be scanned every day.

When I read it, I look for the feature articles on the front page, the feature on the back page, then turn to the commodities section about two-thirds of the way through, and then hit the editorial page, especially the editorials in the left-hand column. Anyone who wants to protect his assets who does not read *The Wall Street Journal* is foolish.

BUSINESS WEEK AND FORBES

I wade through all of these magazines as soon as they hit my desk. *Business Week* is a very conservative, somewhat sober, but generally quite accurate analysis of what's going on in the world. I have found a lot of key pieces of data from which very important decisions have been made.

Forbes, even though it has been wrong in many of its editorial conclusions, is a useful source of data. Just ignore their generally anti-hard money stance. They declared gold dead when it was $110 an ounce, so they are not very objective about that precious metal, but it's still well worth reading.

NEWSLETTERS

At the top of my list of suggested newsletters is, of course, *The Ruff Times* (Target Publishers, P.O. Box 172, Alamo, CA 94507. $105 per year. Write for free samples). We publish twice a month and I keep you posted on all the changes in strategy and what's going on in the world. We give a lot of helpful advice to our subscribers relative to personal security, survival, privacy, government regulation, with frequent re-assessments of the investment implications of political and economic events. My principal function, however, is to apprise you of structural changes in the economy. I'm not publishing a tip sheet for short-term speculators, although I guess much of the information would be useful in that respect. It is written for the cautious, careful guy who wants to protect what he has against all onslaughts, whether from our inflationary or deflationary flanks. We also provide all of our subscribers with a Toll-Free number which can be used to deal with individual problems. Our Member Services Department has both generalists and specialists in almost any subject of interest to our subscribers. This Toll Free number can be used without limit. I think it is the best newsletter in the business, but I'm humble about it. In any event, if you don't like it after 90 days, you get your money back.

Next on my list is Richard Russell's *Dow Theory Letter* (P.O. Box 1759, La Jolla, CA 92038, 36 issues per year, $150). Dick Russell writes in the context of the fundamentals but is the best technical analyst of the stock market and the economy. He has a vast fund of common sense and nothing much gets by him. When he makes a strong judgment call on the marketplace or the economy, I have to listen. He and I have had some vigorous debates on some issues but I respect him immensely and he is tremendously readable, although it may take two or three issues before you catch up on the language he is using and learn to read his charts, but it's great stuff. I wish every person in America had his letter.

Gary North is the only other person I've ever allowed to write for my own newsletter.

He was head of the research staff of Congressman Ron Paul, has a doctorate in economic history, and is a major contributor for many conservative and libertarian publications including the *Wall Street Journal*. His newsletter, *The Remnant Review* (713 W. Cornwallis, Durham, NC 27707), is a one-subject-per-issue, in-depth discussion of issues of interest to the hard-money fan. Most of the time it is outstanding. He has a mind like a humorous computer and is one of the most brilliant people I know. He also is a consultant in our Member Services Department. His publication is well worth the $60 per year.

The Reaper, by R. E. McMaster, is another dandy (P.O. Box 39026, Phoenix, AZ 85061, $195 per year). Not only does he give you detailed information on the commodities market, but I am always interested in what he says the markets are telling him about the future. The markets not only are means of making money but also have great predictive value. R. E. is an expert on cycles, and his book, *Cycles of War*, is one of my most important library fixtures. He believes, and his track record proves it, that cycles have predictive value, and they are predicting war before 1982. He has done a beautiful job of calling both short-term, intermediate and long-term trends in the commodities market. In the first six months of 1978, if you had bought all of his recommended trades, just one contract each time, you would have made $54,000. His accuracy ratio is about 70%—the best I've seen. He is hard-money oriented, understands the philosophy of this book and agrees with it.

Daily News Digest (Johnny Johnston, P.O. Box 39027, Phoenix, AZ 85069, 2 years $210), is the best capsule summary of news items that would be of interest to the hard-money fan. I don't always agree with the conclusions that Johnny draws from the articles, but ideologically we are pretty much in the same camp and he has a tremendous knack for ferreting out news items from obscure publications, digesting them and putting them in context. It's not so much an advice letter as it is a capsule clipping service, and it's well worth the money.

The View From the Pit (1595 Little John Court, Highland Park, IL 60035, 12 issues per year, $96, or special 6-issue trial subscription, $54) is published by Maury Kravitz, who is a member of the Board of Governors of the Chicago Board of Exchange and trades gold on the floor—"The Pit." He knows more about gold than almost anybody. He is very perceptive and had the courage to stand firm in predicting the U.S. Treasury gold auctions when everybody else was wavering. He is my personal broker for my own trades and I would not think of making an investment in gold without consulting Maury or his staff. His publication is a bit verbose but always interesting and belongs in any investor's information stream.

Personal Finance Letter (formerly *Inflation Survival Letter*) is the granddaddy of the hard-money newsletters. It takes a totally different approach from my letter in that it is loaded with detailed "how to" articles without any particular editorial focus. Sometimes I think it's dull, but just when I'm about ready to despair, the editors come up with a beautiful article of immense value. It's technically and economically sound and indispensable reading (P.O. Box 2599, Landover Hills, MD 29784).

Spotlight is a publication of Liberty Lobby, an extreme right-wing organization. When you talk about *Spotlight* there's good news and bad news. The bad news first. It is the most blatantly biased publication around, and its political point of view is somewhere to the right of Genghis Khan. Every issue is into tax revolt, white supremacy, international conspiracy, anticommunism, and the Trilateral Commission, along with arguments that Hitler really wasn't that bad after all.

And now the good news. It does some of the darndest investigative reporting I've seen. It uncovered the drug connections of Carter's drug abuse advisor, Peter Bourne, many months before he was fired from his White House position for writing fraudulent drug prescriptions. It detailed Jimmy Carter's Trilateral Commission connection long before anyone in the news industry was interested or concerned. It has taken the lead in pointing out the excesses of the Federal tax collection system, and exposed examples of I.R.S. Gestapo behavior that need exposure. *Spotlight* has truly done the world a great service in that respect.

If you read *Spotlight*, prepare to be outraged, offended and informed. There are some things which I detest about it, but I wouldn't be without it.

TIME, NEWSWEEK, AND U.S. NEWS AND WORLD REPORT

These are the standard news magazines. I don't read them for opinion. I read them for information and then I apply my own standard of judgment as to how objective they are. Their liberal bias is considerable, but on the whole, I find them useful, and everyone should read them.

BARRON'S

Barron's is a weekly financial paper, published by Dow Jones. It's full of useful investment summaries and insightful articles.

There's a whole bunch of secondary publications that I find useful. Jim McKeever, former editor of *Inflation Survival Letter*, publishes *McKeever Investment and Survival Letter*. It's a lot like *Inflation Survival Letter*, in that, just as I'm about to despair, he comes up with some important stuff. His investment track record is like everybody else's in this business —pretty good and sometimes embarrassing, but again, he is well worth listening to.

Knowledge is indeed power. As we move into our difficult future there are three things that are going to get you through in good shape—knowledge, money, and courage. Knowledge and money are what this book has been about. But courage and character are more important. I hope you have them, because those who take my advice and survive personally and financially will be tomorrow's leaders, and I hope it's the "good guys" who get through with the judgment and the assets to influence our national future, because my children and I will have to share that future with you.

Table #4—SAMPLE PORTFOLIO (FAMILY OF THREE)*
Rising Inflation and Interest Rates

	$10,000	$50,000	$100,000
Food Storage	3,000	3,000	3,000
Silver Coins	3,300	10,000	13,000
(pre-1965 U.S.)	(¼ bag)	(¾ bag)	(1 bag)
Cash (Demand deposits, concealed cash, T-bills or Money Fund)	2,200	5,000	9,000
Gold Coins (survival)	-0-	15,000	15,000
Diamonds, Gold, Silver, Rare Coins, Real Estate, Antiques, Stamps, Swiss Francs, etc.	1,500	12,000	50,000
Speculative Funds (Future contracts, gold shares, etc.)	-0-	5,000	10,000
	$10,000	$50,000	$100,000

Table #5—SAMPLE PORTFOLIO (FAMILY OF THREE)
Falling Inflation and Interest Rates

	$10,000	$50,000	$100,000
Food Storage	3,000	3,000	3,000
Silver Coins	3,300	10,000	13,000
(pre-1965 U.S.)	(¼ bag)	(¾ bag)	(1 bag)
Cash (Demand deposits, concealed cash, T-bills or Money Fund)	2,200	5,000	9,000
Gold Coins (survival)	-0-	15,000	15,000
Bonds	1,500	12,000	50,000
Speculative Funds (Stocks, "Junk bonds" on margin, etc.)	-0-	5,000	10,000
	$10,000	$50,000	$100,000

*Changes in the prices of investments, footnoted elsewhere in the book, have resulted in these updated portfolios.

NOTE: Here are my newsletter and vendor recommendations as of March, 1981. However, names, phone numbers or addresses of companies change from time to time, or, as a matter of policy, I may alter my recommendations. Therefore, for an updated list of vendors, call or write my office (800-227-0703, P.O. Box 2000, San Ramon, CA 94583).

APPENDIX

Goods and Services
for Your Consideration

In several instances you will note a "Recommended" firm and a list of others which are "Also Reputable."

The Recommended firms are those which I have personally researched, negotiated favorable arrangements for those who choose to take my advice, and monitor on a regular basis. As my recommendation provides a substantial portion of the business of these Recommended firms, this gives me considerable clout if any problems arise.

The "Also Reputable" firms also occupy an integral niche in The Ruff Times family of services, but time limitations preclude my monitoring them as closely.

In some instances there is only one Recommended firm, and none is listed as Also Reputable, because the industry in question has a great many problems or because I have not had time to dig any deeper. Perhaps this list will be expanded in subsequent editions.

Prices subject to inflationary change.

NEWSLETTERS AND ADVISORY

Recommended:

The Ruff Times, P.O. Box 2000, San Ramon, CA 94583, $145 per year, call Toll-Free 800-227-0703 (USA) or 800-642-0204 (Calif.) or call Collect 415-837-1566 (Alaska, Canada, Hawaii).

Ray Anderson's Taxflation Fighter, New Capital Publications, P.O. Box 3000, San Ramon, CA 94583; annual subscription rate—$195, introduction rate—$145.

Douglas R. Casey's Investing In Crisis, New Capital Publications, P.O. Box 3000, San Ramon, CA 94583; annual subscription rate—$195, introduction rate—$145.

Richard Russell's Dow Theory Letters, P.O. Box 1759, La Jolla, CA 92038, 24 letters per year—$185, 6 months, $105.

Gary North's Remnant Review, P.O. Box 35547, Phoenix, AZ 85069, $95 per year. 602-252-4477.

The Reaper, P.O. Box 39026, Phoenix, AZ 85069, $225 per year, 5 issue trial—$25. 602-993-1626.

Daily News Digest, P.O. Box 39027, Phoenix, AZ 85069, $150 per year, 5 week trial—$15.

Personal Finance Letter (formerly *Inflation Survival Letter*), P.O. Box 2599, Landover Hills, MD 20784, 24 issues—$54.

Gold Newsletter, 8422 Oak, New Orleans, LA 70118, $39 per year in the U.S.; overseas, $49.

Harry Browne Special Reports, 207 Jefferson Square, Austin, TX 78731, 512-453-7313, $195 per year.

Mark Skousen's Forecasts & Strategies, Phillips Publishing, 7315 Wisconsin Ave., Suite 1200 N, Washington, D.C. 20014; $95 per year.

Robert Kinsman's Low Risk Advisory Letter, 1700 So. El Camino Real, Suite #408, San Mateo, CA 94402; Phone: 415-574-7174. Published 17 times annually at $125.

McKeever's Misl, Contact—Omega Services, P.O. Box 4130, Medford, OR 97501; Phone: 503-773-8575; $165 per year; 6 months, $90.

Tax Angles, 901 North Washington St., Suite 605, Alexandria, VA 22314; 12 issues, $36.

The Retirement Letter, 7315 Wisconsin Ave., Washington, D.C. 20014; $49 per year.

Myers' Finance and Energy, 642 Peyton Building, Suite 418, Spokane, WA 99201, 509-747-9371; 14 issues, $200, 3 issues, $25.

World Money Analyst, 927 S. Walter Reed Dr., Arlington, VA 22204 or 1914 Asian House, One Hennessy, Hong Kong; $135 per year.

World Market Perspective, P.O. Box 91491, West Vancouver, B.C., Canada V7V 3P2; $96 per year; 3 months' trial, $36.

The International Harry Schultz Letter, P.O. Box 2523, Lausanne 1002, Switzerland; Phone: 392918; $258 per year.

Precioustones Newsletter, P.O. Box 4649, Thousand Oaks, CA 91359; Phone: 213-889-4367; $125 per year (12 issues) USA; $149 out of USA.

OTHER PUBLICATIONS

Acres, USA, 10227 E. 61st Street, Raytown, MO 64133.

Small Town, USA, Woods Creek Press, P.O. Box 339, Ridgecrest, CA 93555, $24 per year, Sample Copy—$1.00.

Mother Earth News, P.O. Box 70 Hendersonville, NC 28739, 704-693-0211.

Organic Gardening & Farming, 33 East Minor Street, Emmaus, PA 18049, 215-967-5176.

Prevention Magazine, Rodale Press, Inc., 33 E. Minor St., Emmaus, PA 18049; $10 for 12 months. Phone 215-967-5141.

Let's Live Magazine, 444 No. Larchmont Blvd., Los Angeles, CA 90004; $9 for 1 year. Phone 213-469-3901.

Creative Real Estate Magazine, Box 2446, Leucadia, CA 92024; $33 per year. 714-438-2446.

FOOD STORAGE

Recommended:

Martens Health and Survival Products, Inc., P.O. Box 359, Lafayette, CA 94549. Phone: 415-283-2257 (Lafayette); Toll Free 800-824-7861 (USA); or 800-822-5984 (CA).

Also Reputable:

Sam Andy Foods, 1770 Chicago Ave., Riverside, CA 92507; Phone: 714-684-9003.

Intermountain Freeze-Dried Foods, 3125 Washington Blvd., Ogden, UT 84401; Phone: 800-453-9210.

The Simpler Life (Arrowhead Mills), P.O. Box 671, Hereford, TX 79045; Phone: 806-364-0730.

Frontier Foods Association, 7263 Envoy Ct., Dallas TX 75247; Phone: 214-630-6221.

Oregon Freeze-Dry Food, P.O. Box 1048, Albany, OR 97321; Phone: 503-926-6001.

Rainy Day Foods, P.O. Box 71, Provo, UT 84601; Phone: 801-377-3093.

The Grover Company, 2111 South Industrial Park Ave., Tempe, AZ 85282; Phone: 800-528-1406 (USA); 602-967-8738 (AZ, HI, Canada, Alaska).

The Survival Center, 5555 Newton Falls Rd., Ravenna, OH 44266; Phone: 216-678-4000 or Toll Free 800-321-2900 (USA).

COIN DEALERS

Recommended:

Investment Rarities, 1 Appletree Square, Minneapolis, MN 55420; Phone: Toll Free 800-328-1860 (USA) or Call Collect 612-853-0700 (Minn., Alaska, Canada, Hawaii).

Deak-Perera, 1800 K. Street NW, Washington, D.C. 20006; Phone: 202-872-1233 or Phone: 800-424-1186 (USA WATS) (202-872-1630) (Recorded currency quotations).

Also Reputable:

Camino Coin Company, 851 Burlway Road #105, P.O. Box 4292, Burlingame, CA 94010; Phone: 415-341-2925 or 415-343-1837.

C. Rhyne and Associates, 110 Cherry St., Suite 202, Seattle, WA 98104; Phone: 206-623-6900 or (USA) 800-426-7835.

Joel D. Coen, Inc., 39 W. 55th St., New York, New York 10019; Phone: 800-223-0868 (USA) or 212-246-5025.

Lee Numismatics International, Executive Place, 60 Mall Rd., Burlington, MA 01803; Phone: 800-343-8564 (USA) or 617-235-9033.

Numisco, 1423 W. Fullerton, Chicago, IL 60614; Phone: 800-612-5272 or 312-922-3465.

North American Coin and Currency, Ltd., Suite G2, 100 West Washington St., First National Bank Plaza, Phoenix, AZ 85003; Phone: 800-528-5346 (USA) or 602-257-0873.

DIAMONDS

Recommended:

Reliance Diamonds, 1990 North California Blvd., Suite 400, Walnut Creek, CA 94596; Phone: Toll Free 800-227-1590 USA; CA 800-642-2406; collect 415-938-6510 (Calif., Alaska, Canada, Hawaii).

Also Reputable:
Gemstone Trading Corp., 30 Rockefeller Plaza, New York, NY 10020; Phone: 800-223-0490.

COLORED GEMSTONES

Recommended:
Investment Rarities, 1 Appletree Square, Minneapolis, MN 55420; Phone: USA 800-328-1928 or collect 612-853-0700 (MN, AK, Canada, HI).
H. Stern Jewelers, Inc., 645 Fifth Ave., New York, NY 10022; Phone: 212-688-0300 (USA) 800-221-4768.

Also Reputable:
Precision Gems, Santa Helena Financial Square, P.O. Box 1047, Solana Beach, CA 92075; Phone: (CA) 800-542-7283; (USA) 800-854-7099; 714-481-1101.

FOOD SUPPLEMENTS

Recommended:
Martens Health and Survival Products, Inc., P.O. Box 359 Lafayette, CA 94549; Phone: 415-283-2557 or Toll Free 800-824-7861 (USA); 800-822-5984 (CA).

COMMODITY BROKERS

Maury Kravitz, Rufenacht, Bromagen and Hertz, 222 S. Riverside Plaza, Chicago, IL 60606; Phone: 312-648-0180 or Toll Free 800-621-0003.

GOLD STOCK BROKERS

Rauscher, Pierce, Refsnes, Inc., 2 Houston Center, Suite 3400, Houston, Texas 77010; Phone: 713-652-3033.
T. E. Slanker Company, 9450 SW Commerce Circle, 300 AGC Center, Wilsonville, Oregon 97070; Phone: 503-682-4000.
Saunders & Taylor, P.O. Box 61642, Marshalltown 2107, South Africa; Phone: 834-6811.

FINANCIAL AND INVESTMENT PLANNERS

Financial Planners International, 1926 Tice Valley, Walnut Creek, California 94595.

MONEY MARKET FUNDS

Recommended:
Capital Preservation Fund, 755 Page Mill Road, Palo Alto, CA 94304; Phone: 800-227-8380 (USA); 800-982-6150 (CA) or collect 415-858-2400 (Alaska, Canada, Hawaii); for info packet 800-982-5873 (CA) or 800-227-8996 (USA).

SURVIVAL PRODUCTS (MAIL ORDER)

Recommended:
Reliance Products, 1990 North California Blvd., Suite 400, Walnut Creek, CA 94596; Phone (USA) 800-227-0414 or collect 415-938-1650.

Also Reputable:
SI Outdoor Food & Equipment by Mail, 16809 Central Ave., Carson, CA 90746; Phone: 800-421-2179 (USA) or 213-631-6197.

The Grover Company, 2111 South Industrial Park Ave., Tempe, AZ 85282; Phone: 800-528-1406 (USA); 601-967-8738 (AZ, HI, Canada, Alaska).

The Survival Center, 5555 Newton Fall Rd., Ravenna, OH 44266; Phone: 216-678-3000 or (USA) 800-321-2900.

REAL ESTATE

Real Estate Investment Training:
Dr. Albert Lowry, Educational Advancement Institute, 50 Washington St., Reno, NV 89503; Phone: 800-648-5955 or 702-322-1923.

Professional Educational Foundation, Box 2446, Leucadia, CA 92024; Phone: 714-438-2446.

Fortune Seminars, Inc., 1938 Ringling Blvd., Sarasota, FL 33577; Phone: 813-366-9024.

STORED FUEL PRESERVATIVES

Recommended:
Bob Hinrichs, Fuel-Mate, P.O. Box 3471, Santa Barbara, CA 93105; Phone: 805-682-6919 or 801-976-7914.

WATER PURIFIERS

Recommended:
American Water Purification Company (Water Washer), 115 Mason Circle, Concord, CA 94520; Phone: 415-825-9100.

BARTER

Comstock Trading Company, P.O. Box 8020, 1926 Tice Valley Blvd., Walnut Creek, CA 94596; Phone: 415-939-9292.

SURVIVAL HOMES

Joel Skousen Survival Homes, Inc., 4270 Westcliff Drive, Hood River, OR 97031; Phone: 503-386-6553.

RETREAT and SURVIVAL COUNSELING and SURVIVAL HOMES

Don Stephens, Drawer 1441, Spokane, WA 99210; Phone: 509-838-8222.

14 KARAT GOLD JEWELRY

Ounce O' Gold, 6 D 88 Apparel Mart, 2300 Stemmons Freeway, Dallas, TX 75207; 800-527-9846 (USA); 214-637-2083.

FINE ARTS

Fine Arts, Ltd. (Limited edition prints), 1955 Jackson Street, San Francisco, CA 94109; Phone: 415-775-2722.
Dr. Wesley M. Burnside (American Painting & Sculpture), Art Department, BYU, Provo, Utah 84602; Phone: 801-378-2881.

SECURITY STORAGE VAULTS

Perpetual Storage, Inc., 3322 South 3rd East, Salt Lake City, UT 84115; Phone: 801-486-3563.

BOOKS

(All available from Target Publishers, P.O. Box 2000, San Ramon, CA 94583—add $1.00 postage handling for each item ordered. California residents add 6.5% sales tax.)

BOOKS

(All available from Target Publishers, P.O. Box 2000, San Ramon, CA 94583—add $1.00 postage handling for each item ordered. California residents add 6.5% sales tax.)

Howard J. Ruff from A to Z, Howard J. Ruff, $25 (an alphabetized collection from the first four years of *Ruff Times*, arranged by subject matter for ready reference).

How You Can Become Financially Independent by Investing in Real Estate, Albert J. Lowry, Simon & Schuster, $11.95.

Cycles of War, R. E. McMaster, War Cycles Institute, $10.00.

War on Gold, Antony Sutton, 76 Press, $12.50.

The Insider's Banking & Credit Almanac, Mark Skousen, Kephart Communications, $14.95.

Mark Skousen's Guide to Financial Privacy, Mark Skousen, Kephart Communications, $14.95.

How You Can Profit From the Coming Price Controls, Dr. Gary North, American Bureau of Economic Research, $14.50.

How to Successfully Manage Real Estate in Your Spare Time, Albert Lowry, Capital Printing, $19.95.

How I Turned $1,000 Into Five Million in Real Estate, William Nickerson, Simon & Schuster, $14.95.

Home For Sale by Owner, Gerald M. Steiner (paperback) Hawthorn Books, $7.95.

Common Sense Economics, John Pugsley, Common Sense Press, $14.95.

The Biggest Con, Irwin Schiff, Freedom Books, $5.95.

The Great Inflation, William Guttman & Virginia Meegan, Saxon, $4.95.

Harry Browne's Complete Guide to Swiss Banks, Harry Browne, McGraw Hill, $19.95.

The ABC's of Home Food Dehydration, Barbara Densley, Horizon Publishing, $4.50.

Just in Case—A Manual of Home Preparedness, Barbara H. Salsbury, Bookcraft, $5.50.

Field Guide to Edible Wild Plants, Bradford Angier, Stackpole Books, $6.95.

Making the Best of Basics, James Talmage Stevens, Peton Corporation, $6.95.

The International Man, Douglas R. Casey, Kephart Communications, $14.95.

The Survival Home Manual, J. Skousen, Survival Homes, $25.00.

Stocking Up, Editors, Organic Gardening and Farming, Rodale Press, $13.95.

New Profits From The Monetary Crisis, Harry Browne, William & Morrow, $12.95; Paperback: Warner Books, $2.95.

Skill For Survival, Esther Dickey, Horizon Publishing, $6.95.

Energy—The Created Crisis, Antony C. Sutton, Books In Focus, $10.95.

The Invisible Crash, James Dines, Ballantine Books, $10.00.

The Age of Inflation, Hans Sennholz, Western Islands, $8.95.

The Robert Kinsman Guide to Tax Havens, Robert Kinsman, Dow Jones-Irwin, $17.50.

Finding and Buying Your Place in The Country, Leo Scher, Macmillan Publishing, $6.95.

The Mother Earth News Handbook of Homemade Power, The Staff of Mother Earth News, Bantam Books, $2.50.

Sunbelt Retirement, Peter Dickinson, E. P. Dutton, $8.95.

How to Use Interest Rate Futures Contracts, Edward W. Schwarz, Dow Jones-Irwin, $17.95.

The Dow Jones-Irwin Guide to Commodities Trading, Bruce Gould, $17.50.

The Coming Currency Collapse, Jerome Smith, Books in Focus, $12.95.

Crisis Investing, Douglas R. Casey, '76 Press, $14.95.

How You Can Use Inflation to Beat the IRS, B. Ray Anderson, Harper & Row, $12.95.

INDEX

Adams, John, 159
American Water Purification, 316
Anderson, Arthur, 157
Anderson, B. Ray (Bill), 210
Angier, Bradford, 282
Ayers, Samuel, 293–94

Banking system, 28–29, 44, 126–43
  failures, 128–35
  condition of, 135–40
  consumer protection, 129–30, 140–43, 151–52
  and foreign depositors, 60–61, 125–127, 136–37
  loans abroad, 62, 133–34
  safe deposit boxes, 142–43
Barron's, 366
Barter, 239–41, 243–44
Beame, Abe, 96, 100
Benham, James, 356–57
Bicknell, Franklin, 303
Black markets, 29, 77, 80, 238–46
Bonds, 62–64, 68–74, 323–30, 356–60
  municipal, 138
  U.S. Government, 327, 328

Borrowing
  inflation and, 53–54, 60–61
  by foreign countries, 62
  to invest, 191–93
  and paying off, 30, 49–50, 73–74, 193–94
  personal, managing, 191–94
  See also Mortgages; Real estate, financing
Bronfenbrenner, Urie, 161–62
Browne, Harry, 181, 247, 324, 325
Browning, Iben, 260
Bryson, Reed, 260
Building supplies, 241
Burke, Edmund, 159
Burns, Arthur, 44
Burns, Walter X., 118
Business Week, 114, 131, 361

California Vegetable Concentrates, 283–284, 286
Capital Preservation Fund, 355–56
Carter, Jimmy, 27, 80–81, 168

Carson, Johnny, 250
Cash
  reserves, 193, 232
  transactions, 150, 151–52, 188
Central Selling Organization, 348–49
Certificates of deposit, 141
Cities, problems of, 98–100
  business climate, 107–109
  debt, 104–06
  deterioration, 103–14, 244–45
  federal programs and, 109–14
  real estate, 122–24
  rent controls, 28–29, 107–09
  safety of surrounding areas, 115–16
Clothing, 238–41
Coins, 178–90, 244–46, 329–30, 338–41, 358, 359–60
  buying, 183–90, 329–330
  payment in the taxes, 221–22
  rare ("numismatic"), 341–46
  selling, 189–90, 339–340
Commemorative medallions, 344–45
Commodities market, 152, 331–32
  gold futures, 333–38, 358
  silver futures, 332, 333–35
Consumer Price Index, 80
Cooperative League of America, 240
Cooperatives, for buying, 240, 299
Cornish, Jesse, 89
Crane, Phil, 157–58
Crime, urban, 103–09, 112

Daily News Digest, 364
Dallas Morning News, 119
Debt, 25–26
  government, 51–53, 59–62, 72–74, 78–80, 153–58
  indexing, 192, 193
  municipal, 105–06
  personal, 191–95. *See also* Mortgages
Deflation, 28, 56–64, 244–46
Densley, Barbara, 311
Depression, 29–30, 238–246
  coping with, 30–31, 33–37. *See also* specific subjects
  deflation and, 28–29, 56–64
  and Executive Orders, 144–52
  imminence of, 27

inflation and. *See* Inflation
Diamonds, 52, 245, 329, 347–52
Dicky, Esther, 273, 299
Diocletian, 38–39
Dow Theory Letter, 362
Dreyfus Liquid Assets Fund, 355–56
Dumpson, James, 111

Economy
 durability of American, 25–26, 31–32
 morality and, 159–71
 See also specific subjects
Education for survival, 238–39, 240, 360–367
Eisenhower, Dwight D., 59
Energy self-sufficiency, 313–15
Equipment, for self-sufficiency, 238–39, 240
 replacement parts, 241–42, 316–17
Erdman, Paul, 359–60
Executive Orders, 145–152

Farms and farming, 243, 261–62
 as investments, 200–202, 230, 245
Federal Deposit Insurance Corporation, 129–30, 136, 141–142, 143
Federal Preparedness Agency, 145
Federal Reserve, 41–42, 45, 136
Federal Trade Commission, 286–87
Ferguson, Adam, 244
Food, 248–63
 allergies, 310–11
 analogues (imitations), 300–05
 condiments and seasonings, 300–05
 buying, 240, 271, 274–80, 298–99
 canned, 274–75, 277
 cost of year's supply, 269–71
 dehydrated and freeze-dried, 240, 264, 272–74, 283, 300, 301–09
 dehydrating at home, 310–12
 frozen, 274, 275
 growing own, 239, 241, 272
 hunting and fishing for, 318
 morality of storing, 267–69, 312–14
 need, individual for year, 312
 and nutrition, 274–292, 312
 packaging and quality, 309–11

379

prices, 258–59
protein powders, 286–292
rotation of supplies, 279–80
self-protection and stocking of, 266–68
shelf life, 269, 276–79
staples, 297–300
storage, 36, 239, 255–314
storage facilities, 269, 272–73
storage plans, 273–74
supplements, 278–79, 282–92
sweeteners, 291–93, 304–05, 306
vitamins and minerals, 279, 286, 292–97, 306–08
wild plants, 282
Food and Drug Administration, 277–78, 287–92, 295
Forbes, 135–36, 361
Fortune magazine, 105
Fredericks, Carlton, 291
Friedman, Milton, 28–29, 44
Fuel, 241
Futures. *See* Commodities market

Gemological Institute of America, 349–51
General Services Administration, 146, 149

Gold
coins, 178–79, 186–190, 323–24, 328–330, 340–41, 358–360
coins, rare ("numismatic"), 341–44
futures contracts, 331–38, 358
Keogh plan using, 51
mining stocks, 334–36
standard, 41–43, 189–90
Government, U.S.
bonds, 327–28
and cities, 109–14
debt and credit commitments, 51–53, 59–63, 72–73, 74, 128–30, 154–58
Executive Orders, 145–52
Treasury bills, 141, 353–57

Hardy, Jerome, 356
Hensel, John, 129–30
Hoarding, 240
Household supplies, 240
Huber, Don, 275
Hunting and fishing, 318

Indianapolis Star, 256
Inflation
borrowers and, 53–54, 72–73
cities and, 98–116, 244–45

and deflation, 56–64, 244–46
experience in other countries, 28, 38–42, 53, 56, 59–60, 62, 72–73
government obligations and, 51–53, 72–74, 178–80
and interest rates, 49–50, 57–58, 69–73
and investments, 49–50, 54–55, 62–63, 65–74
and lenders, 30, 49–50, 72–74
money values and, 28–30, 38ff.
and pension and retirement plans, 51–53, 78–80, 82–97
and savings, 27, 50, 72–73
and stocks and bonds, 62–64, 65–74
as taxation, 43–49, 69–72
Inflation Survival Letter, 364–66
Insurance, cash value, 69–70, 71–72
Interest rates
bond market, 68–74, 324–30
inflation and, 49–50, 57–58, 69–73
and real estate, 229, 232–34
Investment Rarities, 189–90
Investments, 33–35
borrowing for, 191–193
and inflation, 49–50, 54–55
leverage and, 121–22, 193
margin buying, 329
portfolios, 65–74, 356–60
reading for, 359–67
See also specific subjects
I.R.A. plans, 34, 51
Jennings, Isabel, W., 294
Johnston, Johnny, 364
Journal of Commerce, 96
Journal of Pharmaceutical Services, 296
Journal of the American Medical Association, 293

Kemmerer, E. W., 73
Keogh and Investment Rarities, 51–52
Keogh plans, 34, 51–52
Kirkpatrick, Charles D., 118
Kraft, Joseph, 103
Kravitz, Maury, 364

Lappe, Frances Moore, 285
LeBon, Gustave, 250–51
Liberty Lobby, 365
Lowry, Albert J., 196, 218, 227, 234, 236
Lyons, John, 136

Magy, Marguerita, 293
Marten's Health & Survival Products, Inc., 292
McKeever's Investment and Survival Letter, 366
McMaster, R. E., 363
Medications, stocking, 318
Merchandising, 55
Millar, Thomas, 114
Money, 28–30, 38ff
  in deflation, 56–64, 244–46
  flight abroad, 148–50
  gold-backed, 30, 41–43, 189–90
  in inflation, 28–29, 38–39, 43–45. See also Inflation
  leverage, in investing, 120–22
  supply, 28–29, 40–45, 56–64, 77–78
  Swiss francs, 323–25
  See also Coins
Money Market Funds, 354–57
Montgomery, Forest D., 221–22
Mo-peds, 317
Morality
  and economy, 159–71
  and food storage, 267–69, 312–14
Mortgage
  vs. cash payment, 203–05, 211–12
  and cash reserves, 232
  on home, 53–54, 193–94, 197, 203–205, 226
  inflation and, 53–54
  as investment–money source, 212–13
  liability protection, 201–02
  purchase money or second, 204–12
  refinancing, 202–04
  rates, fixed vs. variable, 232–34
  taxes and, 206–10
Motels and trailer parks, 232
Mother Earth News, 238

Newsweek, 366
New York City, 95–96, 98–114, 137
Nickerson, 236
Nixon, Richard M., 77
North American Newspaper Alliance, 46–47
North, Gary, 78, 241, 313, 340, 362

Organic Gardening and Farming, 238–39

Parade magazine, 264
Pensions and retirement plans
  funding, 84–88, 94, 96
  inflation and, 27, 51–52, 78–80, 82–97
  investments of, 95–96

Preston, Robert, 181
Prices
  controls, 28–29, 75–77, 80–81, 149, 238–43
  deflation and, 56–64
  food, 258–60
  inflation and, 36, 46, 58–59, 78–80. *See also* Inflation
Proxmire, William, 82–83, 131

Rationing, 243
Real estate, 196–237, 244–46
  brokers, 235–37
  cash reserves and, 232
  exchanges, 222–24
  farms, 200–01, 230–231
  financing, 53–54, 197, 203–15, 229, 232–35. *See also* Mortgages
  homes, 53–54, 117–124, 193–94
  land, 217–18, 226
  loans on, 226, 234–235
  location criteria, 197–201, 214–15
  motels and trailer parks, 232
  mountain retreats, 214–15
  prices, 201–03, 227–228
  pyramids, 229–31, 245–46
  residential income property, 197, 216, 217–19, 229
  sales, as career, 232
  and self-sufficiency, 219–21
  small-town, 55, 117–124, 195–97, 200–201, 219–21
  speculation, 218–19
  taxes, 28, 46, 60–63, 206–10, 221–26, 246
  urban, 107–12, 122–124, 195–96, 202–203, 225–26, 230–231
Real Estate Exchange Counselors, 222
Reaper, The, 363–64
Reliance Diamond, 52, 352
Reliance Products, 300, 310–11
Remnant Review, The, 363
Rent controls, 29, 107, 109
Roche Chemical Division, 295
Rogers, Will, 63–64
Ruff Times, The, 229, 358, 361
Russell, Richard (Dick), 68, 156, 247, 262

Schuck, Peter, 167–68
Schultz, Harry, 247

383

Safe deposit boxes, 142–143
Savings, inflation and, 26–27, 50, 72–73
Silver
  coins, 178–86, 189–190, 244–46, 339–340, 358–59, 360
  coins, rare ("numismatic"), 340–44
  commemorative medallions, 344–45
  futures market, 331–332, 333–35
Skousen, Joel, 239
Social Security System, 27, 78–80, 82–97, 155
Spotlight, 365
Stein, Benjamin, 54
Steiner, Gerald M., 235–236
Sternleed, George, 102
Stevens, James Talmage, 272–73
Stock market, 65–69, 334–35
Stoves, 314–15
Super Ease, 292
Swiss francs, 324–25

Taxation
  of business, urban, 107–09
  and coins as payment, 221–22
  deflation and, 246
  inflation as, 43–49, 69–72
  limitation movements, 28–29, 45–46, 61–62
  property exchanges, 223–24
  property sales, 206–10
  recipients of tax money, 46–49
  shelters, 224–25
  Social Security, 84–87
  urban, 112
Tiffany, 351
Time magazine, 366
Tools, 238–39
Transportation, 317
Treasury bills, 141–42, 353–57
Tytler, Alexander, 42–43

U.S. News and World Report, 366
View From the Pit, The, 364
Von Mises, Ludwig, 40

Wachter, Michael, 96–97
Wall Street Journal, The, 360
Water storage, 315–17
Welfare, 101–02, 106–111
Wheeler, Emma, 311
Wille, Frank, 130
Wilson, Esther, H., 275